'Post Demonetization Budget-2017-Expectations, Apprehensions and Reality'

By Ajit Kumar Roy

Disclaimer: The Editor of this book has no political or business affiliation and no overt or covert agenda. The purpose of the writing is to make people aware of the facts and figures in a light-hearted manner based on secondary information. The views and opinions expressed in this book are those of the original contributors and do not necessarily reflect the views of Editor.

Dedication:

Dedicated to my granddaughter
'ANGANA'

PREFACE

India's Budget for 2017-18 remained one of the most awaited budget presentations in recent decades where finance minister Arun Jaitley started by underlining the current government's efforts in putting India on a "transformative mode" through a series of reforms initiated over the last three years. The backdrop to the Budget was a fairly volatile past few months with multiple issues such as (a) demonetization; (b) ambiguities on indirect transfer taxes; (c) treaty changes to India-Mauritius Treaty ("**Mauritius Treaty**"), India-Singapore Treaty ("**Singapore Treaty**") and India-Cyprus Treaty ("**Cyprus Treaty**"); (d) application of General Anti Avoidance Rules ("**GAAR**") from April 1, 2017 along with other macro global changes, all of which were on top of investors' minds.

The economic assessment of demonetization offered in this year's Economic Survey is perhaps the first official government account that objectively seeks to analyze a set of broader questions raised in recent months by the public debate on demonetization; on assessing the administrative design and implementation of the initiative, the short and long run impact, and "its implications for the broader vision underlying the future conduct of economic policy".

"What is positive is that the middle class, for once, also gets a break through reduced taxes, as well as the small and medium enterprises (SME) sector. India will ramp up spending on rural areas, infrastructure and fighting poverty. Finance minister Arun Jaitley added that the impact on growth from the government's cash crackdown would wear off soon as well as hardship to people. So he's trying to mitigate that as much as possible, with some rural schemes and reduction in taxation for low income people."

"Affordable housing is a priority for this government and it was expected to get infrastructure status. Addressing parliament, Jaitley called his fourth Budget one for the poor. Yet, while vowing prudent fiscal management, he also raised his 2017/18 federal deficit target to 3.2% of GDP to cover his spending promises.

Calling the Budget "mildly growth supportive," rating agency Crisil notes: "The Union Budget 2017 has performed a balancing act. With an eye to reducing deficit and simultaneously improving growth prospects, the budget refrained from stretching its fiscal coffers to give a steroidal push to the economy. Yet, sectors like transport and affordable housing received a shot in the arm, which in turn, is expected to push demand in areas such as cement and steel, generating positive multiplier effects in employment and incomes. This, to an extent, will help alleviate some stress in rural areas which were hit hardest by the demonetization drive."

The budget has others who see both positive and negative features. This budget, like all budgets, is a mixed bag, with what appears to be a greater thrust on long-term, systemic reforms than on ensuring growth per se. The priority is on digital transactions and broader digitization of India. The government is betting big on the BHIM app which according to Jaitley has now been downloaded by 125 lakh users. India hopes to create a cleaner, more transparent economy via digitalization that will lead to an improved climate for foreign investment, boost economic growth, and ultimately propel the country to the next chapter of its emerging markets story.

The Budget announcements by finance minister Arun Jaitley clearly reflect Modi's confidence that the *aam aadmi* would support the "bigger moral purpose" behind demonetization, which now guides various policy measures aimed at "cleansing the economy".

The compiled book entitled *'Post Demonetization Budget-2017- Expectations, Apprehensions and Reality'* presents in-depth analysis, insights and key highlights from experts. For convenience of readers the book is divided into the following chapters. *Chapter-1: Expectations from Budget-2017, Chapter-2: Economic Survey 2017, Chapter-3: Budget-2017- Opening Speech of President of India, Chapter-4: Fiscal and Deveopment Issues and Chapter-5: Union Budget 2017.* Thanks to the original contributors of the articles that are presented in the book for bringing awareness among the interested readers.

AJIT KUMAR ROY

ABOUT THE BOOK

The Prime Minister's announcement of the withdrawal of ₹1000 and ₹500 notes ranks amongst the most significant economic measures taken by his government. The audacious move has given birth to hopes of a decisive blow to the black economy, terrorism and counterfeit currency. It is also being lauded for its potential to convert India into a cashless economy.

The economic survey prepared by the chief economic advisor Arvind Subramanian and his team presents a roadmap for the finance minister and his team in announcing various fiscal outlays and tax proposals in line with the broader macroeconomic realities listed in the survey's analysis. The backdrop to the Budget was a fairly volatile past few months with multiple issues such as (a) demonetization; (b) ambiguities on indirect transfer taxes; (c) treaty changes to India-Mauritius Treaty etc.

Union finance minister Arun Jaitley stepped into Parliament on February 1, 2017, the weight of an entire nation and the world rested on his shoulders as he unveiled India's first Budget post demonetization. Many people have questioned if this move is the biggest disruption for electronic payments in 2016. Remonetization has made a difference to the situation on the ground in the recent months with cash being inducted back into the system easing the pain and discomfort associated with missing cash for large segments of a cash-dependent population.

It is a digital economy budget. Government has pushed the digital theme in every area of the budget. Every person from small shops to consumers is pushed towards the digital economy. Tax benefits, incentives to use digital payments and extending loans based on a digital footprint will create a larger merchant ecosystem for digital Payments highlighting that the focus of this budget was the digitization of the Indian economy.

The Budget announcements by finance minister Arun Jaitley clearly reflect Modi's confidence that the *aam aadmi* would support the "bigger moral purpose" behind demonetization, which now guides various policy measures aimed at "cleansing the economy".

Among the many firsts that the Union Budget 2017 has been associated with policy and budget measures to construct a digital economy stand out as original and groundbreaking, especially for a growing economy with tremendous competition for financial resource allocations in the sectors of poverty alleviation, education, infrastructure development, health, etc.

Focusing on Digital Economy for speed, accountability, and transparency Government has pushed the digital theme in every area of the budget. Every person from small shops to consumers is pushed towards the digital economy. Tax benefits, incentives to use digital payments and extending loans based on a digital footprint will create a larger merchant ecosystem for digital payments. *The BHIM app has been launched. It will unleash the power of mobile phones for digital payments and financial inclusion.*

Affordable housing, spending on rural areas, infrastructure and fighting poverty are noteworthy steps. The two big economic efforts of the Budget were towards housing and a tax break for Micro and Small Medium Enterprises (MSMEs).

Many have damned the Union Budget 2017-18 with faint praise: "Workmanlike", "conservative", "middle of the road", "does no harm", "please-all" and so on. Calling the Budget "mildly growth supportive," rating agency Crisil notes: "The Union Budget 2017 has performed a balancing act".

Prime Minister Modi's attempt to formalize the economy through the Goods and Services Tax and the demonetization drive, could be the only solution to India's jobs problem. Undoubtedly GST and demonetization will go a long way in creating jobs but Budget 2017 may have failed to remove the regulatory hurdles that hamper creation of jobs, especially in the education sector, according to some expert.

The compiled book entitled *'Post Demonetization Budget-2017- Expectations, Apprehensions and Reality'* presents in-depth analysis, insights and key highlights. For convenience of the readers the book is divided into the following chapters **Chapter-1: Expectations from Budget-2017, Chapter-2: Economic Survey 2017, Chapter-3: Budget-2017-Opening Speech of President of India, Chapter-4: Fiscal and growth Issues and Chapter-5: Union Budget 2017.** It is expected that the book with latest information about post demonization budget will generate interest among potential researchers/readers.

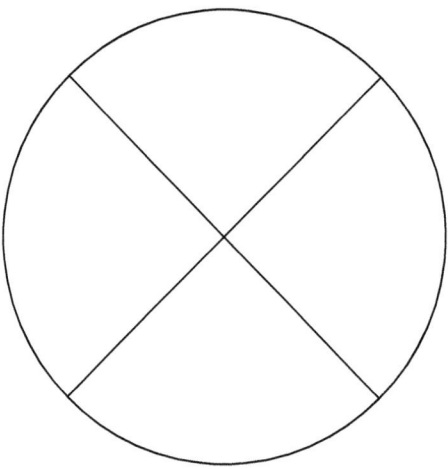

Contents

Chapter-1: Expectations from Budget-2017

Many have damned the Union Budget 2017-18 with faint praise: "Workmanlike", "conservative", "middle of the road", "does no harm", "please-all" and so on. This is unfair. Had this been a normal year, then these descriptions may have been closer to the mark. But the times are far from normal. The circumstances for Budget-making were extraordinarily difficult, perhaps the most challenging since the summer of 1991. For Finance Minister Arun Jaitley and his team to have delivered a decent Budget in these trying times deserves high praise.

1.1 Demonetization, Budget and Expectations
By Dr. Martin Patrick: 28/01/2017

The Central Government will present the budget for 2017–18 on February 1, 2017. The decision to present the budget a month in advance is praiseworthy; normally the budget is presented on the last day of February. Another salient feature of the impending Union Budget is that the Railway Budget has become part of it. Expectations about the budget are unparallel this time, especially when the country faces considerable challenges from the demonetization-induced demand shock leading to uncertainties in the economy. The problem is crucial in the rural sector of the country. Even before demonetization, the economy was suffering from certain concerns such as increasing non-performing assets, poor investment activity, weak industrial production, rising core inflation, FII outflows and rupee depreciation. Adding fuel to fire, demonetization has accentuated the crisis. Hence, the Government will stay away from hard measures, which may further affect the economy adversely.

Sops for Poor and MSME

Rural India, with little access to digital and plastic money, seems to be the worst hit by demonetization. There is every chance that farmers may be given some relief to compensate for their pains. What experts believe is that the capital expenditure may rise in rural areas, particularly for roads, housing and irrigation.

Another sector adversely hit by demonetization is MSME. There is a short-term liquidity crunch and hence more sops will be announced for the uplift of this sector. Yet, an honest approach cannot be expected in this segment; all steps will be political gimmicks.

Sector-wise Focus

In respect of sectoral impact of demonetization, agriculture, cement, automobile, fertilizers, textiles, real estate and retail have faced a negative impact, whereas, power, pharmaceuticals, oil and gas, IT and electronics and infrastructure have had a positive impact, which is not substantiated properly.

The real estate sector that was a major contributor to GDP has been on a downslide for the last two years. Demonetization has created a cash crunch in this sector, apart from the damage created by RERA. Having grown the housing finance market at 30 per cent CAGR in the last 30 years, there is scope for further growth considering increasing urbanization, lower interest rates and demographic dividend. Better incentives and policies will be rolled out in the budget for the developers of the affordable housing segment. The slogan 'Housing for all by 2020' being a goal of the Government, one can expect some positive announcements for the benefit of the housing sector, particularly for the lower income groups. Relaxation in interest rate, hike in HRA deduction limit for salaried class, measures to standardize construction material cost etc will be part of the announcements in the budget.

With regard to other industrial sectors, the metal industry expects protectionism measures so that it can compete with cheaper imports. The cement industry expects lower excise duty as the Government moves towards providing affordable housing, whereas, the automobile sector expects special dispensation as its sales have been hit due to demonetization. The investment in infrastructure will be very high this time, as railway becomes part of the budget. The banking sector needs special mention, as it is blessed with huge volumes of deposits. There will be additional measures in the budget to provide growth in the credit. Recapitalization of banks may not get adequate attention this time.

Social Sector Spending

India's spending on human capital, education and health to GDP ratio is the lowest among BRICS and lowers than OECD and emerging market economies averages. It is even lower than that of comparable per capita GDP economies such as Vietnam, Bolivia and Uzbekistan. Bangladesh performs better than India in this segment. There is no expectation that the Government will reverse the trend and attitude; no surprise can be expected in the budget allocation for social sector spending. The point often ignored by all governments is that social sector spending can play a leading role in realizing higher growth, lower inflation and lower public debt so that macroeconomic stability can be maintained. No doubt, PM Suraksha Bhima Yojana, Jeevan Jyoti Yojana and Atal Pension Yojana will get some allocation, which will be a continuation of the existing strategy.

Digitalization

There will be announcements for moving the society from cash economy to less cash economy. The Government has already announced certain measures like discounts on card payments, discounts on tollbooth payments using cards, waiver of merchant discount rates when using debit cards at POS machines etc. In continuation, there will be more announcements relating to the use of debit cards, credit cards, mobile wallets and apps. There are chances for measures to provide greater access to cashless transaction modes in rural areas, especially for farmers. The companies that manufacture POS machines, finger print cards, biometric cards and micro ATMs may be given some incentives through cutting or eliminating excise duty on these items. The excise duty exemptions that will cease to exist by March 2017 may be extended. It is rumoured that import duty on the components required for manufacturing the above products may be reduced.

The question is how far the Government will address the issue of commissions and charges collected by banks and service providers, thereby lessening the burden on the customers.

Tax Rationalization and Fiscal Consolidation

One of the key agendas of the Government has been to improve India's ranking on the World Bank's Ease of Doing Business index. Simplifying and streamlining tax policies will be continued. There is a possibility that corporate tax may be cut from 30 per cent to 28 per cent, as part of the stated objective of reducing it to the level of 25 per cent. MAT rate is also expected to be reduced from 18.5 per cent to 15 per cent. On the direct tax front, there is a possibility for raising the 80 C limit from Rs 1.5 lakh to Rs 2–2.5 lakh. There could be an increase in the tax rate for short-term capital gains from 15 per cent to 17.5 per cent. Reducing lock of bank deposits in tax rebates, raising the threshold for mandatory TDS on interest income etc are other expectations. Service tax may be hiked to 18 per cent in line with the GST proposals.

It is expected that the Government will stick to the 3 per cent of GDP target for the core fiscal deficit. According to the global financial services major, the Government should continue with its fiscal consolidation in a 'practical fashion' and stick to the 3 per cent pre-announced fiscal deficit for 2016–17, but give itself headroom for compensating states for revenue losses once GST is in place. The report of the high-level committee headed by N K Singh on 'Fiscal Responsibility and Budget Management' is pending with the Government. The recommendations of the committee may be included in the budget proposals. If so, the result may be a fiscal deficit target of 3.3 to 3.5 per cent of GDP. GAAR [1] will also be rolled out in the next fiscal.

Conclusion

The Government going for populist announcements amidst elections declared for five state assemblies, as they restrict the freedom to announce sops for the poor and rural sector, is a major challenge. At the same time, Indian economy needs consumption-led stimulus now, as investment is a long cycle. No doubt, investment in Research and Development must be encouraged at a higher pace. But consumption based on the strategy of social sector spending should be the spirit of the budget proposals. Sector-specific expenditure along with social sector spending is required to reverse slump in demand and not a single sided thrust on investment boost.

The anti-globalization developments around the world must be heeded. The Brexit vote and the victory of Donald Trump in the US presidential elections are some events that would lead to a host of protectionist policies. The FM will have to evaluate the situation, while making budget proposals. Considering all these, it is apt to say that, "… it will be an unprecedented budget," as one official spokesperson said.

[1] GAAR (General Anti-avoidance Rule) is a set of general rules to check tax avoidance. These rules target any transaction or business arrangement that is entered into with the objective of avoiding tax. It was introduced by then FM Pranab Mukherjee on March 16, 2012 during the budget session.

Dr. Martin Patrick is Chief Economist at CPPR.

http://www.thedialogue.co/demonetisation-budget-and-expectations/

1.2 Budget 2017: This is what India Inc expects from the Finance Minister

"We are expecting favourable change in the Income Tax slabs and rates in Union Budget 2017, as customer spending is still anticipated to decline for short term due to demonetization," said the CFO of Acer. - By: **Express Web Desk** | New Delhi | Updated: January 20, 2017 2:27 pm

Expectations from Finance Minister Arun Jaitley are high at a time when the ban on high value currency notes have led to chaos and cash crunch across the country. 2016 saw two major economic decisions by the government, one was the Goods and Services Tax and the other, demonetization, announced on November 8. While people are still uncertain about the impact of both decisions, it is the budget of 2017 that is most awaited and will determine the government's way of dealing with the situation.

Apart from expectations from the government to address the problems caused by demonetization, the two other issues the Union Budget 2017 will witness are the merger of the Railway budget with the Union budget, and the change of date of the budget from end February to February 1.

Here is what India Inc expects from budget 2017:

TRANSPORT

Uber India - Shweta Rajpal Kohli, Head Public Policy, Uber India: "We hope that the government announces measures that can ease the friction experienced by users while executing digital transactions. While the efforts of the government on this front are laudable, we would like to see an enabling framework that allows innovative and seamless solutions to be operationalised for digital transactions. This would include permission to allow merchants and/or card networks to authenticate digital transactions in the background while providing users the ease of a one-click payment. Further, as a fledgling industry which has already created hundreds of thousands of economic opportunities across the country, we would hope for concessions in the form of tax rebates under the proposed GST regime. This would be imperative for sharing economy players such as us to realize the market potential in India and contribute to India's growth story."

Shuttle – Bus aggregator in NCR Amit Singh, Co-Founder, Shuttle: "The present Union government has taken some seminal initiatives towards creating a digital economy and promoting the start-up culture in the country through the Digital India and Start-Up India programmes. We look forward to improvements in regulatory framework particularly addressing of issues like ambiguity and multiplicity of regulations. This will help in realizing the benefits of digital economy in urban mobility and turn our cities in truly world-class Smart Cities."

Finance Minister Arun Jaitley Lauds Demonetization Move at Vibrant Gujarat Summit in Gandhinagar.

WELLNESS

Qtrove.com: Online market place - Vinamra Pandiya, CEO and Founder, Qtrove.com: We are very keen about the 2017 budget and are excited about Mr. Jaitley's announcement of the same on 1st Feb. As an e commerce startup, we look forward to receiving some more clarity for FDI in B2C e-commerce through an automatic route. We also hope for a provision of enabling marketplaces to give a discount from their side. Besides this, we are also expecting relaxation of the rule of 'not more than 25% of the business coming from one vendor for marketplaces.' And lastly, I feel quite a lot of entrepreneurs are awaiting the implementation of GST at the earliest to enable cross state logistics with minimum constraints and friction.

The Man Company: Premium Men's Grooming brand - Rohit Chawla, CEO and Co-Founder, The Man Company: The last couple of months have definitely created an impact for most ecommerce and FMCG brands selling online. In this budget, we are expecting the government to take steps that will boost consumption and sales. How the government goes about digitization of the economy will be interesting to know. We hope that there are provisions that encourage digital payments over cash transactions. We are also expecting a smooth execution of GST.

TECHNOLOGY

SpiderG: India's first e-invoicing technology provider for SMEs - Ashwani Rathore, CEO and Co-Founder, SpiderG: "As a startup we face various tax and regulatory issues and I am hoping that this union budget will address some of these issues. Last financial year was tough for Indian startup ecosystem and to make the situation better Employee Stock ownership (ESOP) plans for the startups should be taxed at the time of sale which would help in paying their taxes as they would have greater liquidity and the instruments could also get a fair valuation. Government should announce a series of initiatives to support the startups, including widening of the tax-free regime to five years from three years and faster procedural clearances. Such announcements will boost our honorable PM's Startup India movement. I am also expecting some announcements at the backdrop of demonetization to promote the digital economy where online payment transaction charges would be reduced."

Intex Technologies Ltd.: Rajeev Jain, CFO, Intex Technologies Ltd.: "The mobile handset industry is the fast growing Industry and has become an imperative part of our everyday life. India is moving towards a digital economy and mobile banking. Smart phones will play a crucial role in supporting this vision. The recent demonetization reform by the Government has further laid the ground for setting a cashless economy. The entire country is looking forward towards mobile banking which shall create a new user base and fuel the growth in mobile Industry. As an industry, we expect a long-term and stable policy on mobile manufacturing in India. The industry has huge potential and can supplement government initiatives of 'Make in India' with highly technical product if focused. Incentives to create sufficient technical manpower will lay the foundation of a strong and robust manufacturing base in India. Further, a clearly laid out research and development policy is necessary to succeed in a highly technical industry like ours and will help bring component manufacturing base in India to save precious foreign exchange. In the end, to create a truly inclusive digital economy, affordable mobile handset or consumer durable items up to certain value should be given a concessional duty treatment."

ACER: **Alok Dubey, CFO, ACER**: "The Union Budget for the year 2017-18 is likely to be unique as many prime factors like demonetization, GST, cashless economy measures, will play a key role this year. We are expecting favourable change in the Income Tax slabs and rates, as customer spending is still anticipated to decline for short term due to demonetization. We also expect the budget to focus on shaping the IT infrastructure and urge the government to provide tax deductions on purchase of PC for consumers as well providing easy short-term loans for retailers for working capital requirement. This is required to accompaniment India's emergent IT sector and further help the industry make improved technology more accessible to Indian market to fulfill government's push for a digital economy."

OnePlus: **Vikas Agarwal, GM, OnePlus India:** "After Make in India and demonetization, the next big disruption is GST. The government has to carefully take measures to remonetize the economy to return to high GDP growth while maintaining cost competitiveness. From policy perspective, the tax structure should be rationalized and land acquisition policies should be simplified to enable local manufacturing at a larger scale."

Directi: A group of tech businesses: Bhavin Turakhia, Co-Founder and CEO, Directi: "2016 saw a slew of announcements made by the government. With the goal of putting our country on the path towards a cashless economy, the Union Budget 2017-18 should include definitive SOPs and tax rebates to encourage and boost e-payments. Moreover, to achieve the goal of financial inclusion, the government should also rationalize indirect taxes and charges levied with respect to digital payment transactions, and further incentivize companies operating within this space. To adapt to the need of time, government should also rationalize income tax provisions including provisions related to employee tax benefits such that payments / documents in the digital medium are treated at par with physical instruments. As a natural corollary to the demonetization process, the time is ripe to increase the tax exemption limit and also the corporate tax limits. Steps should also be taken to help startups tide over its immediate effects. Furthermore, with the increase in cash flow within banks, advanced technological infrastructure will help facilitate seamless transactions and improve the overall banking system as we enter into the new financial year. A startup hub, India is currently home to the third largest number of technology driven startups in the world. The previous year witnessed multiple markdowns in the country's startup ecosystem and, therefore, to propel this forward, the PM's flagship 'Startup India' project should receive an impetus in the upcoming budget."

Vertoz Media Pvt. Ltd.: Ashish Shah, CEO and Founder, Vertoz Media Pvt. Ltd: "There is hope that there will be some incentive announcements to further popularize the digital initiatives of the government. Being a pure Ad-Tech firm we are very optimistic on the government's vision of 'Digital India'. We expect to see a growth oriented budget on February 1, 2017. The government has been encouraging entrepreneurship among the younger generation with its flagship initiative – 'Startup India' and keeps up the momentum this time as well. More entrepreneurs in the ecosystem will drive sustainable economic growth and generate more job opportunities."

INFORMATION TECHNOLOGY

NetApp India & SAARC: Anil Valluri, President – NetApp India & SAARC: "The previous two budgets have systematically gone about creating frameworks and processes to give wings to the dreams of multiple sections of the society like Startup India, Standup India and shrink wrapped with a larger vision of Digital India. With the recent move of demonetization trying to shift our cash driven economy of 1.2 billion people and getting them to leap frog to the digital world is unprecedented in history. This is a significant leap towards becoming a digital economy and the budget now needs to focus on how digital can become entrenched and become a way of life, while continuing to focus on growth and providing adequate support to the various pillars of each program so that the economy is on a sustained growth path," said Anil Valluri, President, NetApp India & SAARC.

Grey Orange - Designs, develops and deploys advanced robotics systems: Yaduvendra Singh, Vice President & Global Head – Sales, Marketing & Solutions – Grey Orange Pvt. Ltd.: "We expect the Union Budget 2017 to have significant growth-centric announcements that help put India's economic performance back on track. Given India's medium to long-term prospect as a manufacturing destination, we foresee the manufacturing sector to be a key contributor to India's GDP in the coming years. Hence, the Union Budget should encourage manufacturing in the country. Players offering niche solutions – such as smart manufacturing and industrial automation – that help India achieve global standards of manufacturing and be recognized as a strong manufacturing hub, should be provided regulatory encouragement. Most companies in this space are very young and therefore there should be public spending to develop the right infrastructure for such companies to grow. Tax Holiday could be an effective incentive by the Government to encourage young companies with high potential. There should also be relaxations with respect to the qualifying criteria of working on State/Central Government projects. High threshold of parameters such as bank guarantee, number of years of experience, and number of employees often prevents young but deserving companies from working on large government projects, thereby depriving them of some much-needed experience. Efforts and investments are also required on similar lines as developing Information Technology parks across the country couple of decades back. Large manufacturing parks where all ecosystem players such as component suppliers, logistics support, consultants, and talent are available within the designated locality, will promote access and provide the necessary boost to the industry. Another important aspect that the budget should address is skill development in technology. Currently, we face a problem of having a large army of 'unemployable' engineers. On the other hand, the manufacturing sector is seriously short of skilled workforce. We expect the government to set aside an appropriate proportion of the budget to bridge this skill gap. This can be done through starting more institutions such as the IITs and NITs. Overall, making manufacturing easier in the country not only helps upcoming and innovative firms to prosper but will also accelerate the country's economic growth."

Indus Net Technologies: Abhishek Rungta, CEO, Indus Net Technologies: "Withdrawal of withholding tax for overseas service purchase. In a globalised world, such taxes impact competitiveness of IT businesses from India. Labor law reform is awaited for years. We cannot treat blue collar labors and white collar executives in the same way. There should be tax breaks on R&D investments out of the profits, so that companies focus on IP creation. This can be linked with measurable results. Angel investing is not tax efficient. It needs to be structured such that successful entrepreneurs and executives find it easy to invest and startups are not penalized when raising money from these sources. IP related disputes need a very different expertise and hence a separate bench or court shall be put in place to quickly and appropriately handle IP related disputes. Incubation and acceleration centers by corporate should be encouraged and the investments made in the same should be exempted from tax. IT and digital adoption is extremely poor in SMEs in India. Government shall subsidize that for micro industries to get them to adopt technology at an early stage and become more competitive. It will also encourage and increase internal adoption of IT and hence growth of the industry."

EDUCATION

Aakash Educational Services Pvt. Ltd.: Aakash Chaudhury, Director, Aakash Educational Services Pvt. Ltd.: Access to basic quality education is still a bigger challenge in India, especially in rural areas. With digitization and innovation seeping in to bridge this gap, there is still room for financial and statutory incentives from the government to motivate private organizations to invest their efforts and time into it, apart from money. Further standardization of curriculum across states and boards will enable cheaper access to education, with large number of facilitators in the market. Leveraging of technology is vital to gain access to progress of delivered education; hence developments and additional benefits around education technology will be a welcome step.

The Anita Borg Institute India: Geetha Kannan, Managing Director of ABI India: "Last year the Sixth Economic Census released by the Ministry of Statistics and Programme Implementation had revealed that women constituted only 13.76% of the total 58.5 million entrepreneurs. Despite these low figures, ABI is hopeful that slowly but surely these numbers will improve in the coming years. Unless the Government continues to step in and is highly committed to creating an ecosystem that nurtures and supports women entrepreneurs, all efforts such as 'Startup India', 'Make in India' and 'Stand-Up India' will not achieve the desired goals that implied empowerment and financial stability for women. Our Finance Minister, Mr. Arun Jaitley in the previous budget had allocated Rs. 500 crores under the 'Stand-Up India' scheme, which among other categories included women entrepreneurs. This was a welcome move. We are keen that in the coming budget the Government has plans to expand such schemes and finds more ways to ensure it is reaching the targeted beneficiaries. Women entrepreneurs in technology are on the rise and strong initiatives from the Government could really help in building successful businesses. The Indian economy is anticipated to grow at a slower rate this year due to world politics, global financial fluctuations, and demonetization and so on. We hope the Budget 2017 is able to resist all these and yet provide a stable socio-economic environment. Technology is undoubtedly at the core of most growth and development. Tax reforms, initiatives and policies to further boost the technology sector are always a priority on the budget wish-list."

PAYMENTS

Worldline: Deepak Chandnani, CEO of Worldline South Asia and Middle East: "The government is taking many steps to further the cause of digital payments and move towards a less-cash economy. However, with the reduction in MDR and other short-term measures, the acquiring business is losing its profitability. In the upcoming budget, we hope that the government takes a long-term perspective and brings in measures that make the business viable again. Also, the industry would benefit from the proposed Acceptance Development Fund (ADF), which in turn will accelerate the growth in the acceptance infrastructure of the country."

MobiKwik: Bipin Preet Singh, CEO and Founder, MobiKwik: "The Budget must announce measures to upgrade digital infrastructure across the country. This will encourage more merchants and consumers to transact on non-cash, online platforms. Digital India is a laudable initiative. We need to improve digital literacy and connect cities, towns and villages with high-speed internet networks so that every citizen is empowered with access to a mobile broadband connection. Access to online services should actually be a fundamental right. This will move a large portion of cash transactions to formal economy. The Budget must reduce corporate tax for start-ups and companies promoting digital payments ecosystem. At the moment, it is flat at 35 per cent. There should be reduction in income tax for individuals and companies promoting secure digital payments. The Budget should announce sops for fin-tech companies providing data protection. We need to see visible action on government initiatives like Make in India, Skill India, Start-Up India and Stand up India. The Budget must announce steps to tone up physical infrastructure. We need good roads, good connectivity with rural areas where 65 per cent of Indians live. India needs world-class seaports and airports. Implementation of GST from April 1 may be deferred to help businesses and overall economy recover from demonetization. Clear, uniform taxation for all goods and services is important. India should be a tax compliant society. At present, not even three per cent of people pay any income tax. Transactions worth one trillion dollars are done in the country annually. Of these, barely 10 per cent are on digital platforms. Mobile wallet providers have thus clearly a larger role to play. India is poised for high growth. By 2030, it could become the world's third largest economy after the United States and China."

Zeta: Ramki Gaddipati, **CTO & Co-founder** of **Zeta:** "As digital payments take off, we'd like this year's budget to focus on financial inclusion. We hope the Government of India reduces indirect taxes and charges levied on digital transactions. Further, income tax incentives should be provided to people who use digital payment options. It's also time that digital payment and documents be treated legally on par with physical instruments. We also hope that the Government increases the ceilings on employee tax benefits as they're now quite overdue. To aid merchants, the Merchant Discount Rate on card payments should be abolished. The industry can also benefit from tax incentives provided to organizations operating in the digital payments space."

HOME APPLIANCES

Inalsa Home Appliances: Pankaj Gupta, Head Marketing, Inalsa Home Appliances: "Small appliances industry in India is performing on an average growth rate of 5-6 % in last 3-4 years. However this industry has potential to perform much better. The penetration of many categories in Indian household is as low as 5%. Keeping in view the above we look forward to a budget where few upcoming categories like Chimneys, air purifiers, food steamers are given a preferential treatment. The import duties on such products may be reduced. This shall enable these products to be sold at an affordable price. The industry in these categories can grow to the extent of more than 50% too, as the potential of growth in these categories is huge. Manufacturing sector particularly for traditional product categories like Mixer Grinders & Irons needs to be focused to give much required respite to these categories. These categories have huge potential as penetration still is not very huge but these categories have become stagnant as the major players are not pumping in money in these categories. This stalemate is related to competition between organized & unorganized players. If excise duties are lowered, two fold advantages can be attained. One is that operating prices of all major players shall go down & the second advantage shall be unorganized players too shall be forced to enter into the mainstream of excise & VAT. This shall enable to give a level playing field to all. There is every possibility that we may see not only growth in this sector but innovative product introduction. Organized sector in India is looking forward to implementation of GST so that the differentiated market of organized & unorganized players gets narrower. A major expectation from the Budget 2017 is related to the "Make in India" campaign of government of India. We look forward to impressions of the same in the budget so that domestic small appliance market feels comfortable in the time to come. This shall also ensure employment generation & in totality a better nation-India."

Arun Jaitley: Tax Collection Registered Hike in April-December Despite Demonetization.

TRADING

Trade Smart Online: A discount brokerage firm Vijay Singhania, Founder-Director, Trade Smart Online: Expectation from the forthcoming Union Budget, Q3FY17 earnings and forthcoming public issue of BSE will drive the markets in the coming week. The pre-budget market rally has started and investors have started building positions on likely announcements from the budget to be presented on February 1. Q3FY17 earnings from blue-chip companies are set to be the next big trigger for the markets. Reliance Industries and LIC Housing Finance will announce October – December 2016 quarterly results on Monday. While Axis Bank and Yes Bank will announce December 2016 quarterly results on Thursday, Adani Power and RBL Bank will announce quarterly results on Friday. Meanwhile, Asia's oldest bourse BSE will launch its much-awaited Rs. 1,500 crores initial public offering (IPO) on January 23. The public offer of BSE will see sale of 1.54 crores shares by the existing shareholders through the offer for sale (OFS) route. This works out to close to 30 percent of the total holding. On macro front, the government will announce monthly inflation data based on wholesale price index (WPI) for December 2016 on Monday. Inflation based on WPI eased for the third straight month to 3.2 per cent in November 2016 from 3.4% in October 2016.

TELECOM

Solutions Infini: Aniketh Jain, CEO, Co-Founder of Solutions Infini: "The upcoming budget is crucial to honest taxpayers and we look forward to a low taxation system, which will simultaneously promote a robust digital ecosystem. Moreover, the government should simplify the tax regime for ITs and startups to foster innovations and boost a healthy start-up environment in the country. Also, the union budget 2017-2018 should focus on digital inclusion across industries. Simplification of overall processes across all government infrastructures will be key for the success of India and I believe they should ensure that sufficient budget is allocated for the same."

RETAIL

Giftease.com - India's biggest online gifting portal: Vivek Mathur, CEO at Giftease Technologies Pvt. Ltd: "The current financial year has seen some landmark reforms, which should help boost tax collection. Hence, there are strong expectations of a significant cut in income taxes, for both corporate & individuals. Overall, consumption has been severely impacted in the last couple of months, and firm steps to boost consumption & improve consumer sentiment, are crucial for the retail & ecommerce sectors".

Pepperfry.com: Neelesh Talathi, CFO, Pepperfry.com: "E-commerce sector in India continues to grow at scorching pace thereby contributing to Government's ambitious plans around "Make in India" & employment generation. We anticipate that the government will leverage Budget 2017 to provide further impetus to this sector through tax reforms and enhanced level playing field. GST is the cornerstone to releasing the dream of one-country one-market, as it can potentially resolve impediments in Inter-State movement, unburden e-Commerce of multitude of taxes e.g. Entry Tax etc. All Indians aspire to own their home and we hope that the Budget 2017 accelerates development of urban infrastructure and provides incentive to home buyers. It will also support our mission of helping 20 million customers create beautiful homes by 2020."

REAL   ESTATE,   CONSTRUCTION, INFRASTRUCTURE

House of Hiranandani: Mr. Surendra Hiranandani, CMD, House of Hiranandani: "The real estate sector certainly awaits an accommodative stance by the government in the upcoming budget. Even as the GST rates have been finalized and the slabs fixed at 5%, 12%, 18% and 28%, the real estate sector waits to know which tax rate will be applied to the industry. A 12% slab is preferred by the sector as it will reduce the cost of apartments and increase affordability for end users. Developers too stand to gain as this would positively impact sales in the market. A higher rate of 18% is expected to increase the cost of homes, especially in under construction projects, unless there is clarity provided on the composition scheme (abetment of cost of land), VAT charges if they have been paid by developers for under construction properties). Apart from this we hope the government raises HRA deduction and provides tax incentives for first time home buyers. The corporate taxes need to be reduced and Dividend distribution tax must be scrapped. To get returns one has to pay over 55% in taxes which is the highest in the world. It is more profitable today to trade in shares than to invest in creating a business. Entrepreneurs are presently being penalized while trading is encouraged."

Berger Paints India Limited: Abhijit Roy, CEO & MD of Berger Paints: "Demonetization has affected consumer sentiment with some withholding of purchase decision specially in the discretionary category. We expect the Government to give a boost to the consumer sentiment by lowering taxes and giving tax breaks for buying affordable houses."

Mjunction - An e-marketplace for steel: Vinaya Varma, CEO, mjunction: "I look forward to a budget which carries forward the Prime Minister's vision of a Digital India in the truest sense of the term. Let e-governance be the order of the day, and let e-payments and digital wallets be more incentivized in order to eradicate corruption from its very roots. I am also looking forward to implementation in letter and spirit of the Prime Minister's Startup India programme. This will boost innovative thinking and fresh ideas so crucial for India's economy now."

OTHERS

Denave - A global sales enablement company: Snehashish Bhattacharjee, Global CEO, Co-founder, Denave: "With demonetization significantly altering the dynamics of the entire national economy, expectations are high from the upcoming budget. Alongside countering black money practices, this move has helped the government in expanding the bracket of tax-paying population. This in-turn, equips the government to offer considerable tax rebates and SOPs focused towards societal development and growth. The ambiguities present in the modern-day service sector operations can be lessened with apt reform provisions in the budget. In line with the gradual industrial revamp, we are at interesting junctures wherein artificial intelligence and machine learning are steadily changing the long-established industrial norms and challenging the cheap-labor tag which our country has borne for long now. This technological disruption has created the need for R&D support in the ITES/ BPO industry. The industry needs more government support to build state-of-the-art R&D to eventually create alternate solutions and get back into the game. Lastly, for a holistic growth and development, focus on building a world-class infrastructure and real-estate industry is also critical. Both these sectors require better regularization and standardization support in order to foster an efficient business environment. I expect the upcoming budget to cater to this as well, through incentivized SOPs and other measures."

Tenon - Facility Management and Security Company: Major Manjit Rajain, Group Chairman, Tenon: "The forthcoming Union Budget is expected to unveil reform-centric policies and an action plan that would help boost the growth. The security industry is the second largest employment generator in India, which provides fresh workforce through facilitating pre-job and on the job training. Considering recent initiatives taken by the current government in the areas of agriculture, job creation, skill development and education, we hope this budget to be beneficial for companies like us. We expect new tax incentives in the areas like skill development & job creation and are very optimistic about new policies. Through this Union budget'17, we would request the government to categorize the private security guard under skilled and highly skilled workers under minimum wages Act, while providing with more tax incentives for such trainings. In addition to this, we are expecting simple tax compliances under proposed GST environment. Furthermore, we hope the reduction in custom duty on the electronic security products for the growth and expansion of the industry."

The Akshaya Patra Foundation - Not for profit organization running food program of mid-day meals: Sri Madhu Pandit Dasa, Chairman, The Akshaya Patra Foundation: "The upcoming budget has raised expectations on various significant points. We are hopeful of an increase in allocation of funds in child welfare and educational sector – both primary and secondary. On income tax exemption for charitable activities, we hope that the exemptions already in effect will continue. Withdrawal of these exemptions is expected to discourage such donations, adversely impacting voluntary contributions. Overall we expect that the budget creates a positive environment for child welfare and development, education and the social sector as a whole."

AMD: Vinay Sinha, Head of Sales – India, Director – Commercial Business, AMD Asia Pacific-Japan (APJ) Mega

Region: "Last year's budget saw the Government focus on digital literacy by setting up a scheme to cover 6 crores rural households. Along with the 'national digital literacy mission' and 'digital saksharata abhiyan', these schemes will help democratize use and familiarity with digital devices such as computers, tablet PCs, and smart phones, as well as internet usage. As a result, these trained workers can more actively and effectively participate in the cycle of development, thereby empowering start-ups and large organizations to experience digital transformation. The rapid adoption of the Digital India policy aided by the strong, decisive, and time bound rollout of each of the related pillars fueled the demand for computers and mobility devices in the country. The government must continue to push these programs that proliferate digital services and digital inclusion to the common man. The demonetization move resulted in slowdown of cash purchases; however, the balance of slowdown on cash purchases was offset to a small extent by increased online and B2B growth. The robustness of the digitization move and its impact will only be understood once we have enough data to measure the market movement."

http://indianexpress.com/article/business/budget/union-budget-2017-india-inc-expects-from-finance-minister-arun-jaitley-narendra-modi-4477164/

1.3   2017-Budget Expectations of Financial Inclusion for Women Entrepreneurship

A surge in Indian startups has led to a revolution in women entrepreneurship in India. From Swati Bhargava's Cash karo to Sairee Chahal's Sheroes, women are spreading wings of business ambitions rapidly. With the Union Budget set to be announced in February, women entrepreneurs across the country are hoping for a long list of expectations with the government to be met. Union minister Anupriya Patel vehemently favoured for establishing quotas for women in BIMSTEC-SAARC Women's Economic Forum that will help them compete in mixed gender environments. But will the central government strike out gender-specific policies and measures in this year's Budget?

These #3 women leaders tell us what could be the possible financial inclusions for women entrepreneurship in 2017-Budget.

- **Preeti Sinha, Yes Bank Ltd.**

Though, the government has been supportive in promoting women entrepreneurship, but what most women need is an easy access to funds says Preeti Sinha, Senior President of Yes Institute. An initiative of Yes Bank, Yes Institute educates women and other aspiring entrepreneurs how to lead a sustainable business with the inclusion of socio-economic development and growth.

'With many women showing interest in entrepreneurship should be facilitated by government with better options of loan and other banking policies that could help them to start their small business smoothly.'

- **Dr Monisha Borthakur, Infosys Ltd.**

Women have definitely come a long way fighting all odds in way to attain their goals and objectives. From technological to traditional businesses, women are no behind in race, and ramping up with an unstoppable speed. Since there are a lot of aspiring women entrepreneurs who struggle with finances while starting up a business, Dr. Monisha Borathakur from Infosys Ltd. emphasized on simpler access to funding for aspiring women entrepreneurs.

'*A lot of initiatives of government are helping aspiring women entrepreneurs, but to yield even better results the access to funding should be made simpler for aspiring women entrepreneurs.*'

- **Sonu Iyer, Partner and leader, India Region Ernst & Young**

Accentuating the fact that a lot of women coming up with new ideas and hunches to experiment in market, Sonu Iyer, Partner and Leader of Indian region Ernst & Young shares her view of financial inclusion to be made in 2017 Financial Budget.

'*Since the implementation of GST will be on table for 2017-Budget, government will come up with the new rationalized tax structure. Women entrepreneurs should definitely be a part of consideration in corporate taxes and loans.*'

https://www.entrepreneur.com/article/287946

1.4   Budget 2017: Ten Things to Look Out For

The impact of demonetization on economic growth, fiscal deficit, and jobs and taxes are set to feature prominently in Arun Jaitley's budget speech

1. Carrying forward the demonetization initiative

The Union Budget 2017 will be unveiled under the shadow of the government's demonetization of high-value notes. The government has said time and again that demonetization is a first step in the move to flush out black money. Taken by itself, demonetization is certainly not enough to unearth unaccounted wealth. All eyes will, therefore, be on the budget speech, to see how the process of tackling unaccounted wealth will go forward. The estimates of black money unearthed by demonetization may also be furnished along with details of how the tax base is being broadened, as the government has been claiming. The budget speech could include incentives given for moving to digital payments as well as for moving from the informal to the formal sector, another declared objective of the government.

2. Growth

The government has downplayed the impact on growth of the demonetization exercise, claiming that its negative impact has been far less than what the pundits have been estimating, and that it's temporary. The government's estimate of nominal growth in FY18 will, therefore, be watched carefully. The economy was in recovery mode before being hit by the demonetization bouncer, and the government believes it will soon get back to form.

There are some risks to growth in FY18, however. One, the boost to growth from lower crude oil prices will not be there. Two, the environment of rising protectionism is not conducive for export growth. The burden of reigniting growth, therefore, falls almost entirely on domestic demand. And if there is a long-term impact on the informal economy disrupted by demonetization and the goods and services tax (GST), it could lower demand.

3. Investment

The chart shows the steady fall in the economy's investment/gross domestic product (GDP) ratio after reaching a peak in 2011. Getting investment back on track is necessary for a sustained revival of growth. Unfortunately, the government's capex this fiscal for April-November is 10% lower than in the same period of the previous year, as the government had to spend on the implementation of the 7th Pay Commission recommendations and on increased military pensions.

STEADY DECLINE

Investment as % of GDP in 2016 is the lowest since 2003. For a sustainable recovery, investment demand must improve.

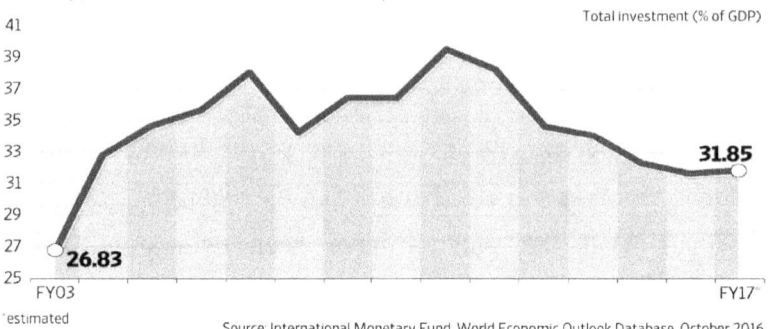

Source: International Monetary Fund, World Economic Outlook Database, October 2016

True, much of the government's capex has been through borrowing by agencies such as the National Highways Authority of India (NHAI); but as the chart shows, it doesn't seem to have made much of a difference. Perhaps, the main reason is the lack of private investment. The budget will be scrutinized to see whether it gives an impetus to investment.

4. Consumption

Government spending on roads and railways and other infrastructure is preferable to boosting consumption, because a big stimulus to consumption runs the risk of igniting inflation, particularly if oil prices remain high. That said, many analysts believe the government will boost consumption, particularly through rural spending.

The budget will tell us whether the government is going to shift its focus to populism, in preparation for the 2019 elections. True, the only way to revive private capex is to increase consumption, which will reduce excess capacity and ultimately lead to investment demand picking up. But if the government is right about the temporary impact of demonetization and consumption is expected to bounce back soon, why do we need to boost it?

5. The fiscal deficit

As in the earlier years, this year, too, there's a lot of talk about postponing the fiscal consolidation targets. Much depends on what the N.K. Singh committee recommends. It's important that the centre's fiscal deficit is reduced, for the simple reason that states may not be able to reduce their deficits as they implement the pay commission recommendations in FY18. Moreover, if the government claims demonetization hasn't really hurt the economy, it cannot simultaneously argue that a fiscal stimulus is needed. The target of 1.8% for the FY18 revenue deficit, in particular, needs to be met.

6. Taxes

This budget may dramatically change the pace of tax reform. Tax rates on individual tax payers could be reduced or at least the threshold and tax brackets changed to provide incentives for declaring income and, perhaps, to boost consumption. Rationalization of corporate taxes will continue and should be aimed at reviving drooping corporate spirits. This is not the time to tinker with capital gains taxes.

7. Jobs

This should perhaps be the No. 1 objective if the government wants to avoid a social and political backlash. That will involve supporting agriculture, but there's not much the central government can do there. Instead, it must find ways of reviving the construction sector, a big source of jobs. Growth in the construction component of gross value added has been falling steadily from 4.6% in 2013-14 to 4.4% in 2014-15 to 3.9% in 2015-16, while the Central Statistics

Office estimates growth of 2.9% this year, and it's likely to be lower. The prime minister, in his New Year's Eve address, had talked of a boost to low-cost rural housing, which could lead to lots of jobs. The budget will tell us whether the government is putting its money where its mouth is.

8. Subsidy reforms

The run-up to the budget has seen a lot of trial balloons being floated about a universal basic income. The budget will tell us whether a beginning is made towards it. Changes in fertilizer and liquefied petroleum gas (LPG) subsidies, if any, and signs of progress towards direct benefits transfer will also be awaited.

9. Banking system

The banking system remains the Achilles heel of the Indian economy and although banks' profits may have gone up due to treasury gains, demonetization may have led to more distress among industries, especially small-scale industries that could result in an increase in bad loans. The budget will tell us whether the government will do more to recapitalize banks.

10. Administrative reforms

The slogan of 'minimum government' seems to have been forgotten and the reform of the bureaucracy and talk of a smaller government has been put aside. A. Prasanna, economist at ICICI Securities Primary Dealership, says fundamental changes are needed in the bureaucracy and in labour laws and regulations. It's doubtful if any of that will happen, and this budget could finally lay to rest any hopes on that front.

http://www.livemint.com/Opinion/fu7hSC6zSMKVLJs8LEG1ZN/Ten -things-to-look-for-in-Budget-2017.html?li_source=LI&li_medium= news_rec

1.5 Demonetization and Budgets: All in the Mind

Arun Jaitley will soon be presenting the 2017-18 budget and his well-laid plans may have to incorporate demonetization-induced changes.

Its 690 seats this year; another 964 seats are up for grabs next year, with the general election to follow in 2019. This inescapable political imperative will weigh on finance minister Arun Jaitley's mind when he drafts India's economic policy. The battle for occupying popular mind space over the past two months is now telescoping into a two-year battle. And if the vast majority of Indians feel confounded after Prime Minister Narendra Modi's surgical excision of 86% of currency, they shouldn't despair: They are in the distinguished company of Jaitley who, presumably, is equally disconcerted.

Jaitley will soon be presenting the 2017-18 budget and his well-laid plans may have to incorporate demonetization-induced changes, over and above those included for introducing the goods and services tax (GST) system. What's worse, with the GST start likely to be postponed, revenue projections may now have to be recast along traditional lines. Two huge changes in three months is more than just a rude disruption.

Arun Jaitley has little option in slashing the outlay for social sector schemes, especially when demonetization has eroded rural incomes.
Photo: Pradeep Gaur / Mint

Two other elements add to the confusion. One, the railway budget will be merged with the Union budget this year in a meaningful break from a meaningless tradition. Also, the traditional expenditure reporting format under the broad heads of Plan and non-Plan expenditure will be jettisoned.

Standing for a moment in Jaitley's shoes, what's likely to be more worrying is how the economic slowdown affects revenue growth and how that shapes spending plans—especially committed social sector or infrastructure expenditure—that cannot be trimmed, leave alone eliminated. Jaitley has already **promised** higher government pump-priming to boost economic growth. Many new variables have cropped up in the meantime, further skewing the math. Modi contributed gamely during his 31 December speech with promises to increase social spending under both new and old schemes.

For example, new interest subventions on small housing loans and farm loans or increases in the number of rural houses built for the poor under the Pradhan Mantri Awas Yojana are some of the schemes which might expand both capital and revenue expenditure bills for 2017-18. It is clear that Jaitley has little option in slashing the outlay for social sector schemes, especially when demonetization has eroded rural incomes and the ruling Bharatiya Janata Party is unable to dismount the election treadmill. Apart from state assembly elections for Uttar Pradesh, Punjab, Goa, Uttarakhand and Manipur in less than a month, next year will see elections in Tripura, Rajasthan, Madhya Pradesh, Karnataka, Chhattisgarh, Nagaland, Mizoram and Meghalaya.

With the political economy constraining deep spending cuts— at the most, outlays might be shuffled around under different schemes—revenue generation becomes imperative for meeting many of the grand spending plans. This is where rubber hits tarmac.

The demonetization narrative focused on cornering tax evaders and, through legislative amendments, forcing assesses depositing unreported incomes to pay higher penal rates. This would require enhanced tax scrutiny and inevitably involve some element of persecution. But by stating that demonetization was launched to punish currency hoarders, it subjected the majority to widespread suffering for the misdemeanors of a few. The messaging was subsequently imbued with nationalist overtones and repurposed to focus on moving India to a less cash economy.

Enter the good cop: News reports claimed that Jaitley had hinted at lower tax rates in a meeting with tax officers, citing how similar attempts earlier had met with success. News leaks from unidentified finance ministry sources also made similar claims.

Jaitley later seemed to deny his statement without actually denying it. There's no text of Jaitley's speech; only a summary is available, which has him stating there was an urgent need for a change of mindset: "India has to move towards a mindset of voluntary compliance…payment of legitimate taxes should be considered as part of the process and nobody should think that tax evasion is acceptable."

This is where things get muddied up. By using the term "mindset", Jaitley pivots seamlessly into the arcane world of behavioural economics. It is reassuring to note that Jaitley recognizes the importance of mindset in correcting tax compliance behaviour. But his public musings betray a contradiction. Initiating mindset change is a long-term project which involves altering social norms using a combination of psychological and social forces. The post-demonetization regime instead uses a carrot-and-stick approach: simultaneously offering incentives (aka the Laffer curve) and disincentives (penalties).

The World Bank's World Development Report 2015—titled "Mind, Society and Behavior"—states clearly that penalties or incentives have failed to improve tax compliance across the world. The UK government's behavioural insights team, also known as the "nudge unit", claims to have used behavioural sciences successfully to improve tax compliance in the UK and other countries. Jaitley will do well to remember that like liquor prohibition failed to stem alcoholism and related social problems, a one-time demonetization (or a subsequent penal regime) might not be enough to raise tax revenue on a sustainable basis. While the impact of behavioural sciences in influencing policy outcomes is still imprecise, one thing is clear: lasting changes in social norms require long-term investments.

Rajrishi Singhal is a consultant and former editor of a leading business newspaper. His Twitter handle is @rajrishisinghal.

http://www.livemint.com/Opinion/gQo8ClEWetvp00FMJS6aIL/Demonetisation-and-budgets-all-in-the-mind.html?li_source=LI&li_medium=news_rec

Chapter-2: Economic Survey 2017

2.1 Economic Survey will be tabled in the Parliament shortly. Know your Economic Survey

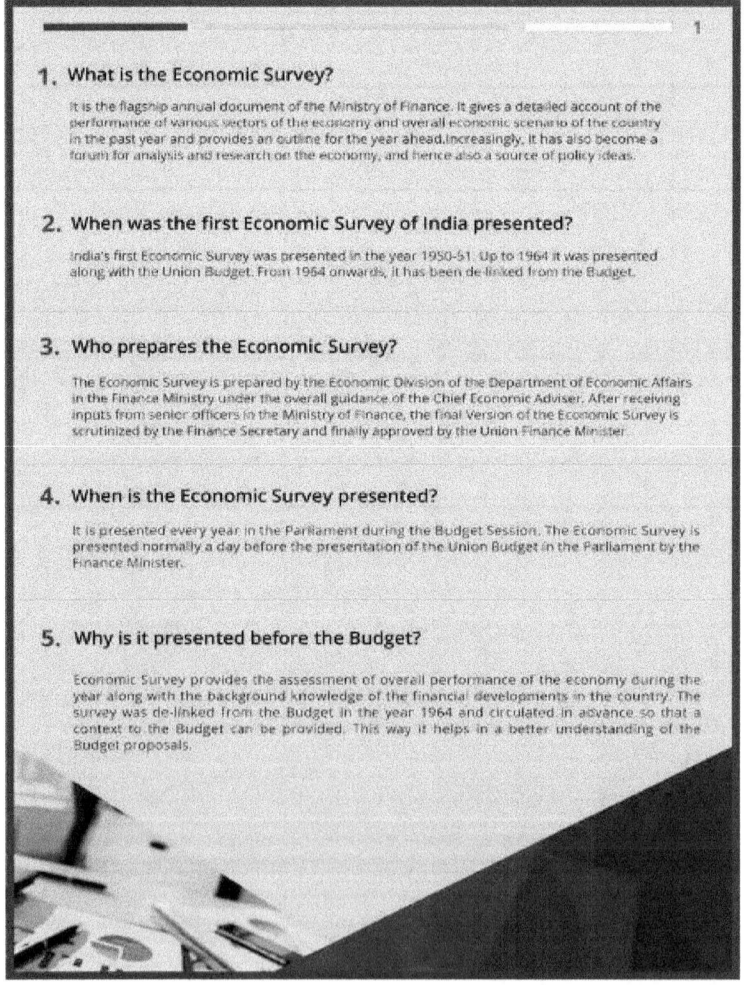

11.06 AM

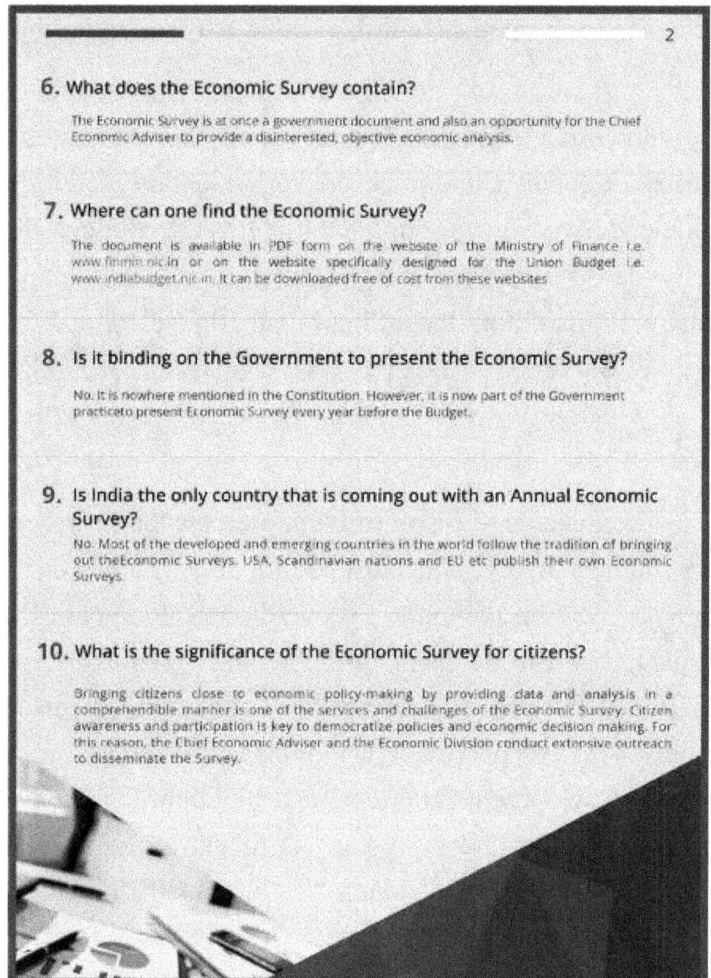

6. What does the Economic Survey contain?

The Economic Survey is at once a government document and also an opportunity for the Chief Economic Adviser to provide a disinterested, objective economic analysis.

7. Where can one find the Economic Survey?

The document is available in PDF form on the website of the Ministry of Finance i.e. www.finmin.nic.in or on the website specifically designed for the Union Budget i.e. www.indiabudget.nic.in. It can be downloaded free of cost from these websites

8. Is it binding on the Government to present the Economic Survey?

No. It is nowhere mentioned in the Constitution. However, it is now part of the Government practice to present Economic Survey every year before the Budget.

9. Is India the only country that is coming out with an Annual Economic Survey?

No. Most of the developed and emerging countries in the world follow the tradition of bringing out the Economic Surveys. USA, Scandinavian nations and EU etc publish their own Economic Surveys.

10. What is the significance of the Economic Survey for citizens?

Bringing citizens close to economic policy-making by providing data and analysis in a comprehendible manner is one of the services and challenges of the Economic Survey. Citizen awareness and participation is key to democratize policies and economic decision making. For this reason, the Chief Economic Adviser and the Economic Division conduct extensive outreach to disseminate the Survey.

10:54 AM

2.2 What is Economic Survey? When will it be presented?

By: FE Online | Updated: January 19, 2017 11:54 AM

The Finance Ministry of India presents the Economic Survey in the parliament every year, just before the Union Budget. This document is presented to both houses of Parliament during the Budget Session.

Throwing some clarity on when the Budget 2017 will be presented, Cabinet Committee on Parliamentary Affairs on Tuesday recommended advancing the holding of the Budget Session from January 31 followed by the presentation of the Union Budget on February 1. Also, both the address of the President and tabling of the Economic Survey will take place on January 31. So, what exactly is Economic Survey? *All those who don't know what it* is, *here is the answer:*

The Finance Ministry of India presents the Economic Survey in the parliament every year, just before the Union Budget. It is the ministry's view on the annual economic development of the country. A flagship annual document of the Ministry of Finance, Government of India, and Economic Survey reviews the developments in the Indian economy over the previous 12 months, summarizes the performance on major development programs, and highlights the policy initiatives of the government and the prospects of the economy in the short to medium term. This document is presented to both houses of Parliament during the Budget Session.

Meanwhile, early presentation of the Budget would mean that the entire exercise is over by March 31 and expenditure as well as tax proposals will come into effect right from the beginning of the new fiscal, thereby ensuring better implementation. As per the earlier practice, the budgetary exercise was completed only by mid-May and with the monsoon arriving in June, most of the schemes and spending by states did not take off until October, leaving just half-a-year for their implementation.

In September last year, ending a nearly a century-long practice, the Cabinet had decided to scrap a separate budget for the railways and merge it with the General Budget, presentation of which was decided to be advanced to spur spending and boost the economy. Earlier, the Budget approval process usually happened in two parts extending to the second or third week of May, hampering early implementation of schemes and spending programmes.*(With inputs from PTI)*

http://www.financialexpress.com/budget/budget-2017-what-is-economic-survey-when-will-it-be-presented-know-here/495185/

2.3 Economic Survey 2017 to be tabled in Parliament today: All you need to know

New Delhi, January 31, 2017 | UPDATED 12:31 IST

Prepared by the government's Chief Economic Advisor, Economic Survey makes recommendations to the government over key economic policies. However, it is for the government to implement or not the recommendations made. According to some reports, Chief Economic Advisor Arvind Subramanian is likely to suggest that the government to reduce corporate tax rates and also loan waivers for farmers.

Economic Survey, the government's economical report card for the financial year, will be tabled in Parliament today. Finance Minister Arun Jaitley will present the Economic Survey after President Pranab Mukherjee's address to the joint session of Parliament marking the beginning of the Budget Session.

HERE'S WHAT YOU NEED TO KNOW:

1. The Economic Survey is a document providing details of the economic performance of the country (the government) in the past one year.

2. The Economic Survey is prepared after the scrutiny of the data supplied by Central Statistical Office of Ministry of Statistics and Programme Implementation. Data can also be sought from other government agencies.

3. The draft Economic Survey is prepared by the department of economic affairs in the finance ministry. This draft is vetted by the Chief Economic Advisor to the government and economic affairs secretary in the finance ministry.

4. Union Finance Minister gives the final approval before the Economic Survey is tabled in Parliament.

5. The purpose of tabling the Economic Survey in Parliament is to explain the backdrop of the Budget for the next one year. Parliament is made aware about the economic and financial health of the country and the government before it scrutinises and clears the Budget.

6. As a practice, the Economic Survey is presented a day before the Budget.

7. Before 1964, Economic Survey document was circulated along with Budget papers. The first Economic Survey was presented in 1951 for 1950-51.

8. The Economic Survey also spells out the economic agenda of the government of the day.

9. Interestingly words Economic Survey and Budget are not mentioned in the Constitution. Though drive their authority from Article 112 of the Constitution, which says that the President (the

government) shall present the "annual financial statement" before Parliament. Such documents are commonly called budget borrowing the term and tradition from Britain.

10. While the Economic Survey is not a statutory obligation of the government, budget is a constitutional foundation for the Executive. Economic Survey is not a secret book as most of the data are already in public domain while the Budget is a confidential document and is prepared in utmost secrecy.

http://indiatoday.intoday.in/story/economic-survey-2017-to-be-tabled-in-parliament-today-all-you-need-to-know/1/870525.html

2.4 Economic Survey 2017: Everything you need to know

By: Express Web Desk | New Delhi | Updated: January 31, 2017 2:09 pm

The annual survey is expected to deliberate in depth on the economic logic behind demonetizing higher denomination notes of Rs. 1000 and Rs. 500 and its repercussions for the economy. Union Finance Minister Arun Jaitley will set the tone for the Union Budget by tabling the Economic Survey in Parliament on Tuesday. Authored by Chief Economic Adviser Arvind Subramanian, the annual survey is expected to shed light on the policy priorities of the government and give a detailed account of the state of the economy especially in the wake of demonetization drive.

What is Economic Survey and What does it feature?

The Economic Survey projects the official version of the state of the economy and is generally presented in Parliament a day before the presentation of the annual Budget. It acts as a precursor to the budget. It discusses the outlook, prospects and challenges of the economy while recommending reform measures that are essential to propel and thrive the economy.

Things to watch out in the Survey

The annual survey is expected to deliberate in depth on the economic logic behind demonetizing higher denomination notes of Rs. 1,000 and Rs. 500 and its repercussions for the economy. It is also expected to project an economic growth trajectory especially after the International Monetary Fund shaved its growth projection for India to 6.6% for 2016-17 and 7.2% in 2017-18 in view of the demonetization fallout. It is widely said that the survey will also be dealt with Universal Basic Income, which guarantees a minimum income to every citizen. In addition, it is expected to mention in detail the policy around various measures and the capacity of the economy to adjust to the new measures.

Are these recommendations mandatory for the government to follow?

These recommendations serve only as a policy guide as the government is not bound to follow them. Earlier, suggestions laid out in the economic survey were not followed in budget proposals on many occasions.

Opposition view point

Earlier on Monday, Congress painted a grim picture of the economy with former finance minister P Chidambaram saying he doesn't expect the economy to grow higher than 6.5 per cent in the next two financial years. He warned the ruling dispensation from projecting a "rosy picture" of the economy.

http://indianexpress.com/article/business/budget/union-budget-economic-survey-2017-everything-you-need-to-know-4500224/

2.5   Highlights Economic Survey 2017 explained in 12 points

BS Web Team | New Delhi January 31, 2017 Last Updated at 14:41 IST

The Economic Survey 2017, tabled in Parliament on Tuesday, projected that the country's gross domestic product (GDP) will grow by 6.75 per cent to 7.5 per cent in 2017-18.

CEA Arvind Subramanian - Photo: PTI

Here are 12 highlights of the Economic Survey 2017:

* **Demonetization impact:** The government says the adverse impact of demonetization on GDP growth will be transitional. Real GDP growth in 2017-18 is projected to be in the range of 6.75 – 7.5 per cent, once the cash supply is replenished.

* Industrial growth to cool: Growth rate of the industrial sector estimated to moderate to 5.2 per cent in 2016-17 from 7.4% last fiscal. The agriculture sector will grow at 4.1 per cent up in the current year than 1.2 per cent in 2015-16.

* Per-capita GSDP: Real per capita GSDP between 1983 and 2014 has shown across-the-board improvement.

* Remonetization: The Economic Survey 2017 has suggested quick remonetization, push for digitization, bringing land and real estate under GST ambit, reduction in taxes and stamp duties and an improved tax administration system as key reform measures to ensure long term economic benefits.

* States' performance: There has been an improvement in the financial position of states over the last few years. The average revenue deficit has been eliminated, while the average fiscal deficit was curbed to less than 3 percent of GSDP. The average debt to GSDP ratio has also fallen. Centre's Fiscal Responsibility and Budget Management (FRBM) Act, mirrored by Fiscal Responsibility Legislations (FRL) adopted in the States.

* NPAs: As per the Survey, gross NPAs have climbed to almost 12 per cent of gross advances for public sector banks at end-September 2016. At this level, India's NPA ratio is higher than any other major emerging market, with the exception of Russia. The consequent squeeze of banks has led them to slow credit growth to crucial sectors-especially to industry and medium and small scale enterprises (MSMEs)-to levels unseen over the past two decades. As this has occurred, growth in private and overall investment has turned negative. A decisive resolution is urgently needed.

* Asset rehabilitation: Survey suggests setting up of a centralized Public Sector Asset Rehabilitation Agency that will look after the largest, most difficult Cases, and make Politically Tough Decisions to reduce Debt.

* **Poor targeting:** According to the Survey, redistribution by the government is far from efficient in targeting the poor. The Survey points out that the capacity of the State in delivering essential services such as health and education is weak due to low capacity, with high levels of corruption, clientelism, rules and red tape. At the level of the states, competitive populism is more in evidence than competitive service delivery.

* **Universal Basic Income:** The Survey has advocated the concept of Universal Basic Income (UBI) as an alternative to the various social welfare schemes in an effort to reduce poverty. The Survey points out that the two prerequisites for a successful UBI are: (a) functional JAM (Jan Dhan, Aadhar and Mobile) system as it ensures that the cash transfer goes directly into the account of a beneficiary and (b) Centre-State negotiations on cost sharing for the programme.

* **Property tax:** A study done for the Survey shows that property tax potential is large and can be tapped to generate additional revenue at city level. Satellite imagery can be a useful tool for improving urban governance by facilitating better property tax compliance.

* **Job creation:** The Survey says Apparel and Leather industry are key to generation of formal and productive jobs: recommends reforms in labour and tax policies to make the Apparel and Leather sector globally competitive. The Survey adds that these sectors provide immense opportunities for creation of jobs for the weaker

sections, especially for women, and can become vehicles for broader social transformation in the country.

* **Labour migration:** New estimates of labour migration in India have revealed that inter-state labour mobility is significantly higher than previous estimates. Relatively poorer states such as Bihar and Uttar Pradesh have high net out-migration. Seven states take positive CMM values reflecting net in-migration: Goa, Delhi, Maharashtra, Gujarat, Tamil Nadu, Kerala and Karnataka. Policy actions to sustain and maximize the benefits of migration include: ensuring portability of food security benefits, providing healthcare and a basic social security framework for migrants – potentially through an inter-state self-registration process.

http://www.business-standard.com/budget/article/economic-survey-2017-explained-in-12-points-117013100579_1.html

2.6 Union Budget 2017: Economic Survey Indicative of Reformative Budget, says India Inc

By: PTI | New Delhi | Published: January 31, 2017 7:24 pm

The industry bodies have pitched for lowering personal as well as corporate income tax to boost demand in the Budget.

India's economic growth has been pegged at 6.5 per cent for the current fiscal, down from 7.6 per cent, but is expected to rebound in the range of 6.75-7.5 per cent in 2017-18. (Illustration by C R Sasikumar)

India Inc on Tuesday said the Economic Survey has correctly assessed challenges facing the country which is indicative of a bold and reformative Budget to be presented on Wednesday. Besides, industry captains feel that the 6.75-7.5 per cent GDP growth estimate for 2017-18 too can be achieved.

"The Survey, points to a likely bold and reformative Budget, which will have a strong focus on infrastructure, employment generation and easing business conditions. The issue of NPAs is most likely to be addressed coherently, along with taking stock of the PPP logjams.

"The survey scores on recognizing the economy's shortcomings, prescribing the required action and setting an optimistic and expectant tone for tomorrow's budget," KPMG India CEO Richard Rekhy said.

The industry bodies also pitched for lowering personal as well as corporate income tax to boost demand in the Budget.

"The Survey has rightly picked up the potential risks to the global economy and its impact on India in the form of higher oil prices, trade tensions from sharp currency movements and geo-political factors. An upsurge in protectionism that could affect India's exports, is surely a matter of concern," Assochem President Sunil Kanoria said.

CII described the 2016-17 report card of the state of the economy tabled by Finance Minister Arun Jaitley in Parliament as a forward-looking, comprehensive and objective analysis.

"We are hopeful that the Budget to be presented tomorrow would deal with the aspects of creating demand, especially through direct tax interventions on the personal income tax and corporate taxation side," CII Director General Chandrajit Banerjee said.

"To reap the long-term benefits of demonetization, there is a need to have follow-up actions such as providing a boost to demand, lowering of tax rates, widening of tax base and reforming the tax administration. We hope that the Union Budget to be presented tomorrow will include measures in these areas," Ficci President Pankaj Patel said.

"We are hopeful that the Budget to be presented tomorrow would deal with the aspects of creating demand, especially through direct tax interventions on the personal income tax and corporate taxation side," Banerjee said.

India's economic growth has been pegged at 6.5 per cent for the current fiscal; down from 7.6 per cent recorded in the last financial year, but is expected to rebound in the range of 6.75-7.5 per cent in 2017-18, according to the Economic Survey.

The Survey lists some of the challenges that might impede India's progress. These include ambivalence about property rights and the private sector, deficiencies in state capacity, especially in delivering essential services and inefficient redistribution.

http://indianexpress.com/article/business/budget/economic-survey-indicative-of-reformative-budget-says-india-inc-4501045/?gclid=COSp3PrngdICFdGKaAodOYQPsA

Has India managed to cushion Modi's note ban blow, will it be able to improve its export competitiveness in an age of protectionism, more importantly, can it keep its growth momentum on? These will be some of questions that today's Economic Survey will reveal. Track it live here.

01:54 AM

Population, performance & pollution find mention in Economic Survey

01:52 AM

Economic Survey: Agricultural growth to accelerate to 4.1% from 1.2% last fiscal

01:51 AM

Replacing PDS with DBT shows mixed results in Economic Survey

01:49 AM

Special category states can be testing ground for UBI

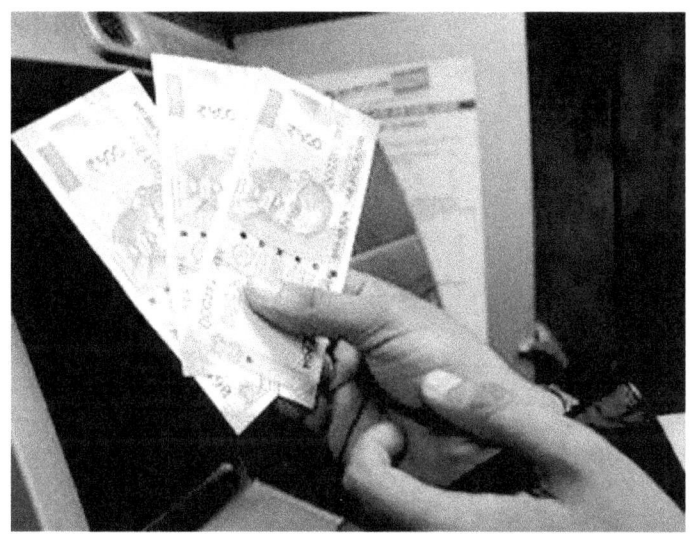

01:46 AM

Economic Survey hints at demonetization 'windfall' doles in Budget 2017

Falling oil prices had yielded an opportunity to raise duties on petroleum products by 1% of GDP in the last two years, but prices are now rising.

01:44 AM

Survey reminds us of Vikram Seth's 'A Suitable Boy' but without any characters

01:42 AM

Demonetization signals an important regime shift: Arvind Subramanian

01:39 AM

Economic Survey: No backing for any big fiscal push

01:33 AM

Private sector fears loom over divestment

The fear of being seen as favouring the private sector is one of the biggest impediments to PSU selloff plans.

01:25 AM

Economic Survey: Right time to outshine China in shoes and clothes

Despite lower wages than China, Vietnam, Bangladesh & Myanmar have outpaced India in apparel, footwear & leather sectors.

01:20 AM

Economic Survey finds rupee to be not so overvalued

01:10 AM

ARC not the most efficient solution: Zarin Daruwala, Standard Chartered Bank

The government should continue its focus on boosting capital investment in sectors with higher multiplier effects on GDP growth: the railways, roads and housing are three such sectors.

01:00 AM

Economic Survey: No credit to global rating agencies

Criticized for methodologies and the differential treatment, it is shown towards India and China.

12:48 AM

Demonetization can yield long-term benefits

Agricultural sowing, passenger car sales and overall excise taxes bear little imprint of demonetization.

12:41 AM

Public Sector Asset Rehabilitation Agency may be set up to buy bad loans

10:34 PM

India ranks fourth globally in wind power installation: Economic Survey

"As a result of various actions in the right direction, India attained 4th position in global wind power installed capacity after China, USA and Germany," it said.

10:29 PM

Resources misallocated under rural employment scheme: Economic Survey

The survey said the poorest areas of the country often obtain a lower share of government resources when compared to their richer counterparts.

09:34 PM

TBS is taking a heavy toll on the health of public sector banks, the Survey presented in Parliament said.

09:21 PM

According to the Economic Survey, in terms of income convergence, Indian states offer a striking contrast to the catch-up that is happening globally -- poorer countries are catching up with the richer ones.

09:14 PM

"Given the pressing need to redistribute, India did not invest sufficiently in human capital - for instance, public spending on health was an unusually low 0.22% of GDP in 1950-51.

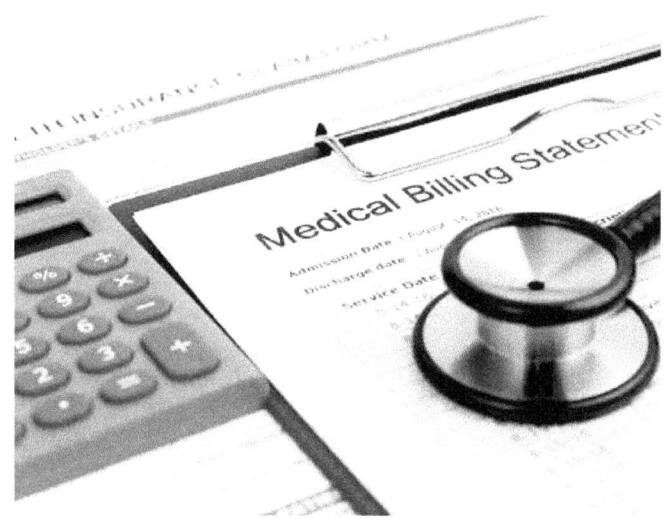

08:43 PM

US fiscal policy will impact capital flows to India: Economic Survey

The pre-Budget document said the markets are factoring in a regime change in advanced countries, especially the US macroeconomic policy, with high expectations.

08:30 PM

Economic Survey 2016-17: Is the rupee overvalued?

Contrary to popular belief that India has been losing competitiveness due to high inflows, the country has maintained its competitiveness.

08:15 PM

India needs to keep close watch on global developments: Economic Survey

From India's perspective, it said, the political carrying capacity for globalization is relevant not just for goods but also services. The world's service exports-GDP ratio is about 6.1%.

07:52 PM

Amazon to take down pirated copies of Economic Survey if GoI complains

Unless there is a flag on the seller about a fraud or abuse by the copyright owner, online marketplaces don't delist products.

07:22 PM

Effort was to make Economic Survey look like Big B blockbuster: CEA

The Oxford-educated economist pointed to a lot of discussion on the role and contents of the Economic Survey in recent times.

07:18 PM

Demonetization stick now needs incentives as carrots: Economic Survey

07:09 PM

Digitalization must be incentivized and the incentives must be borne by the public sector entities (government / RBI) and not the consumer or financial intermediaries.

Economic Survey is being a bit pessimistic: Rajiv Kumar, FICCI

07:06 PM

In a first, FM Arun Jaitley authors a section of Economic Survey

"The Survey has greatly benefitted from the comments and insights of the Hon'ble Finance Minister Arun Jaitley, who also authors a section in the Survey."

07:00 PM

India one of world's largest recipients of FDI: Economic Survey

FDI is running at an annual rate of USD 75 billion, which is not far short of the amounts that China was receiving at the height of its growth boom in the mid-2000s.

05:44 PM

Survey indicative of reformative Budget: India Inc

Besides, industry captains feel that the 6.75-7.5 per cent GDP growth estimate for 2017-18 too can be achieved.

05:28 PM

Try biometric attendance to tackle teacher absenteeism: Survey

Scope of implementation should leave room for flexibility at the local level so the same do not end up as top driven 'Model Schools'.

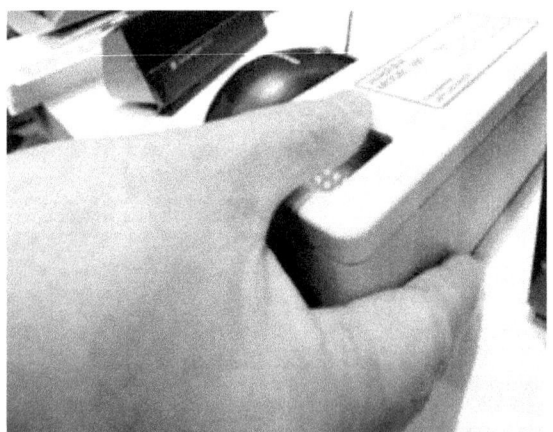

05:28 PM

Highways construction, cargo, power-gen record growth: Survey

Also, customs and port clearances take 6 days here as compared to 1.5 days in China and 3 days in Sri Lanka.

05:12 PM

Major achievements according to Economic Survey this year include:

1. **GST**
2. **Bankruptcy bill**
3. **Monetary Policy Committee**
4. **Aadhaar Bill**
5. **FDI liberalization**
6. **UPI: Inter-Operability and Making the "M" in Jam a reality**
7. **Promoting labour-intensive sectors (apparels and made-ups)**

04:52 PM

CEA Arvind Subramanian 's satellite gaze at Bengaluru: Pay more taxes

The survey stresses the need to adopt the latest satellite based techniques to map urban properties.

04:51 PM

Give workers option to choose social security schemes: Economic Survey

The survey also suggested providing the workers a choice between Employees' Provident Fund Organization (EPFO) and National Pension Scheme (NPS).

04:49 PM

Economic Survey pitches for bringing land, real estate under GST

It went on to term the constitutional bill that enabled GST as "transformational".

04:49 PM

India should reduce dependency on fossil fuels: Economic Survey

On India's fossil fuel use from long-term perspective, the Survey said that so far the country's reliance on fossil fuels remains "well below" China.

04:44 PM

Subsidy bill up by 5 per cent in April-November 2016: Economic Survey

In the Budget for this fiscal, the subsidies on food, fertilizer and petroleum were pegged lower at nearly Rs. 2.31 lakh crores.

03:59 PM

India should play proactive role in promoting open global markets

The environment for global trade policy "has probably" undergone a paradigm shift in the aftermath of Brexit and the US elections, the survey added.

03:56 PM

Full remonetization of economy in 1-2 months: Arvind Subramanian

He said there should be a quick remonetization and the earlier the limits on cash withdrawals are withdrawn, the better.

03:37 PM

Economic Survey 2016-17: Impact of demonetization from the horse's mouth

03:25 PM

The Survey says that post demonetization, real estate prices have declined, as wealth has fallen, while cash shortages impeded transactions.

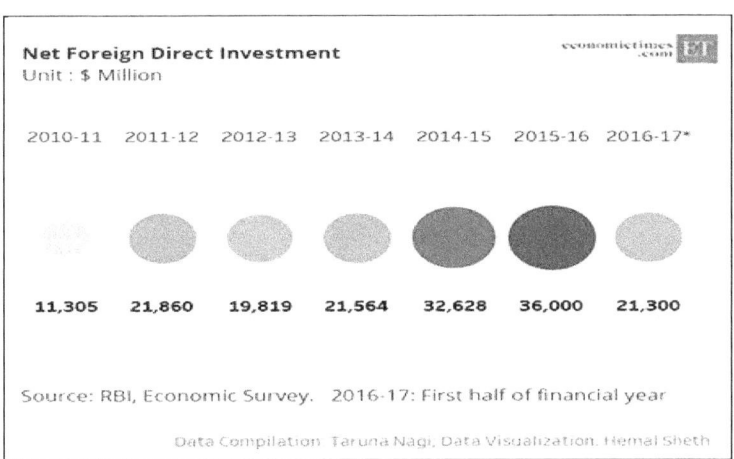

The net FDI flows of US$ 21.3 billion recorded a growth of about 29 per cent over the corresponding period of last year: Economic Survey 2017

03:25 PM

"Demonetization could have the particularly profound impact on the real estate sector," it said in an analysis on the impact of note ban announced on November 8.

03:24 PM

A trend reversal of WPI inflation is seen, from a trough of (-) 5.1 percent in August 2015 to 3.4 percent at end-December 2016, on the back of rising international oil prices: Economic Survey 2017.

03:17 PM

Current account deficit (CAD) narrowed in the first half (H1) of 2016-17 to 0.3% of GDP

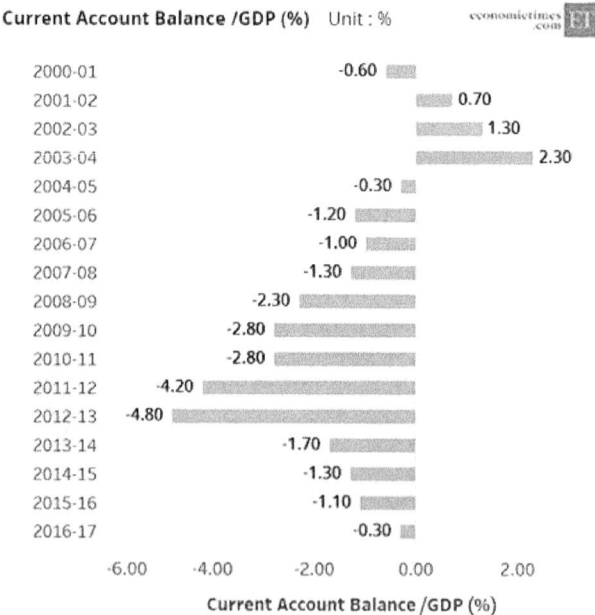

Current Account Balance /GDP (%)   Unit : %

	Current Account Balance /GDP (%)
2000-01	-0.60
2001-02	0.70
2002-03	1.30
2003-04	2.30
2004-05	-0.30
2005-06	-1.20
2006-07	-1.00
2007-08	-1.30
2008-09	-2.30
2009-10	-2.80
2010-11	-2.80
2011-12	-4.20
2012-13	-4.80
2013-14	-1.70
2014-15	-1.30
2015-16	-1.10
2016-17	-0.30

Source: RBI, Economic Survey 2017.
2016-17 :First half of financial year

Data Compilation: Taruna Nagi, Data Visualization: Hemal Sheth

03:06 PM

Argument against Universal Basic Income

02:58 PM

Arguments in favour of Universal Basic Income

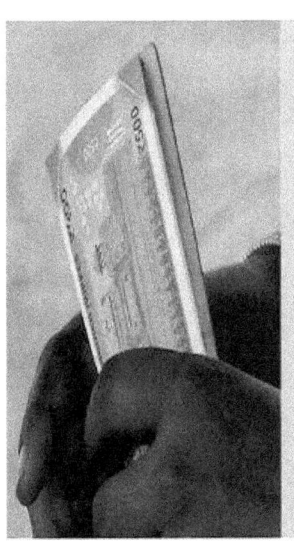

02:53 PM

Eco Survey calls the bluff of rating agencies, says come back to assess us after half a century

The survey talked about 'contrasting experiences' of change in sovereign ratings assigned by rating agencies to China and India over the past couple of years.

02:51 PM

UBI an alternative to subsidies for poverty alleviation: Economic Survey

02:50 PM

Need to modify FRBM Act for tomorrow's India: Economic Survey

It said the country's fiscal experience has underscored the fundamental validity of the fiscal policy principles enshrined in the FRBM Act, 2003.

02:48 PM

CEA Arvind Subramanian estimates basic income for the poor: Rs 7,620 p.a.

Subramanian writes it is not an easy calculation because it depends on a number of objectives and assumptions.

02:46 PM

Gandhi knew better than 'Marxists, market messiahs, materialists and behaviouralists': CEA

Subramanian says UBI provides cash transfers which respects, not dictates, recipients' choices.

02:46 PM

ECO SURVEY CALLS RATING AGENCIES' BLUFF

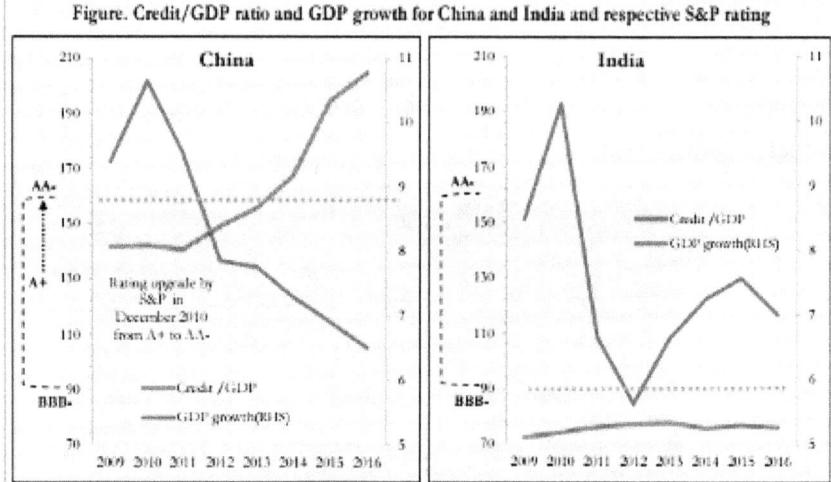

Figure. Credit/GDP ratio and GDP growth for China and India and respective S&P rating

Source: WDI and S&P; for 2016, India's credit data are from RBI and Credit Suisse; for 2016, China's credit number is obtained by adding flows of total social financing (TSF) from the Bank for International Settlements (BIS) to the 2015 stock obtained from the WDI.

02:26 PM

Economic Survey pitches for more local tax on property

The analysis carried out for the survey has found that greater service delivery is correlated with more resources, own revenue, staffing and capital spending per capita.

02:25 PM

Economic Survey moots formation of public sector asset rehabilitation agency

As per the survey, gross NPAs has climbed to almost 12 per cent of gross advances for public sector banks at end-September 2016.

02:24 PM

Was Modi's note ban worth the trouble? Read what Economic Survey says

02:23 PM

Universal income better help than subsidies: Economic Survey

02:22 PM

<u>Real estate prices to fall further; may see some uptick after</u>
<u>GST: Economic Survey</u>

02:20 PM

Potential #UBI cost: 4-5% of GDP. Middle-class & other
subsidies: 2-3%. UBI can't be add-on to other schemes.

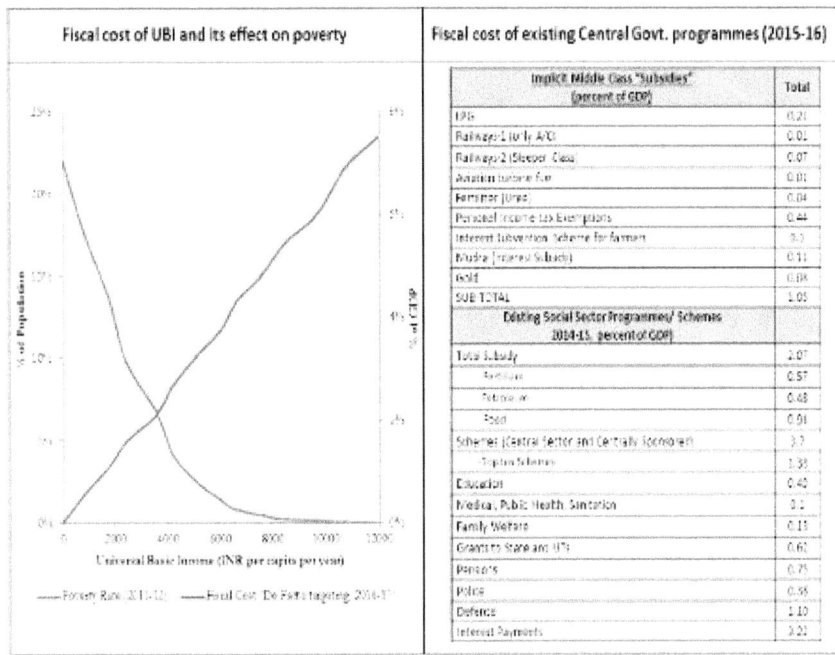

02:20 PM

While the Economic Survey highlighted that recovery from demonetization will need policy stimulus, the focus remains on fiscal prudence as well which bodes well.

- Shibani Kurian, Senior Vice-President & Head of Equity Research, Kotak Mutual Fund

02:19 PM

UBI to overcome weak targeting: for 6 largest schemes, high correlation b/w poverty & resource shortfall.

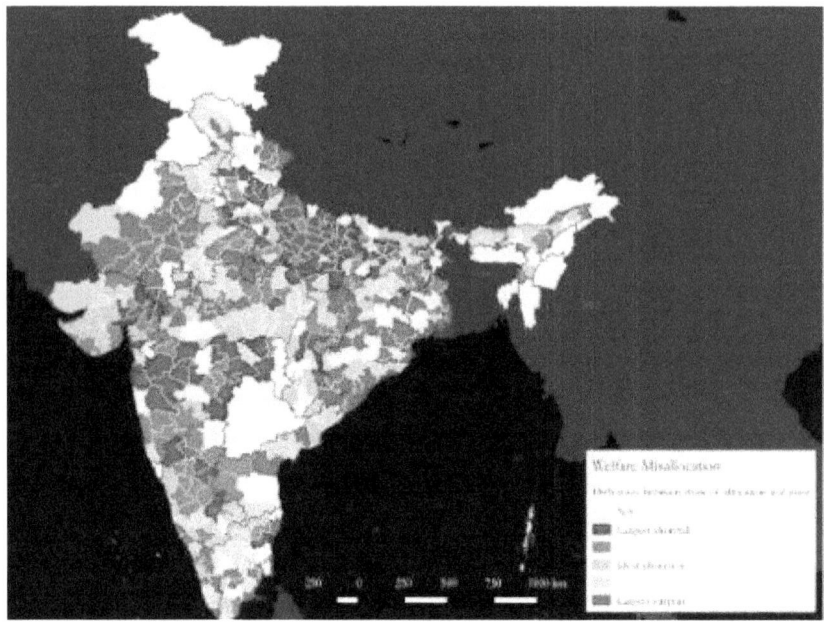

02:18 PM

#UBI to overcome weak targeting: for 6 largest schemes, high correlation b/w poverty & resource shortfall.

02:17 PM

Is it time to consider a Universal Basic Income? What would the Mahatma have thought of the idea?

> *"I will give you a talisman. Whenever you are in doubt, or when the self becomes too much with you, apply the following test. Recall the face of the poorest and the weakest man [woman] whom you may have seen, and ask yourself, if the step you contemplate is going to be of any use to him [her]. Will he [she] gain anything by it? Will it restore him [her] to a control over his [her] own life and destiny? In other words, will it lead to swaraj [freedom] for the hungry and spiritually starving millions? Then you will find your doubts and yourself melt away." -*
> *Mahatma Gandhi*
>
> *"My ahimsa would not tolerate the idea of giving a free meal to a healthy person who has not worked for it in some honest way, and if I had the power I would stop every Sadwarta when free meals are given. It has degraded the nation and it has*

encouraged laziness, idleness, hypocrisy and even crime. Such misplaced charity adds nothing to the wealth of the country, whether material or spiritual, and gives a false sense of meritoriousness to the donor. How nice and wise it would be if the donor were to open the institutions where they would give meals under healthy, clean surroundings to men and women who would work for them... only the rule should be: no labour, no meal." — *Mahatma Gandhi*

02:16 PM

Decay in States' fiscal consolidation; Centre must take lead as fiscal challenges mount (Pay Commission, UDAY bonds etc.)

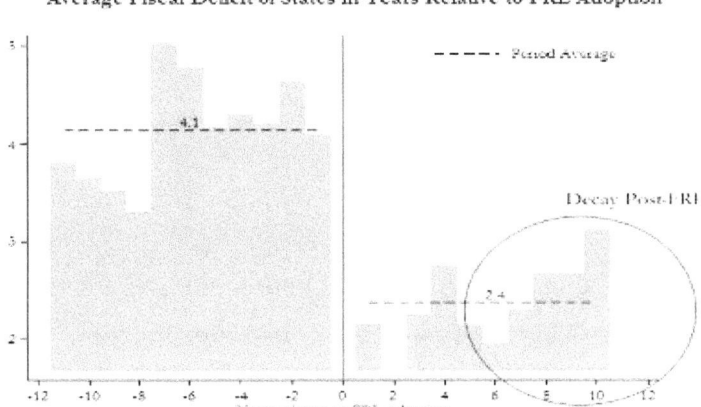

Average Fiscal Deficit of States in Years Relative to FRL Adoption

Note: FRL is Fiscal Responsibility Legislation

02:14 PM

Desisting from splurging not belt-tightening is probably the real contribution of FRL in States' fiscal consolidation.

Figure 9. Decomposition of Change in Deficits before and after FRL

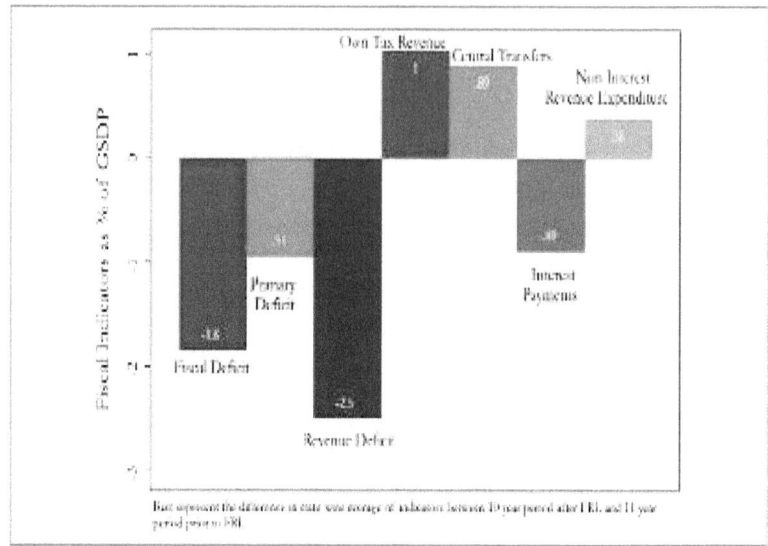

02:13 PM

Stock challenge: debt decline should rely less on favourable growth and more on primary balance adjustment. We will come to know of the benefits and the cons of demonetization, maybe in the next six months or so. It is too premature. Right now, of course, it is anybody's guess. There are people who feel the impact demonetization would be felt after two quarters and that growth will pick up after that. And then there are people who feel the bottom is almost done and we may see a V-shaped recovery starting from this quarter. On top of it, we still have global uncertainties, emerging particularly from west and of course, that will also impact the oil prices -- so that risk always remains.

- Jayesh Mehta, Bank of America-Merrill Lynch

02:12 PM

Figure 4. General Government Debt, Primary Balance and Interest
Rate-Nominal Growth Differential

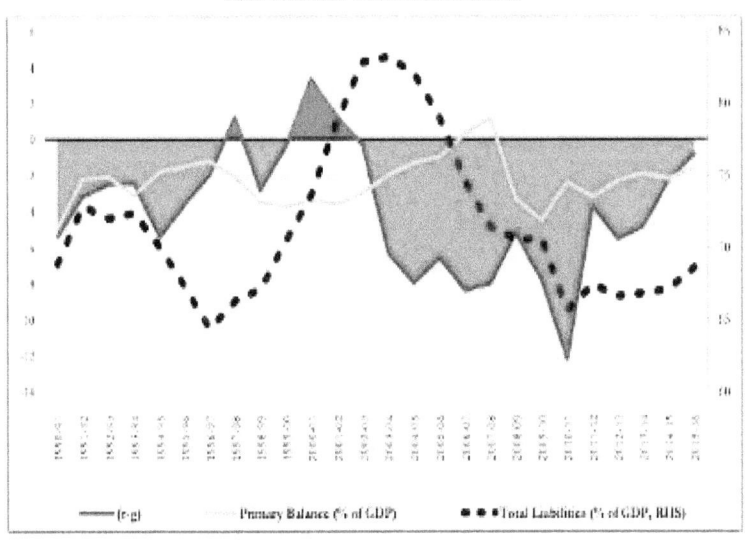

Source: RBI, Budget documents and Survey estimates.

02:12 PM

Economic Survey's headline GDP growth forecast for FY18 at 6.75-7.5 per cent is slightly below market expectations of 7.5-8.0 per cent. The key reason, which the government has given, is demonetization. The other two reasons are higher oil prices and global trade tensions.

- Nikhil Gupta, Economist at Motilal Oswal Financial Services

02:11 PM

Focus on debt resolution. Create a Govt. backed centralized Public Asset Rehabilitation Agency-PARA-to sort most complex cases.

02:10 PM

Steady fiscal consolidation by Centre in last 3 yrs should help address two major fiscal challenges: (1) flow & (2) stock.

Gross Fiscal Deficit of Central Government (% of GDP)

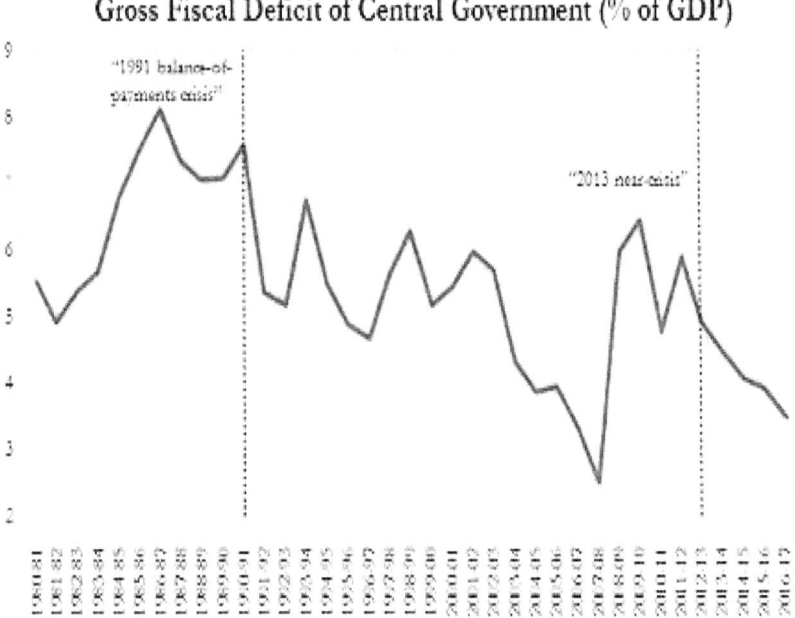

02:10 PM

The festering Twin Balance Sheet problem ails banks` AND companies. Real credit and investment growth negative.

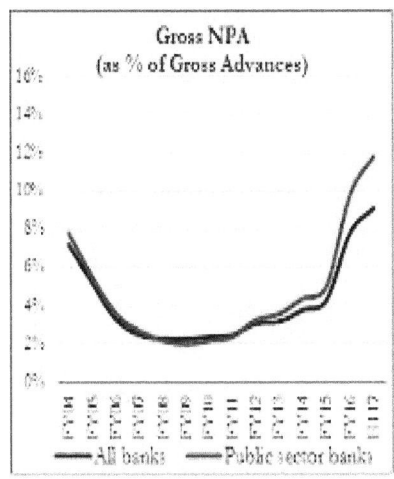 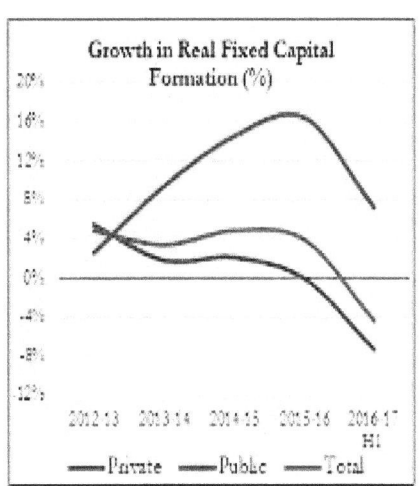

02:08 PM

We should abandon bold changes on the tax rate and we expect that corporate taxes will come down in line with the finance minister's plan a few years ago but hopefully exemptions will close commensurate so that from the government's perspective it is revenue neutral and from the taxpayers perspective it is a much simpler tax system that will hopefully improve compliance.

- Sajjid Z Chinoy, Chief India Economist, JPMorgan

02:07 PM

Demonetization is a very unique move.

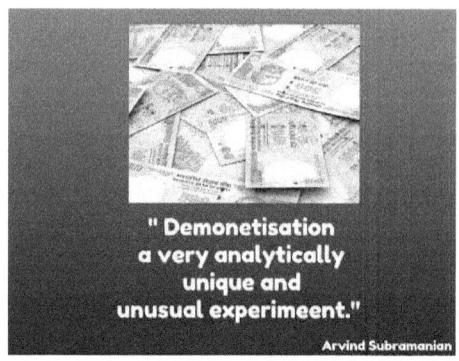

02:06 PM

On another hand, correct to analyze impact in current year, with & without demonetization

- Chief Economic Advisor Arvind Subramanian

02:06 PM

Bank credit affected by demonetization has come down. Overall picture is mixed

- Arvind Subramanian

02:05 PM

Less developed states are likely to grow relatively faster due to the demographic dividend. Exceptions: MP, OD, WB, CHH

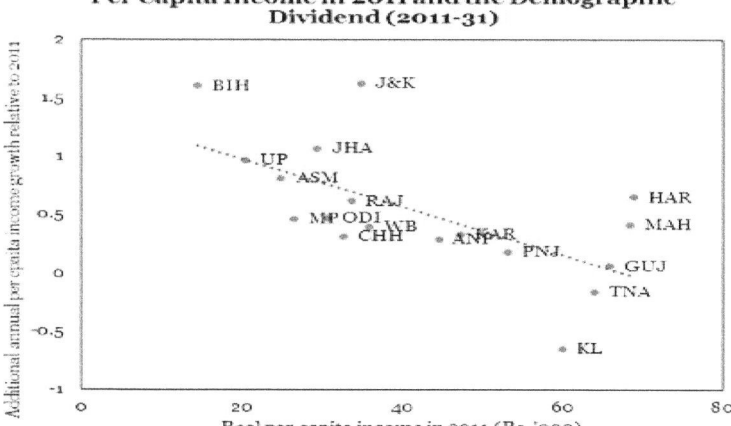

02:04 PM

Aim of demonetization is to bring down real estate prices: Arvind Subramanian

02:02 PM

India's unique demographic dividend 2: large divide in share of work-age pop & fertility b/w peninsular & hinterland states

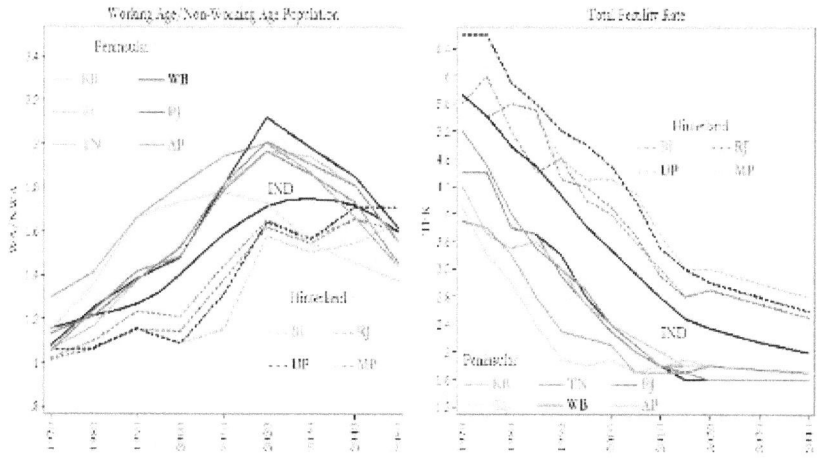

02:01 PM

India's unique demographic dividend 1: peak work-age pop to plateau soon, lower level, but last longer. Cause: slow TFR drop

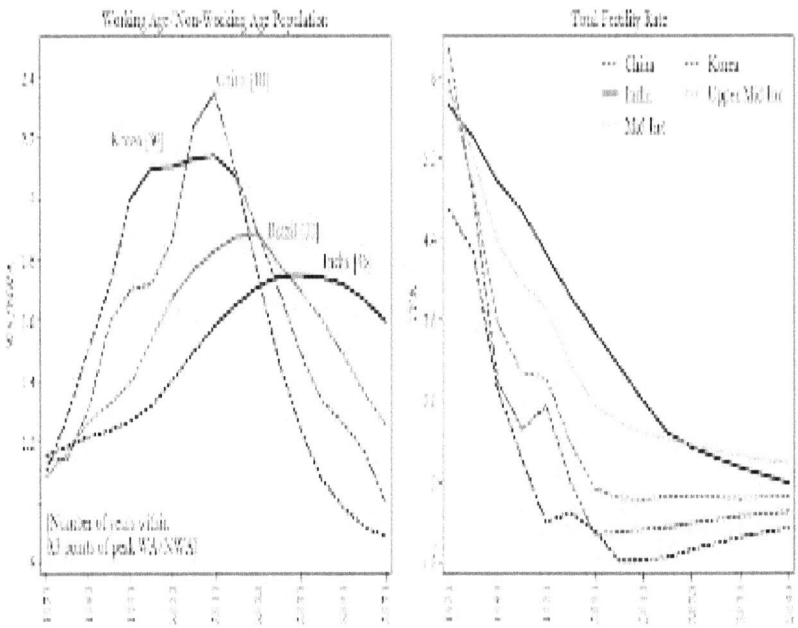

01:59 PM

What demonetization has done is both simultaneously reduced supply of cash, but by the same token it has increased supply of deposits: CEA

01:58 PM

If you could scrap the existing subsidies and just have one targeted universal basic income I have no problems with it but in all likelihood this is going to be one more subsidy and that is an absolute no-no given our fiscal situation.

- Mythili Bhusnurmath

01:58 PM

Economic Survey on note ban: More long-term gain than short-term pain

01:57 PM

Economic Survey cautions on loosening fiscal deficit goals

01:56 PM

Economic Survey points out three threats to India's progress

01:55 PM

Little intrigued by the argument in a survey which talks about a fiscal windfall really from the notes not returned - *Mythili Bhusnurmath*

01:54 PM

Demonetization has affected different forms of money very differently - *Arvind Subramanian*

01:52 PM

Macro stability is fundamental stability any government needs.

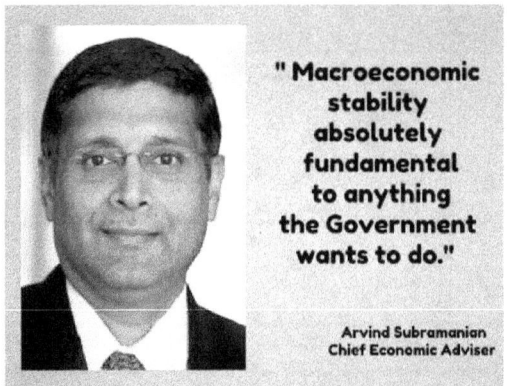

01:51 PM

We have survived two major shocks in 2016; volatility of US elections and demonetization - *Chief Economic Advisor Arvind Subramanian*

01:51 PM

Easy to become complacent about macro eco-stability - *Arvind Subramanian*

01:51 PM

A good economic survey must be purposeful and objective - *Arvind Subramanian*

01:48 PM

Arvind Subramanian said: GST, Bankruptcy Bill, Monetary policy Committee, Aadhaar Bill, FDI liberalization, UPI and promotion of labour-intensive sectors are major achievements of last year.

01:45 PM

The past year has had robust macroeconomic stability - *Arvind Subramanian, Chief Economic Adviser*

01:43 PM

We have survived two major shocks in 2016; volatility of US elections and demonetization - *Arvind Subramanian*

01:42 PM

A good economic survey must be purposeful and objective - *Chief economic adviser Arvind Subramanian*

01:41 PM

CEA Arvind Subramanian addresses media after tabling of Economic Survey

01:39 PM

Demonetization cash squeeze to be completely eliminated by April 2017 unlike February that many spoke about.

01:38 PM

You could still get a good recovery on the product side because there is no real loss. The buildup of inventory is there is postponement of production and sales all that is adjustable but again we do not have any basis in history or past data to be able to say it which is why I have this big band of plus minus 1% uncertainty. - *Dr Arvind Virmani, Former ED IMF & CEA, MoF*

01:37 PM

This is the first time that I am putting a big band of plus minus 1% and that has never happened before, I have been doing forecast for 20 years in and outside the government. - *Dr Arvind Virmani, Former ED IMF & CEA, MoF*

01:37 PM

Capital inflows in India no lower than average emerging market

01:37 PM

The thematic discussion at this point is more meaningful rather than a point estimate which is fraught with uncertainty - *Sajjid Z Chinoy, Chief India Economist, JPMorgan*

01:36 PM

Given the quantum of uncertainty because of the standard errors are going to be very large. We should obsess less about what the exact growth number and focus more on what the growth drivers will be because if exports cease to be a growth driver, where will we get the growth from? - *Sajjid Z Chinoy, Chief India Economist, JPMorgan*

01:35 PM

Average real estate prices in 8 major cities which were on a decline fell further post demonetization

01:31 PM

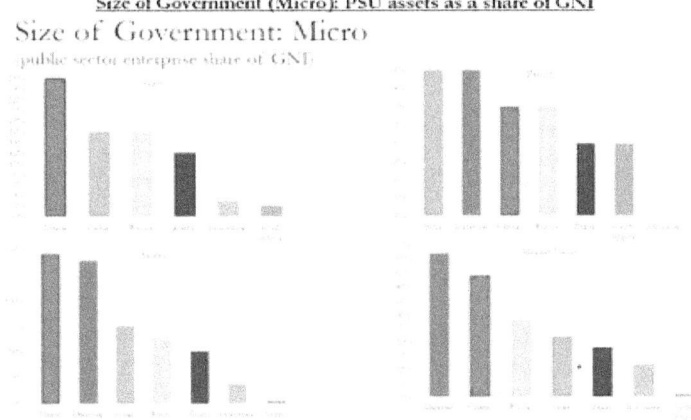

Size of Government (Micro): PSU assets as a share of GNI

Size of Government: Micro
public sector enterprise share of GNI

Size of Indian public sector both in micro-efficiency terms and in a macro-fiscal sense is not large: #Economic Survey

01:30 PM

Capital inflows into India are no lower than in the average emerging market

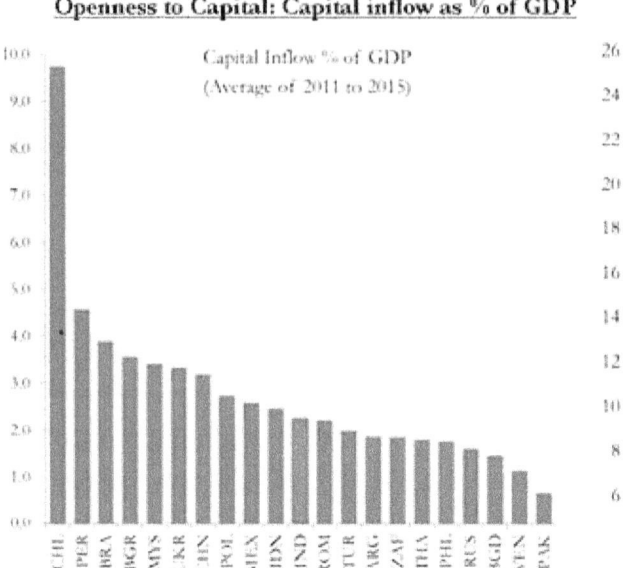

01:30 PM

Size of Indian public sector both in micro-efficiency terms and in a macro-fiscal sense is not large.

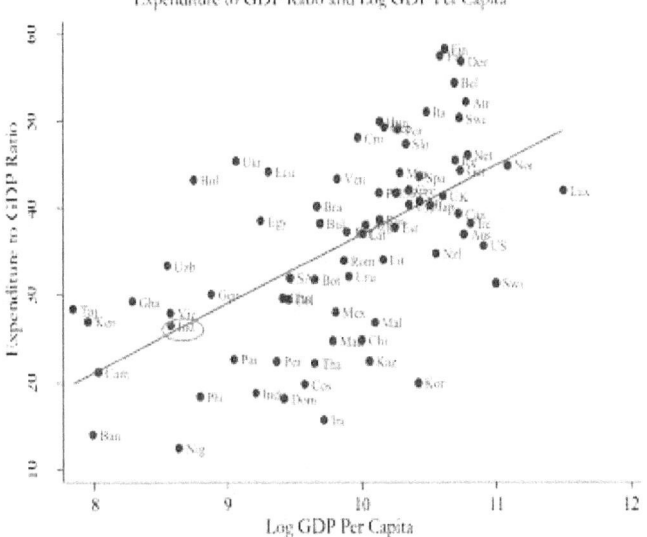

01:29 PM

Eco Survey 2017: FY17 industrial growth seen at 5.2% vs. 7.4% YoY

01:27 PM

As Economic Survey projects slower growth; market recovers a bit

01:26 PM

Economic Survey, however, predicts that it 'Should gradually stabilize as the economy is remonetized'.

01:24 PM

Demonetization has short-term costs but has potential for long term benefits.

01:23 PM

Major challenge to re-establish private investment, exports as drivers of growth; reduce reliance on government, private consumption

01:23 PM

Government made considerable efforts to reduce subsidies in petroleum in past two year.

01:23 PM

India's trade-GDP ratio is now greater than China's: #Economic Survey

01:23 PM

Demonetization: For maximum benefits and minimum costs - fast remonetization, bring real estate into GST, lower taxes, stable tax admin

01:22 PM

The past year witnessed a number of legislative accomplishments, including GST: #Economic Survey'

Demonetization led to an increase in uncertainty leading to firms and households postponing purchases, says Economic Survey

01:20 PM

UPI can unleash the power of mobile phones in achieving digitalization of payments & financial inclusion: Economic Survey

01:20 PM

The year also saw a number of legislative accomplishments. In addition to the GST, the government:

- *Overhauled the bankruptcy laws so that the "exit" problem that pervades the Indian economy – with deleterious consequences highlighted in last year's Survey – can be addressed effectively and expeditiously;*
- *Codified the institutional arrangements on monetary policy with the Reserve Bank of India (RBI), to consolidate the gains from macroeconomic stability by ensuring that inflation control will be less susceptible to the whims of individuals and the caprice of governments; and*
- *Solidified the legal basis for Aadhaar, to realize the long-term gains from the JAM trifecta (Jan-dhan-Aadhaar-Mobile)*

01:20 PM

Macroeconomic Indicators of the economy remain robust.

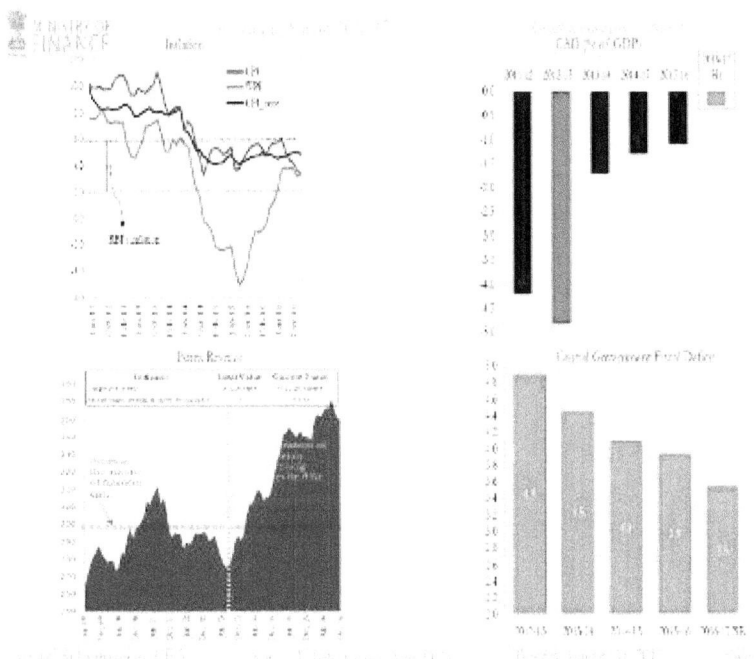

01:20 PM

The past year witnessed a number of legislative accomplishments, including GST

01:19 PM

Credibility will be strengthened if demonetization is accompanied by complementary measures

01:19 PM

Three risks to India's growth in FY18 – note ban, pricey oil, global trade tensions

01:18 PM

Demonetization 4: Temporary? In real GDP growth of ¼ - ½% pt relative to baseline - Growth back toward trend in FY18

01:18 PM

Economic Survey says Demonetization led to job losses, decline in farm incomes, social disruption, especially in cash-intensive sectors

01:17 PM

Demonetization 3: Unusual. Currency declined sharply BUT deposits increased sharply- hence hard to estimate impact Eco Survey

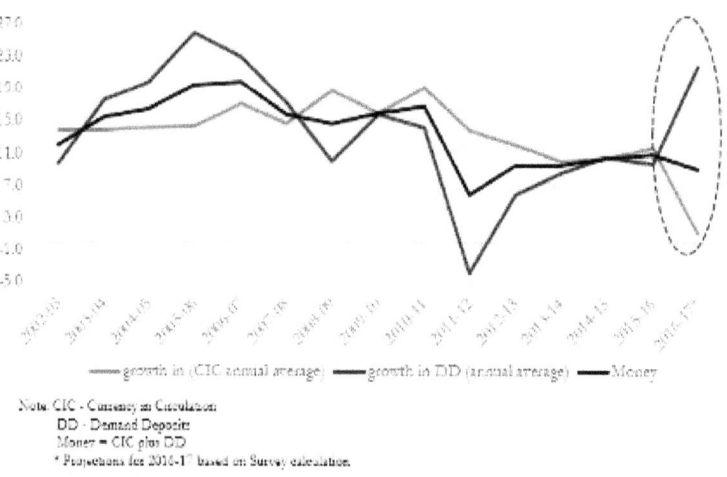

Note: CIC - Currency in Circulation
DD - Demand Deposit
Money = CIC plus DD
* Projections for 2016-17 based on Survey calculation

01:16 PM

Fiscal gains from Goods and Services Tax will take time to realize: Eco Survey

01:16 PM

Demonetization 2: Currency squeezes less acute, but peaked later than perceived. Steady remonetization since December trough Eco Survey

Chart 1 – Market Perception (LHS) versus Survey Calculations (RHS)

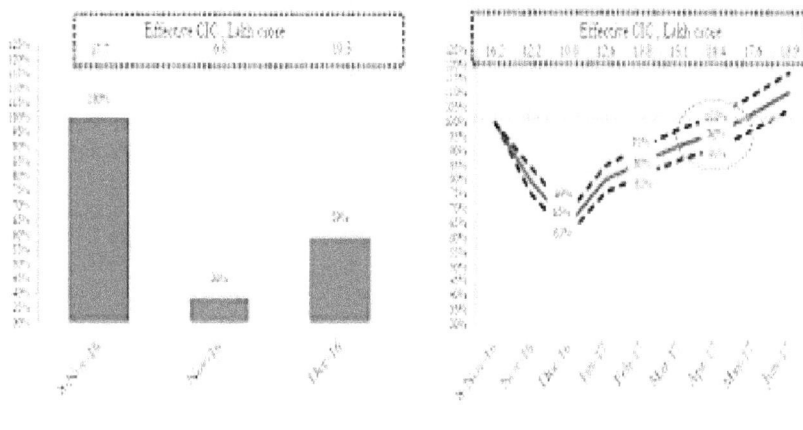

Source: Survey calculations

01:15 PM

Property Tax can be tapped to generate Additional Revenue at City Level, says Economic Survey

01:15 PM

Demonetization 1: Currency + governance + social engineering measure w short-run costs, potential long-run gains #Eco Survey

Remonetization to eliminate cash crunch by April 2017

01:15 PM

India has an opportunity to push leather and apparel exports

01:13 PM

Meta-challenges stem from being early, low income, and a cleavage democracy - Arvind Subramanian

01:12 PM

Sector	Impact	
	Effect through end-December	**Likely longer-term effect**
Money /	Cash declined whereas bank deposits	Cash will recover but settle at a lower

interest rates	increased sharply	level. Similarly, deposits will decline, but probably settle at a slightly higher level
	Interest rates on deposits, loans and government securities declined, implicit rate on cash increased	Loan rates could fall further, if much of the deposits increase proves durable
Unaccounted lessees / black money	Stock of black money fell, as holders cause into the tax net	Power should reduce the flow of unaccounted income
Formalization / digitalization	Digital transactions amongst new users (RuPay / AEPs) increased sharply, existing users' transactions increased in line with historical trend	New-launched digital revolution will continue
Real estate	Prices declined, as wealth fell while cash shortage impeded transactions	Prices could further, as inversing undeclared income in real estate becomes more difficult, but tax component could rise, especially if GST imposed on real estate
Brasher economy	Job losses, decline in farm incomes, social disruption, especially in cash-incentive sectors	Should gradually stabilize as the economy is remonetized
GDP	Growth slowed, as demonetization reduced demand (cash, private wealth), supply (reduced liquidity and working capital and disrupted supply chains), and increased uncertainty	Could be beneficial in the long run if formalization increases and corruption falls
Tax collective	Income taxes rose because of increased disclosure	Indirect and corporate taxes could decline, to the extent growth slows
	Payments to local bodies and discounts increased because demonetized notes remained legal tender for tax payments / clearances of arrears	Over long run, taxes should increase as formalization expands and compliance improves
Uncertainty / credibility	Uncertainty increased, as firms and households were assure of the economic impact and implications for future policy Investment decisions and durable goods purchases postponed	Credibility will be strengthened if demonetization is accompanied by complementary measures. Early and full remonetization essential. Tax arbitrariness and harassment could alternate credibility

01:15 PM

Why is the methodology of ratings agencies not reasonable & consistent?

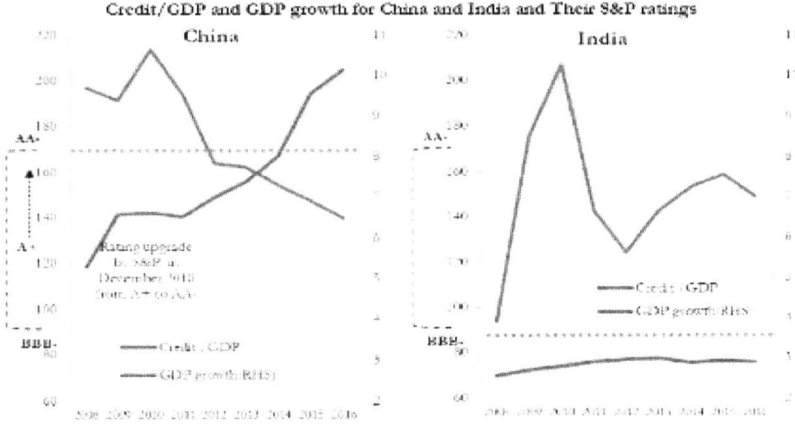

01:10 PM

Economic Survey sees fiscal windfall from Pradhan Mantri Garib Kaayan Yojana, low oil prices

01:09 PM

The decline in Fiscal Deficit has continued.

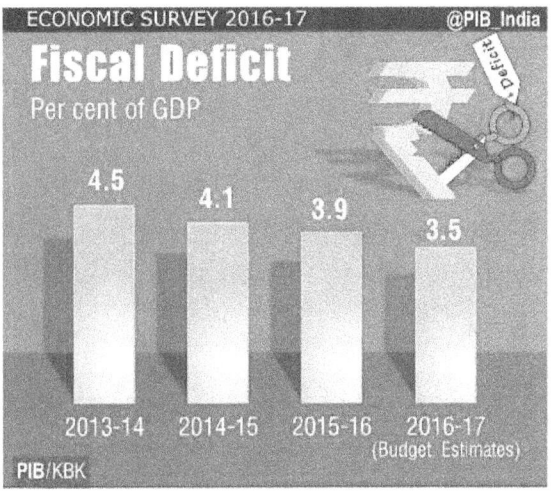

01:07 PM

Inflation is repeatedly being driven by narrow group of food items, pulses being major contributor of food inflation

01:07 PM

Digital Radio platform to promote Digital and Connectivity revolution in the Country

01:07 PM

Inflation based on Wholesale Price Index (WPI) averaged 2.9 per cent during April-December 2016

01:06 PM

Universal Basic Income (UBI) Scheme an alternative to plethora of State subsidies for poverty, advocates reforms to unleash economic dynamism and social justice

01:06 PM

Property Tax can be tapped to generate Additional Revenue at City Level

01:05 PM

Economic Survey 2016-17 suggests setting up of a centralized Public Sector Asset Rehabilitation Agency

01:05 PM

Estimates of annual migrant flows based on railway traffic data

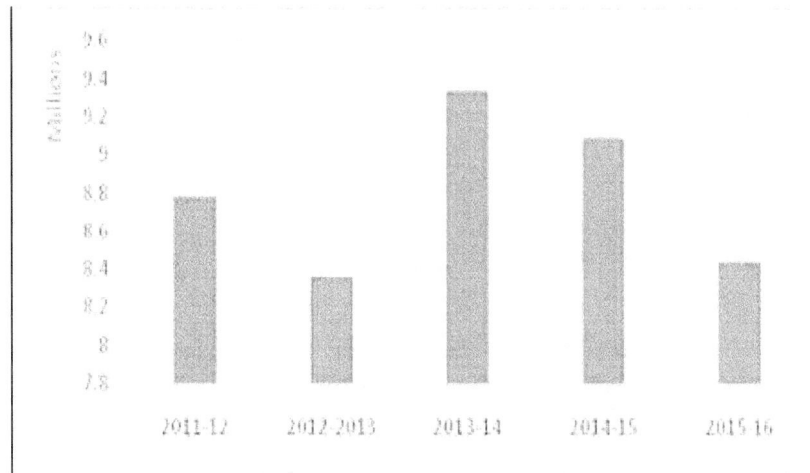

01:04 PM

CPI based core inflation has remained stable in current fiscal year averaging around 5%

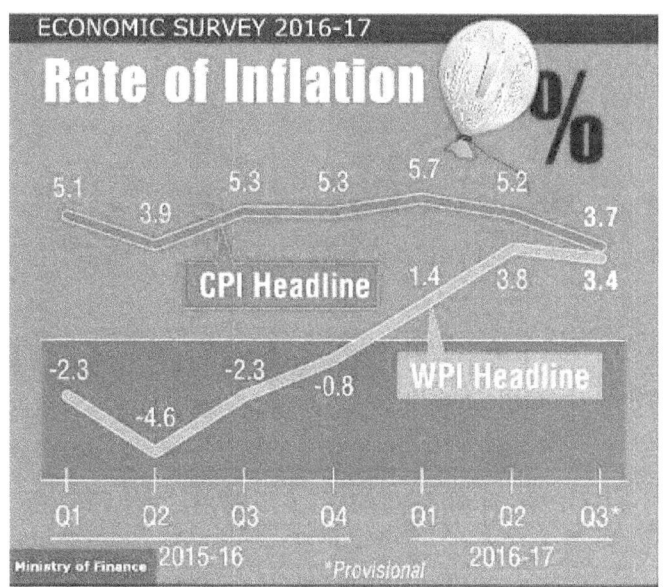

01:03 PM

CPI based core inflation has remained stable in current fiscal year averaging around 5%

01:03 PM

On balance, there is a likelihood that Indian economy may recover back to 6 per cent to 7 per cent in 2017-18

01:02 PM

Service sector estimated to grow at 8.9% in 2016-17

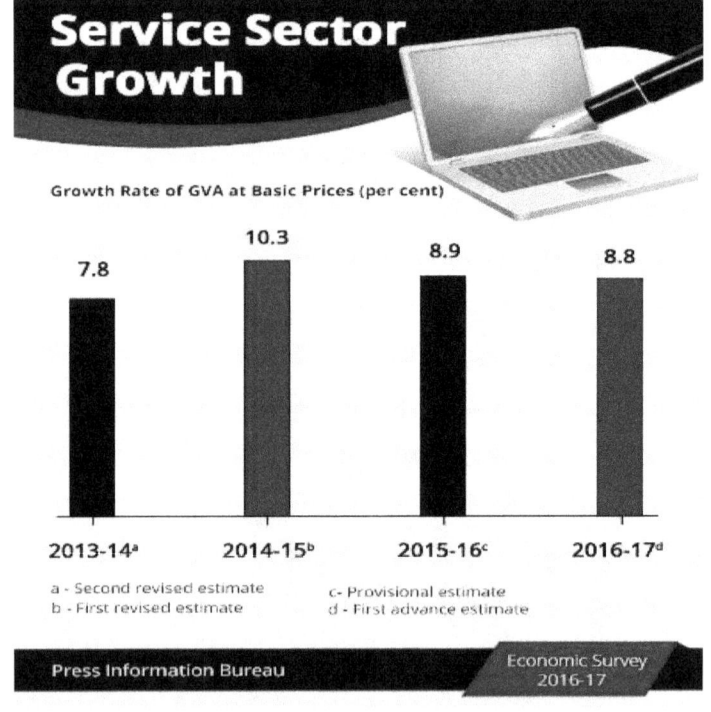

01:01 PM

Need to seriously consider universal basic income data

01:01 PM

Economic Survey: See fiscal windfall from PM Garib Kalyan Yojana

01:00 PM

Growth rate of the industrial sector estimated to moderate to 5.2% in 2016-17 from 7.4% in 2015-16

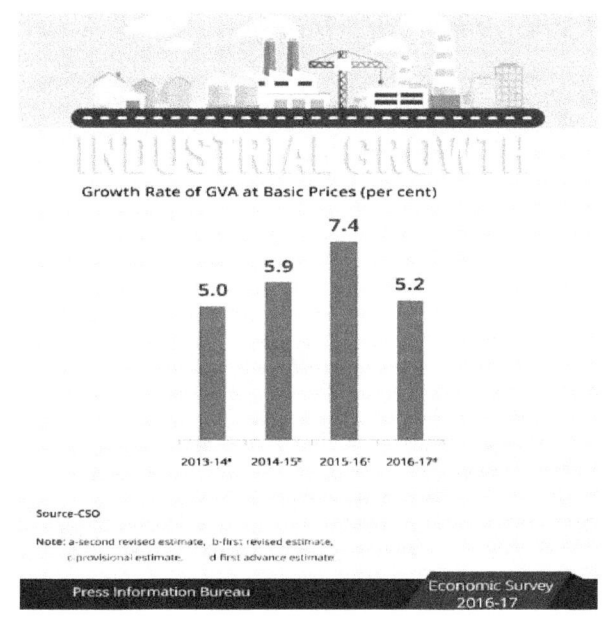

01:01 PM

Sharp rise in prices in FY18 may cap monetary easing headroom

12:59 PM

Economic Survey recommends reforms in labour and tax policies to make the Apparel and Leather sector globally competitive

12:59 PM

Currency shortage to affect supply of some farm products

12:59 PM

Need to modify operational framework of FRBM Act

12:58 PM

Outlook for GST collections must be cautious

12:57 PM

Agriculture sector to grow at 4.1 per cent in the current year up from 1.2 per cent in 2015-16

12:57 PM

Excise related taxes to fall around 0.1% of FY18 GDP

12:56 PM

Lower interest rates in FY18 will boost economy

12:55 PM

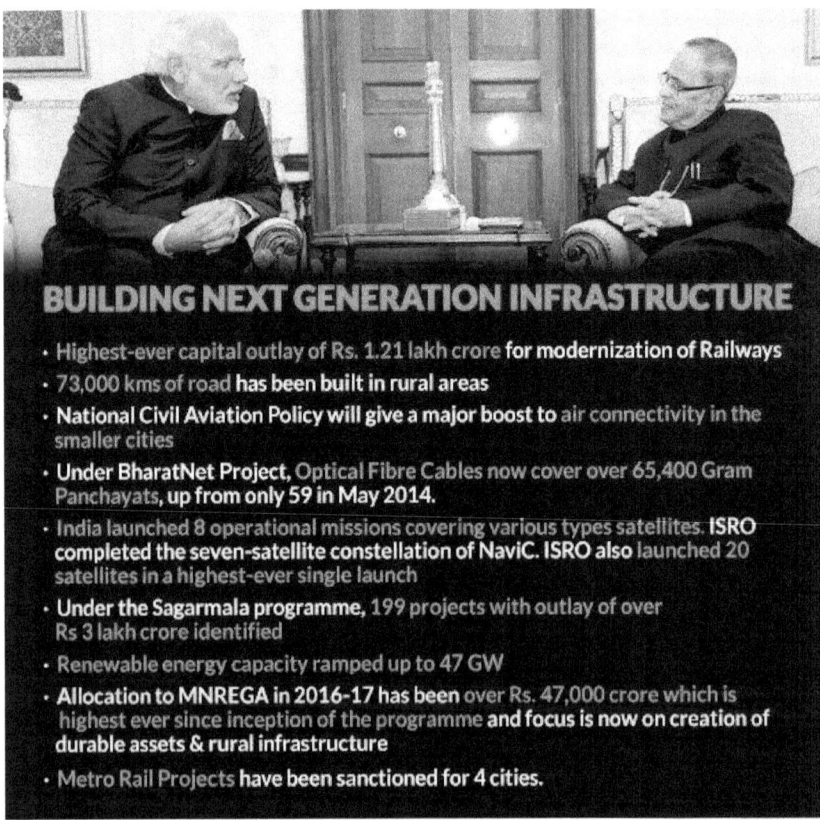

Next-Gen Infrastructure

GDP growth rate at constant market prices for the current year i.e.2016-17 is placed at 7.1 per cent

12:53 PM

Three main downside risks to FY18 GDP growth forecast

12:53 PM

FY18 GDP Growth seen in range of 6.75-7.5%

12:51 PM

FM Arun Jaitley tables Economic Survey in Lok Sabha

12:25 PM

Act East Policy

- Pradhan Mantri Urja Ganga started with 2,500 kms long Jagdishpur-Haldia- Bokaro-Dhamra Natural Gas Pipeline Project. With an investment of Rs. 12,500 crore, it will cater to energy requirements of five states, covering 40 districts and 2,600 villages.
- Opening up road and rail routes to our neighbouring countries to boost the economic development of the region.
- Continued special dispensation in assistance pattern to North-eastern states in the ratio of 90:10 for core central schemes and 80:20 for non-core schemes
- All Meter-Gauge tracks in the north-eastern states will be converted to Broad-Gauge. Arunachal Pradesh and Meghalaya have been put on the rail map
- The Brahmaputra Cracker and Polymer Limited and Numaligarh Refinery Limited's wax unit will create huge employment opportunities in the North East region
- The Govt has approved North East BPO promotion scheme for creation of employment opportunities.
- Ministry of Tourism has identified a thematic circuit for the North East region.

http://economictimes.indiatimes.com/economic-survey-2017-18/liveblog/56869242.cms

Economic Survey 2017: 5 things to watch out for

Chief Economic Adviser Arvind Subramanian is all set to roll out the Economic Survey of 2017. Here are five things to watch out for in this year's Economic Survey.

10:42 AM

Pre-Budget stock-taking: Economic Survey in 7 points

The survey, authored by Chief Economic Adviser Arvind Subramanian, is expected to offer clarity on the policy priorities of the government and some estimate of the impact of demonetization on the economy.

10:26 AM

At what rate can we expect India to grow this fiscal?

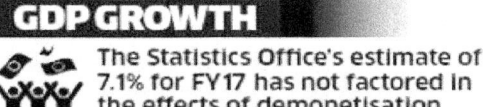

GDP GROWTH

The Statistics Office's estimate of 7.1% for FY17 has not factored in the effects of demonetisation

7.2% FY15

7.6% FY16

7.1% FY17 (Forecast)

CEA's Take ⊗

He will have to give a growth number for the current and next fiscal year that will have to include the demonetisation effect. Could it be less than 7%?

10:26 AM

What will government do to ease demonetization pain?

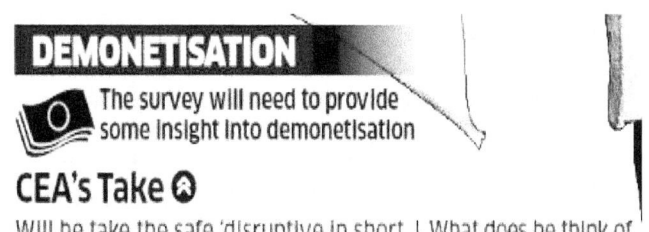

DEMONETISATION

The survey will need to provide some insight into demonetisation

CEA's Take ⊗

Will he take the safe 'disruptive in short run but beneficial in the long term' line? | What does he think of the digital economy?

10:26 AM

2.7   Economic survey 2017: 5 things you need to know

10:26 AM

Does India have enough money for Universal basic Income?

UNIVERSAL BASIC INCOME

Subramanian has already said the survey will examine the issue

CEA's Take ⊘

| He could propose some sort of income for the poorest | May also flag the difficulty of implementation |

10:26 AM

And what is about cash transaction tax?

CASH TRANSACTION TAX

The budget needs measures to build on demonetisation

CEA's Take ⊘

| The survey could offer some suggestions in this regard | Transaction tax on big cash withdrawals seen as a way to encourage digital economy |  |

04:38 PM

2.8 Economic Survey 2017 Tabled; Highlights of the Report

Universal basic income (UBI), demonetization, GDP estimates for FY 2017 and 2018 form part of CEA Arvind Subramanian's Economic Survey 2017.

S V Krishnamachari: January 31, 2017 13:36 IST

People show new currency notes of Rs 500 outside an ATM in Patna on Nov 24, 2016 (representational image). -- IANS

The Economic Survey has been tabled in Parliament. Here are the highlights of the report:

On economic growth rate projections

1. GDP growth estimate for FY2017 slashed to 6.50-6.75 percent from the earlier 7.1 percent.

2. Growth rate for FY2018 pegged at 6.75-7.50 percent.

On remonetization

Cash squeeze will be eliminated by April 2017.

On universal basic income (UBI)

UBI that reduces poverty to 0.5 percent would cost between 4-5 percent of GDP, assuming that those in the top 25 percent income bracket do not participate. It is a powerful idea whose time even if not ripe for implementation, is ripe for serious discussion.

On real estate prices in 8 select cities

The weighted average price of real estate in eight major cities which was already on a declining trend fell further after November 8, 2016 with the announcement of demonetization.

Chief Economic Adviser Arvind Subramanian has started tweeting on Economic Survey 2017 even as the Modi government has released the report. The Survey talks about how universal basic income (UBI) would impact the GDP even as he says it's time to discuss, if not implement, while the GDP growth estimate for FY2017 has been cut to 6.50-6.75 percent from the earlier 7.1 percent.

"The cash squeeze in the meantime will have significant implications for GDP, reducing 2016-17 growth by ¼ to ½ percentage points compared to the baseline of 7 percent."

PM Narendra Modi hoped that the Budget Session will be a fruitful one with debates on all topics including Budget 2017.

The Economic Survey 2017 will be tabled in the Parliament on Tuesday, January 31, coinciding with the commencement of the Budget Session of Parliament that will last till April 12 (subject to exigencies of government business). Here are the top five things to look for in the Survey that is both a review as well as a forward-looking document to make sense of Budget 2017 that will be presented on February 1.

Sensex, Nifty LIVE Updates: Markets in red ahead of Economic Survey 2017; Idea Cellular gains 11%

Demonetization, fiscal dividend and corruption

Till date, there are no authentic estimates on how much of the ~Rs 15.44 lakh crores demonetized money has returned to the banking system. This is crucial, as the difference between the amount returned and the original amount (~Rs. 15.44 lakh crores) would constitute "fiscal dividend" for the Modi government. Of course, the deadline for the return of such banned notes is March 31, 2017 and therefore, it would be inappropriate to expect numbers from the RBI at this point of time. But the Survey can give an update as of January 2017.

FY2017 GDP estimates, fiscal deficit target

The two projections for India's economic growth rate for the current fiscal are 7.1 percent, one by the Central government a few days ago and the other by the Reserve Bank of India (RBI). The Central government estimate explicitly said that it did not factor in the slowdown induced by demonetization. Therefore, it would be interesting to look for the Survey's estimate for this fiscal and the next financial year.

Read: RBI retains repo rate, slashes GDP growth rate forecast for FY2017.

On the fiscal deficit front, it would be interesting to know if the government is confident of achieving its target of reigning in the deficit at 3.5 percent of the gross domestic product (GDP) for the current fiscal as envisaged in the budget presented last year.

Views on universal basic income (UBI)

This could be the theme of Economic Survey 2017 in the context of the concept gaining popularity globally as a tool to address economic inequalities and raise standards of living for those surviving on meager income. In the context of India, there is speculation that the UBI could be repackaged to subsume the rural employment guarantee scheme (MNREGS) and make it populist so as to appeal to voters in the upcoming Assembly elections to five states. It could come with riders such as seeding with Aadhaar and designed so as to boost the digital economy push.

Digital economy push

To counter the cash crunch and nudge people to go digital, the Modi government announced a slew of incentives early last month in addition to lucky draws at the end of December 2016. It would be interesting to see if the Survey — authored by the Chief Economic Advisor Arvind Subramanian — provides insights on how the digital economy could be given a fillip, either with or without incentives.

Disinvestment target

Last year, the Survey scaled down the FY2016 target from disinvestment proceeds from Rs. 69,500 crores to Rs. 25,000 crores in its revised estimates, citing "highly uncertain market conditions prevalent for most part of the year." For the current fiscal, the government has collected Rs. 23,528 crores as against the target of Rs. 56,500 crores, according to a January 3, 2017 finance ministry update.

Besides, the Economic Survey is also expected to throw light on subsidy bill, government debt, trade deficit, non-performing assets of banks, among other aspects of the economy.

The Economic Survey has various chapters including an overview of the economy, public finance, external sector, monetary management and human development indicators.

http://www.ibtimes.co.in/economic-survey-2017-5-things-watch-out-714128

Chief Economic Adviser Arvind Subramanian is addressing the media on the details of the economic survey.

News18.com | January 31, 2017, 2:14 PM IST

Chief Economic Advisor Begins Address

New Delhi: Chief Economic Adviser Arvind Subramanian is addressing the media on the details of the economic survey.

"The economic recovery from demonetization requires policy support," Subramaniam said.

Economic Survey, the government sees FY18 GDP growth in range of 6.75-7.5%. It also outlines three main downside risks to FY18 GDP growth forecast adding that demonetization, raise in oil prices and global trade tensions will affect the growth forecast.

The Survey sees fiscal windfall from invalid notes not returned. Excise related taxes will also fall around 0.1% of FY18 GDP.

Tap for live updates:

Jan 31, 20172:31 pm (IST)

HIGHLIGHTS OF ARVIND SUBRAMANIAN's SPEECH

- Demonetization has affected aggregate demand and aggregate supply

- There is genuine uncertainty on how the economy performing

- Wheat production has gone up to 7%, and main pulse is up by 10%

- Indirect tax collection has seen a dip

- There is a decline in the real estate price, purchase, launches, but that was the aim so that the equilibrium is achieved in India

- Two-wheelers sectors has seen a huge dip because demand for rural India has seen a setback

- Land should be included under the ambit of GST

- Need to reduce tax and stamp duties

- Investments, credit, cash investment, has suffered a setback

- Consumption should increase as remonetization happens

- Consumption and government has been the drivers of growth in India

- There is a festering twin balance sheet problem that is affecting private investments

- Overall private investments declining. Investments are in negative and that is worrisome.

- For bank credit, real credit from corporate sector to industry is declining

- But personal loans to consumers is increasing in double digits

- India may need a Public Sector Asset Rehabilitation Agency.

- Oil prices could go higher. Macro fiscal escalation will also increase.

- Trade tensions with China possible.

- If the world economy picks up, then outlook could be better than what projected so ar.

2.9 Economic Survey Lauds Universal Basic Income: Here's What It Is

Tushar Dhara | News18.com **First published:** January 31, 2017, 1:40 PM IST | **Updated:** January 31, 2017

The Economic Survey is often seen as a signpost to the Union Budget. One of the key take away from the Economic Survey 2017-18 is the mention of Universal Basic Income, a concept that has been in currency recently. The Survey document tabled in Parliament on Wednesday says that "Universal Basic Income an alternative to plethora of state subsidies for poverty."

So can we expect a grand announce by finance minister Arun Jaitley in his Union Budget speech tomorrow on this mother of all social security schemes? Well, let's wait for a day more. In the meantime, News18's Tushar Dhara tells you all that you need to know about Universal Basic Income.

Q) What is a Basic Income?

A) Basic income is a periodic cash payment unconditionally delivered to all on an individual basis, without means test or work requirement.

Q) Why is it Universal?

A) The idea is that every citizen gets it and therefore it is universal. Chief Economic Adviser Arvind Subramanian said last year that the government is considering giving an unconditional cash transfer of about Rs 10,000-15,000 on an annual basis to each and every citizen in the country.

Q) Is it in cash, rather than in-kind?

A) Basic income is provided in cash, without any restriction as to the nature or timing of the consumption or investment it helps fund. In most cases, it supplements, rather than substitutes, existing in-kind transfers such as free education or basic health insurance.

Q) How would it work in India?

A) If implemented in India it could replace numerous poverty alleviation schemes such as Indira Awas Yojna, NREGA and PDS. On the other hand, the idea is that it supplements, rather than substitutes, existing in-kind transfers such as free education or basic health insurance.

Q) What is the rationale for it?

A) The changing nature of job creation – with increasing automation leading to fewer jobs– mean that in the next 20 years as much as 68% of existing jobs in the country will be under threat, hence the need for a guaranteed source of income.

Q) How much would a Universal Basic Income scheme cost in India?

A) This is where the details are not clear. Estimates peg the cost of providing a universal income to 1.3 billion Indians at around 10% of GDP. The government on the other hand could decide to give it to the poorest households, as identified by the Tendulkar Committee-defined poverty line or individuals with Jan Dhan accounts. Arvind Panagariya, NITI Aayog Vice-Chairman, estimates that giving Rs. 1,000 to 130 crores Indians would cost the exchequer Rs. 15.6 lakh crores.

Q) Has it been tried out in India?

A) Yes. In 2011, In eight villages in Madhya Pradesh, every man, woman, and child was provided with a monthly payment of, initially, Rs 200 for each adult and Rs 100 for each child paid to the mother or guardian; these were later raised to 300 and 150 respectively. The two pilot projects were funded by UNICEF.

Q) What were the results?

A) Dr. Guy Standing of the School of Oriental and African Studies, who was involved with the project, has written that the results were positive. Nutrition increased and the better health outcomes led to increased school attendance. The basic income led to small scale investments by the recipients and reduced debt levels.

Q) So is it the right way to go?

A) There is still no consensus on the issue. Critics caution that any scheme that provides an unconditional guaranteed income to a section of the population (as may happen in India) without having to work will create resentment. Also, getting rid of subsidies in kind (food, healthcare, and schooling) may result in decreased outcomes in these areas.

http://www.news18.com/news/india/economic-survey-lauds-universal-basic-income-heres-what-it-is-1343076.html

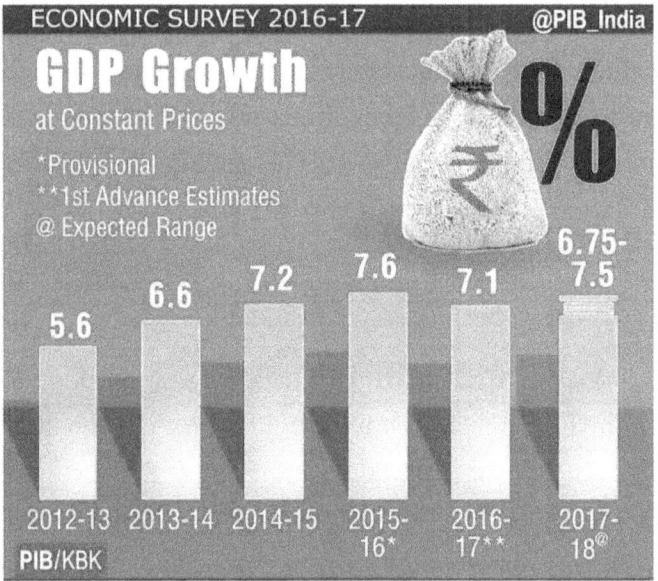

Major Achievements This Year

1. GST
2. Bankruptcy bill
3. Monetary Policy Committee
4. Aadhaar Bill
5. FDI liberalization
6. UPI: Inter-Operability and Making the "M" in Jam a reality
7. Promoting labour-intensive sectors (apparels and made-ups)

2.10 Highlights of Economic Survey 2017

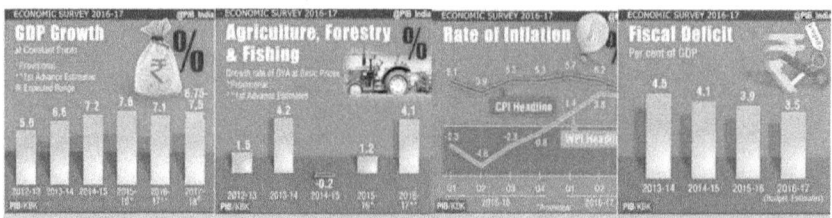

ECONOMIC SURVEY 2016-17
HIGHLIGHTS

- Agriculture sector growth 4.1% in FY 2016-17, up from 1.2% in 2015-16.
- Industrial sector growth to come down to 5.2% in 2016-17 from 7.4% in 2015-16.
- Service sector estimated to grow at 8.9% in 2016-17.
- Economic growth in FY 2017-18 between 6.7% and 7.5%.
- Demonetisation risk to growth in next fiscal year.
- Property tax can be tapped to generate revenue at city level.
- Labour migration increasing at accelerating rate.
- Fiscal activism of advanced economies not relevant to India.
- Universal Basic Income an alternative to plethora of state subsidies for poverty.
- Suggests setting up a centralized Public Sector Asset Rehabilitation Agency.
- Current Account Deficit in 1H of FY 2016-17 narrowed to 0.3% of GDP.
- Headline CPI inflation under control in FY 2016-17.
- Decline in Fiscal deficit has continued.
- GDP estimated at 7.1%

2.11 Economic Survey 2016-17 highlights
REUTERS

Union Finance Minister Arun Jaitley with Chief Economic Adviser
Arvind Subramanian (L) and Economic Affairs Secretary Shaktikanta Das
(2nd L) who authored the Economic Survey 2016-17 -- PTI

The survey was prepared by the Finance Ministry's Chief Economic Adviser Arvind Subramanian on January 31, 2017:

India's economy should grow between 6.75 per cent and 7.5 per cent in the financial year beginning on April 1, Economic Survey, estimated on Tuesday.

The Economic Survey, which sets the scene for Finance Minister Arun Jaitley's fourth annual budget on Wednesday, forecast that Asia's third-largest economy should steady after a hit from the government's shock decision in November to scrap most cash in circulation.

The survey was prepared by the finance ministry's chief economic adviser Arvind Subramanian.

Here are the highlights of the report:

Growth

* 2017/18 GDP growth seen between 6.75 and 7.5 per cent year on year

* GDP growth rate at constant market prices for the current year 2016/17 is placed at 7.1 per cent

* The federal statistics office's estimate of 7.1 per cent growth for 2016/17 likely to be revised downwards

* Service sector is estimated to grow at 8.9 per cent in 2016/17

* Industrial growth rate expected to moderate to 5.2 per cent in 2016/17 from 7.4 per cent in 2015/16

Fiscal Deficit

* Implementation of wage hike, muted tax receipts to put pressure on fiscal deficit in 2017/18

* Need for fiscal prudence for both centre and states for fiscal health of the economy

* Fiscal windfall from low oil prices to disappear in 2017/18 - TV channels

Monetary Policy

* Sharp rise in prices in 2017/18 may cap monetary easing headroom

* Market interest rates seen lower in 2017/18 due to demonetization

Government debt

* Government debt to GDP ratio in 2016 seen at 68.5 per cent down from 69.1 per cent in 2015

Demonetization

* Remonetization will ensure that the cash squeeze is eliminated by April 2017

* Supply of currency should follow actual demand and not be dictated by official estimate of desirable demand

* Government windfall arising from unreturned notes should be deployed towards capital spending

Banks

* Suggests setting up public sector asset rehabilitation agency to take charge of large bad loans in banks

* Central agency with government backing could overcome coordination and political issues on bad loans

Taxation

* Income tax rates and real estate stamp duties could be reduced

* Timetable for reducing corporate tax rate could be accelerated

Universal basic income

* Universal Basic Income (UBI) proposal a powerful idea, but not ready for implementation

* UBI an alternative to plethora of state subsidies for poverty alleviation

* UBI would cost between 4 and 5 per cent of GDP

(This article was published on January 31, 2017)

http://www.thehindubusinessline.com/economy/budget/economic-survey-201617-highlights/article9511608.ece

2.12 Economic Survey 2017 tabled in Parliament: Key highlights

Union finance minister Arun Jaitley tabled the Economic Survey 2016-17 in Parliament during the first day of the budget session. Here are the major highlights from the Survey

Union finance minister Arun Jaitley on Tuesday tabled the **Economic Survey 2016-17** in Parliament budget session. The survey projects the economy to grow in the range of 6.75% to 7.25% in the next fiscal year 2017-18 in the post-demonetization year.

The survey prepared by chief economic adviser in the finance ministry Arvind Subramanian said the adverse impact of demonetization on GDP growth will be transitional. The Economic Survey 2016-17 advocates the concept of Universal Basic Income (UBI) as an alternative to the various social welfare schemes in an effort to reduce poverty.

Here are the major highlights from Economic Survey 2016-17:

■ Gross domestic product (GDP) growth in 2016-17 to dip to 6.5%, down from 7.6% in last fiscal

■ Economic growth to rebound to 6.75 to 7.5% in 2017-18

■ Economic Survey sees fiscal windfall from Pradhan Mantri Garib Kalyan Yojana, low oil prices

■ Farm sector to grow at 4.1% in the current fiscal, up from 1.2% in 2015-16

■ Fiscal gains from Goods and Services Tax (GST) will take time to realize

■ Growth rate of industrial sector estimated to moderate to 5.2% in 2016-17 from 7.4% last fiscal

■ The survey prepared by Chief Economic Adviser in the finance ministry Arvind Subramanian said the adverse impact of demonetization on GDP growth will be transitional.

■ The Economic Survey 2016-17 has advocated the concept of Universal Basic Income (UBI) as an alternative to the various social welfare schemes in an effort to reduce poverty. In his budget speech earlier this month, J&K finance minister Haseeb Drabu said he would want to create a social security fund and provide a UBI to all those living below the poverty line through a direct benefit transfer system.

http://www.livemint.com/Politics/nytAifl9vkKQ0Zd9fKKzYJ/Econo mic-Survey-2017-tabled-in-Parliament-Key-highlights.html

2.13 Economic Survey 2017 explained in 12 points

BS Web Team | New Delhi January 31, 2017 Last Updated at 14:41 IST

Here are the highlights of the Economic Survey 2017:

The Economic Survey 2017, tabled in Parliament on Tuesday, projected that the country's gross domestic product (GDP) will grow by 6.75 per cent to 7.5 per cent in 2017-18.

Here are 12 highlights of the Economic Survey 2017:

* Demonetization **impact:** The government says the adverse impact of demonetization on GDP   growth will   be   transitional.

Real GDP growth in 2017-18 is projected to be in the range of 6.75 – 7.5 per cent, once the cash supply is replenished.

* **Industrial growth to cool:** Growth rate of the industrial sector estimated to moderate to 5.2 per cent in 2016-17 from 7.4% last fiscal. The agriculture sector to grow at 4.1 per cent in the current year up from 1.2 per cent in 2015-16

* **Per-capita GSDP:** Real per capita GSDP between 1983 and 2014 has shown across-the-board improvement

* **Remonetization:** The Economic Survey 2017 has suggested quick remonetization, push for digitization, bringing land and real estate under GST ambit, reduction in taxes and stamp duties and an improved tax administration system as key reform measures to ensure long term economic benefits.

* **States' performance:** There has been an improvement in the financial position of states over the last few years. The average revenue deficit has been eliminated, while the average fiscal deficit was curbed to less than 3 percent of GSDP. The average debt to GSDP ratio has also fallen. Centre's Fiscal Responsibility and Budget Management (FRBM) Act, mirrored by Fiscal Responsibility Legislations (FRL) adopted in the States.

* **NPAs:** As per the Survey, gross NPAs has climbed to almost 12 per cent of gross advances for public sector banks at end-September 2016. At this level, India's NPA ratio is higher than any other major emerging market, with the exception of Russia. The consequent squeeze of banks has led them to slow credit growth to crucial sectors-especially to industry and medium and small scale enterprises (MSMEs)-to levels unseen over the past two decades. As this has occurred, growth in private and overall investment has turned negative. A decisive resolution is urgently needed.

* **Asset rehabilitation:** Survey suggests setting up of a centralized Public Sector Asset Rehabilitation Agency that will look after the largest, most difficult Cases, and make Politically Tough Decisions to reduce Debt.

* **Poor targeting:** According to the Survey, redistribution by the government is far from efficient in targeting the poor. The Survey points out that the capacity of the State in delivering essential services such as health and education is weak due to low capacity, with high levels of corruption, clienteles, rules and red tape. At the level of the states, competitive populism is more in evidence than competitive service delivery.

* **Universal Basic Income:** The Survey has advocated the concept of Universal Basic Income (UBI) as an alternative to the various social welfare schemes in an effort to reduce poverty. The Survey points out that the two prerequisites for a successful UBI are: (a) functional JAM (Jan Dhan, Aadhar and Mobile) system as it ensures that the cash transfer goes directly into the account of a beneficiary and (b) Centre-State negotiations on cost sharing for the programme.

* **Property tax:** A study done for the Survey shows that property tax potential is large and can be tapped to generate additional revenue at city level. Satellite imagery can be a useful tool for improving urban governance by facilitating better property tax compliance.

* **Job creation:** The Survey says Apparel and Leather industry are key to generation of formal and productive jobs: recommends reforms in labour and tax policies to make the Apparel and Leather sector globally competitive. The Survey adds that these sectors

provide immense opportunities for creation of jobs for the weaker sections, especially for women, and can become vehicles for broader social transformation in the country.

   * **Labour migration:** New estimates of labour migration in India have revealed that inter-state labour mobility is significantly higher than previous estimates. Relatively poorer states such as Bihar and Uttar Pradesh have high net out-migration. Seven states take positive CMM values reflecting net in-migration: Goa, Delhi, Maharashtra, Gujarat, Tamil Nadu, Kerala and Karnataka. Policy actions to sustain and maximize the benefits of migration include: ensuring portability of food security benefits, providing healthcare and a basic social security framework for migrants – potentially through an inter-state self-registration process.

   http://www.business-standard.com/budget/article/economic-survey-2017-explained-in-12-points-117013100579_1.html

2.14 Economic Survey may focus on Cashless Economy

RISHI SHAH | Tue, 31 Jan 2017 07:30am,   DNA

The survey could shed some light as to how the government intends to do a tight rope walk of managing its finances while giving a boost to growth

   Will it be an Economic Survey of a changing India or a developing economy?

   The last few years have been marked by volatile economic situations in the domestic and global economy. While the developed economies grapple with bringing sustainable growth, the domestic economy continues to move towards its potential rate of growth, while being careful of the excesses of the past.

In such a scenario, the Economic Survey to be published today would present an important insight into the government's thought process.

In general, the survey itself has undergone a change over the last couple of years as the government has released two documents instead of one. While the first one retains its essence from the past, the second one has more of technical speak with economic models assessing policy choices. It also, sometimes, explores the performance of certain marquee programmes while at the same time warning on the pitfalls of certain macroeconomic policies as well as the emerging signals from the data.

Coming to the present, developments over the past few months have had a bearing on economic activity and the economy is slowing down in the near term. The most obvious policy response would be to increase government spending support spending as demand levels came back to the norm. However, given the chosen path of fiscal consolidation for the central government, any increase in expenditure has to be well founded in the fundamentals. Any increase in revenue expenditure is unlikely to be appreciated by ratings agencies that are likely to highlight that the combined (state and central) deficits are still high, and any increase in capital expenditure would help growth albeit more slowly. The survey could shed some light as to how the government intends to do a tight rope walk of managing its finances while giving a boost to growth.

The second important aspect to watch out for will likely be the impact assessment of implementation of GST. As such, there is consensus that a sweeping tax reform like the GST could affect businesses in the short term; there could also be some disruption in government revenue streams. The last year's survey showed how India was under-taxed with the average of emerging market's tax to GDP ratio at 21.4% and India's ratio at 16.4%. The survey could also weigh on demonetization and its effects on the economy while providing policy options to encourage taxpaying in the future. There might be relevant policy discussions and examples from across the globe that can be used in India to give tax collection a fillip. The Indian economy is in a peculiar situation wherein indirect tax accounts for the majority of tax collections as against direct taxes.

The survey would also possibly highlight the requirements from a macroeconomic perspective to create a system where cash requirements would be lower than the present. A move towards the cashless or less-cash economy cannot be an immediate one and there would need to be adequate incentives and infrastructure put in before the transition can be made in a meaningful sense. In the ongoing attempt to go digital, the government has decided that the economic survey and budget documents will also made available only in an electronic form.

Lastly, one of India's shortcomings has been the lack of export competitiveness in the economy. For the success of the 'Make in India' scheme, there has to be concerted push to exports and manufacturing for domestic markets. Creating such circumstances has become trickier due to the rise of protectionism in the world markets. The existing powerhouses of trade are unlikely to cede space in an environment where growth is at a premium. The survey could explain some of the policy imperatives in the current situation.

The survey also springs up some surprises every year and we can expect this year to be no different. As such, it is likely to set the stage for some policy debates in the coming months.

The writer is economist at Deloitte

http://www.dnaindia.com/money/report-budget-2017-eco-survey-may-focus-on-cashless-economy-2301844

2.15 Macro woes on Arun Jaitley's mind, ahead of Budget 2017

The broad expectations from the budget are that the finance minister will present a broad-ranging stimulus package.

Jaitley may unveil measures to soften the blow of demonetization and revive investments to return the economy to a higher growth trajectory - Photo: Reuters

As finance minister Arun Jaitley prepares to present his fourth budget, he is confronted with a bleak macroeconomic backdrop. Jaitley may unveil measures to soften the blow of demonetization and revive investments to return the economy to a higher growth trajectory. Accordingly, the broad expectations from the budget are that the finance minister will present a broad-ranging stimulus package.

INFLATION THREAT RECEDES...

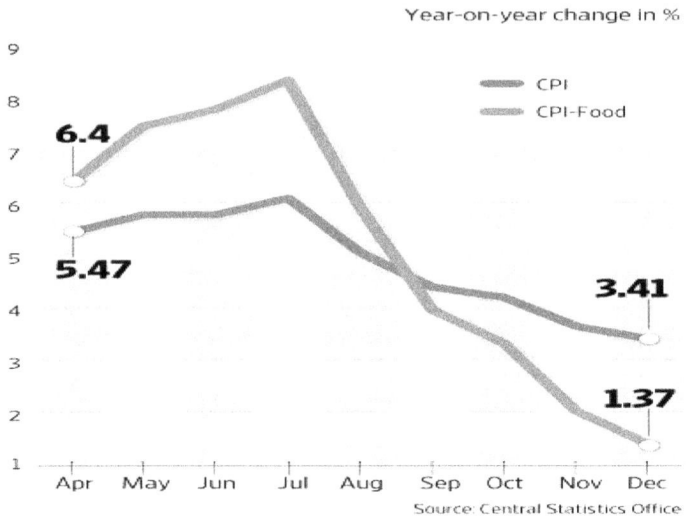

Year-on-year change in %

— CPI
— CPI-Food

6.4

5.47

3.41

1.37

Source: Central Statistics Office

...BUT UPWARD PRESSURE REMAINS

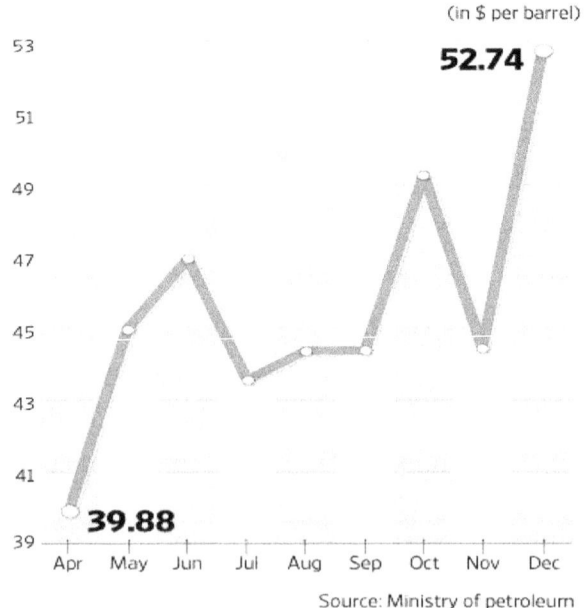

(in $ per barrel)

52.74

39.88

Source: Ministry of petroleum

DECLINE IN EXPORTS REFLECT TEPID GLOBAL DEMAND

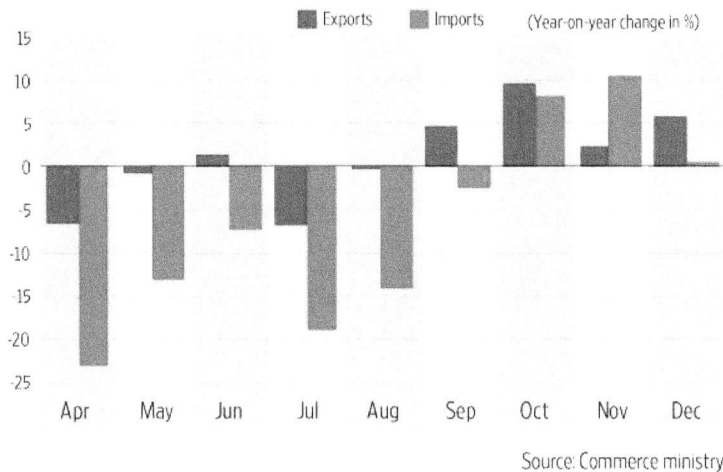

Source: Commerce ministry

INVESTMENT IN DOLDRUMS

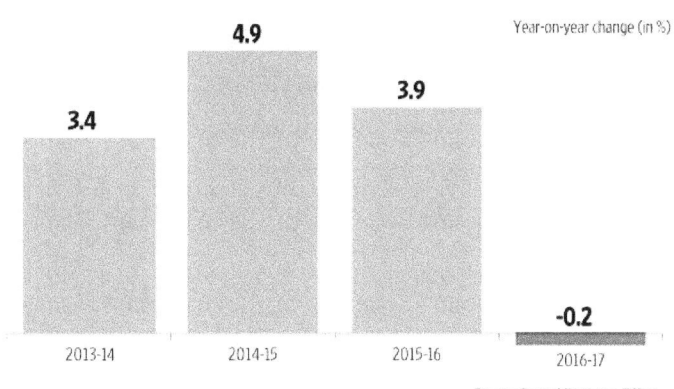

Source: Central Statistics Office

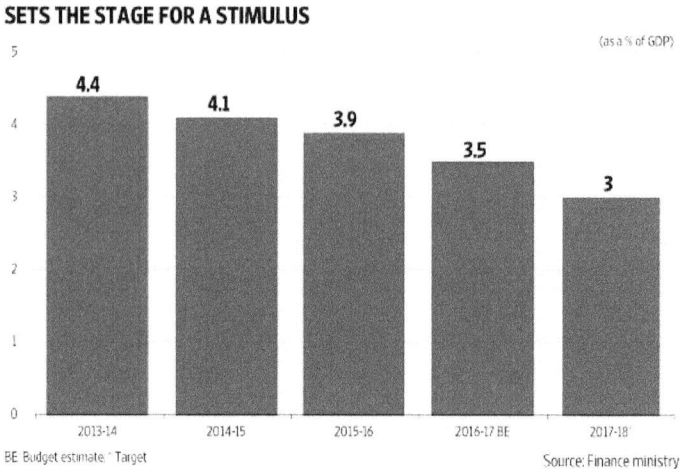

SETS THE STAGE FOR A STIMULUS

(as a % of GDP)

Source: Finance ministry

BE: Budget estimate; * Target

http://www.livemint.com/Politics/xXtYhSWUZ5yCOFZydRY4WI/Macro-woes-on-Arun-Jaitleys-mind-ahead-of-Budget-2017.html?li_source=LI&li_medium=news_rec

Chapter-3: Budget-2017-Opening Speech of President of India

3.1   President Pranab Mukherjee kicks off Budget session: 15 key points from his opening speech

The President, in his speech, stressed on issues 'financial inclusion', 'social schemes' and 'women power'. Here are 10 big takeaways from his speech.

Govt. committed to growth, 'sabka saath, sabka vikaas':
President Pranab Mukherjee

"The government has taken many initiatives to improve the quality of life of the poor and financial inclusion is key to poverty alleviation," President said.

12:01 PM

My government has simplified procedures, repealed obsolete laws and eliminated scope for corruption: Pranab Mukherjee

12:00 PM

My government is committed to combat terrorism, and ensure that perpetrators of these acts are brought to justice, says President Pranab Mukherjee

11:59 AM

India is facing the great challenge of terrorism from past 4 decades. India will actively collaborate with other nations to actively defeat these terrorist groups: Pranab Mukherjee

11:58 AM

My government is thankful to the GST council for working to resolve the outstanding issues: Pranab Mukherjee

11:58 AM

The National Civil Aviation Policy, will give a major boost to air connectivity in the smaller cities and towns: Pranab Mukherjee

11:57 AM

Under the Bharat Net Project, Optical Fiber Cables now cover over 75,700 Gram Panchayets - Pranab Mukherjee

11:57 AM

BHIM has become one of the most customized payment system in the country - Pranab Mukherjee

11:55 AM

Under Ek Bharat, Shreshtha Bharat Program, entwine two diverse states so that each state can inherit the cultural spirit of the other state - Pranab Mukherjee

11:54 AM

Over Rs 2 lakh crores sanctioned under Mudra scheme: President Pranab Mukherjee

President Mukherjee on Tuesday said the government has provided over Rs two lakh crores through 5.6 crores loans sanctioned under the Pradhan Mantri Mudra Yojana.

11:51 AM

Universal Account Number has ensured portability of EPF accounts and has safeguarded the interest of crores of workers - Pranab Mukherjee

11:51 AM

Implementation of the 7th Pay Commission has benefited 50 lakh employees and 35 lakh pensioners, says President Mukherjee

11:48 AM

To combat black money, corruption, counterfeit currency and terror financing, government took decision on November 8, 2016 to ban Rs 500 & 1000 notes - Pranab Mukherjee

11:47 AM

Metro rail projects sanction for four cities included to Nagpur, Ahmedabad and Pune with Chennai Metro expansion - Pranab Mukherjee

11:43 AM

Under Sabarimala program, 199 projects with outlay of 3 lakh crores has been identified for implementation over the next 3 years, says Pranab Mukherjee

11:40 AM

North East BPO promotion schemes under Digital India program for employment schemes - Pranab Mukherjee

11:39 AM

Railways have undertaken major expansion in North East region at the cost of Rs. 10,000 crores. Tripura has been connected with broad gauge line and Arunachal Pradesh has been connected to Meghalaya - Pranab Mukherjee

11:36 AM

By year end, all the meter gauge tracks in the North East will be converted into broad gauge lines - Pranab Mukherjee

11:33 AM

National Apprenticeship Promotion Scheme has been launched with a budget outlay of Rs 10,000 crores - Pranab Mukherjee

11:32 AM

Pradhan Mantri YUVA Yojana launched for promoting entrepreneurship education and training amongst 7 lakh student - Pranab Mukherjee

11:31 AM

The Pradhan Mantri Ujjwala Yojana will make clean energy accessible to the poor - Pranab Mukherjee

11:31 AM

The revision of Maternity Benefit Act will support pregnant women at the workplace - Pranab Mukherjee

11:30 AM

Over 20 lakh youth have benefitted from the PMKVY, says President, says Pranab Mukherjee

11:28 AM

Through Stand up India initiative, over 2.5 lakh SC/ST women entrepreneurship launched with RS 490 crores - Pranab Mukherjee

11:27 AM

Interest rate for senior citizen has been fixed at 8 per cent monthly for a period of 10 year - Pranab Mukherjee

11:26 AM

11000 of 18000 villages which were in darkness since independence electrified in record time, says President Pranab Mukherjee

11:24 AM

Minimum wages increased by 42 per cent, both agricultural and non-agricultural sector: President Pranab Mukherjee

11:24 AM

Package of Rs 6000 crores will boost employability of youth. And also add 1.1 crores jobs: President Pranab Mukherjee

11:22 AM

Soaring prices of pulses was the matter of great concern around this time last year, my govt. took proactive steps, it is now under control: Pranab Mukherjee

11:21 AM

After consecutive years of drought, farmer oriented schemes have been increased. 6 per cent increase has been seen from last year: Pranab Mukherjee

11:20 AM

37 per cent of 1.5 crores beneficiaries of Ujjwala scheme to provide free LPG cylinder to the poor, belong to the SC/ST category: Pranab Mukherjee

11:19 AM

Nari shakti is an integral part of our development journey. They deserve equal opportunity - Pranab Mukherjee

11:18 AM

With objective of digitization of all the live Kisan credit cards, 3 crores cards will be converted to RuPay card soon - Pranab Mukherjee

11:17 AM

My government is committed to provide shelter to every houseless poor household through the Pradhan Mantri Aawas Yojana - Pranab Mukherjee

11:16 AM

At the core of all my government policies, is the welfare of 'gareeb', 'peedit', 'Dalit', 'vanchhit' - Pranab Mukherjee

11:14 AM

Over Rs 2 lakh Crores has been provided through 5.6 crores loans sanctioned under Pradhan Mantri Mudra Yojana - Pranab Mukherjee

11:13 AM

Gas connections are being provided to 5 crores households-Pranab Mukherjee

11:12 AM

My Govt. has taken many initiatives to improve quality of life of the poor, committed to provide shelter - Pranab Mukherjee

11:11 AM

Under Deen Dayal Upadhyaya Yojna, chain to empower women, from the deprived section, over Rs. 16,000 crores has been made available to SHG - Pranab Mukherjee

11:10 AM

An unprecedented 26 crores plus Jan Dhan accounts have been opened for the unbanked - Pranab Mukherjee

11:09 AM

Resilience demonstrated by our countrymen particularly the poor, in the fight against black money and corruption, is remarkable - President Pranab Mukherjee

11:09 AM

Over 1.2 crores consumers have given up their LPG connections: Pranab Mukherjee

11:08 AM

This is a historic session heralding advancement of budget cycle, merger of general budget with rail budget for first time in independent India: President Mukherjee

11:07 AM

President Pranab Mukherjee addresses joint session of Parliament.

3.2 Budget 2017: Here is what we can expect from the Upcoming Financial Year

By: **Express Web Desk** | New Delhi | Published: December 19, 2016   6:15 pm

The budget of 2017 is most awaited in determining the government's way of dealing with the current situation of chaos and expectations in the country.

The 2017 budget might see a number of welfare measures and pro-poor schemes which could see a surge in social spending expenditures.

This financial year is about to end on a heavy note with the ban on high value currency notes leading to chaos and cash crunch across the country. The year 2016 has seen two major economic decisions taken by the government, one being the Goods and Services Tax and the second being the demonetization move announced on November 8. While people are still uncertain about the impact of both these decisions, it is the budget of 2017 that is most awaited in determining the government's way of dealing with the current situation of chaos and expectations in the country.

Apart from the expectations from the government to address the issues raised by demonetization in the upcoming budget, there are two major changes which the Union Budget 2017 will witness. First is the merger of the Railway budget with the Union budget, and second being the change of date of announcement from the end of February to February 1.

Here are some of the major changes and expectations from budget 2017:

Departing from the colonial era tradition

The tradition of passing the budget on the last working day of February was part of the British administration in India that the Indian government inherited post independence. In November 2016, Prime Minister Narendra Modi announced a shift in date of budget. In 2017 therefore, the budget would be presented on February 1.

The change in date is expected to speed up the process of financial decision making for the upcoming year. The budget session in the parliament is expected to start from the second week of January. With the early planning and presentation of the budget, the government would get more time to efficiently implement financial decisions by April 1 without any delay.

However, the flip side to the decision is that with the advancement of the date by a month, there is less time for the various departments to collect data for the sake of budgetary planning.

Merger of Railway budget with Union budget

Marking a dramatic move away from the 92-year-old practice of presenting a separate Railway budget ahead of the Union budget, the railway and Union budget will be presented together. The process of preparing the Railway budget remains unchanged. A single appropriation bill would be prepared with the estimates of the Railway budget as well. The reasoning behind the move is to save time for the government by not having to hold consideration for two separate bills.

Expected tax changes

Ever since the planning of the 2016 Union budget, expectations have been high regarding changes in the existing tax structure. The 2016 budget was expected to raise the tax exemption bar from the current level of Rs. 2.5 lakh to 3 lakh per annum. Since, the change could not be carried out in the existing budget; it is expected to be announced in 2017. Further, with the grievances and pain inflicted upon the common man with the note ban move, the expectation of a raise in tax exemption rate is ripe.

Moreover, we might also see a reduction in tax rates that is currently at 10 per cent for incomes above Rs. 2.5 lakh, 20 per cent for those earning above Rs. 5 lakh and 30 per cent for those earning above Rs. 10 lakh.

Welfare benefit measures

With the politics surrounding demonetization being extremely critical to the government, particularly pointing at the difficulties faced by the poor, the ruling party is in an urgent need to devise policies that benefit the poor. This is already evident from the Pradhan Mantri Garib Kalyan Yojana that was announced by Prime Minister Narendra Modi on November 29. As part of the scheme, those with large amounts of unaccounted wealth can deposit the same with a penalty of 50 percent on it as opposed to tax rate of 85 percent for those who do not opt for the scheme.

Keeping in mind the government's need to please the poor, the 2017 budget might see a number of welfare measures and pro-poor schemes which could see a surge in social spending expenditures.

The other aspect of benefit measures can take the form of incentives for digital payments. With the rhetoric of a cashless economy taking centre stage in the aftermath of demonetization, the government has already taken a number of steps to encourage electronic payments. Service tax on payments made through debit and credit cards up to Rs. 2000 have been removed. More recently, Finance Minister, <u>Arun Jaitley</u> announced a list of measures as incentives for digital payments which include cheaper petrol and diesel when paid for electronically, discounts on railway tickets and highway tolls.

Given the trend of incentivizing cashless transactions, we might expect a number of sops encouraging e-payments in the 2017 budget.

http://indianexpress.com/article/business/budget/budget-2017-here-is-what-we-can-expect-from-the-upcoming-financial-year-4435513/

Chapter 4: Fiscal and Growth issues

4.1 Budget 2017: A Case for Aggressive Fiscal Stimulus

India will have to depend largely on domestic initiatives for 8%-or-above GDP growth rate, given the global growth slowdown and threats to globalization

A comprehensive calculus of demonetization's net gains, if any, can await the release of appropriate data. The priority is to uplift the economy from its current contractionary phase. Given the global growth slowdown and the inward orientation of major developed countries, India will have to depend largely on domestic initiatives to reach and sustain its potential growth of 8% or above. The Union budget of 2017-18 provides a significant opportunity for a substantive push to growth.

Slowdown preceded demonetization

An economic slowdown clearly preceded demonetization. By the second quarter of fiscal year 2017 (Q2FY17), investment demand as measured by gross fixed capital formation had already been contracting for three consecutive quarters. As shown by year-on-year negative growth rates of -1.9% in Q4FY16, -3.1% in Q1FY17 and -5.6% in Q2FY17, this contraction has increased in magnitude. Growth in exports had been negative throughout FY16. It was near zero in Q2FY17. The growth, year-on-year, of the centre's gross tax revenues in Q2FY17 fell to 8.7%, compared to 24.1% in Q2FY16. This was mainly due to corporate and personal income tax, and customs duties. The Central Statistics Office's Advance Estimates for FY17 indicate that even private final consumption expenditure has slowed down. Without taking into account the effect of demonetization, its FY17 gross domestic product (GDP) growth estimate at 7.1% is 0.5 percentage points lower than that in FY16.

Available evidence indicates that demonetization has accentuated these contractionary trends. At 49.6 for manufacturing and 46.8 for services in December 2016, the Purchasing Managers' Index (PMI) has gone below the threshold of 50, indicating contraction. The services PMI showed contraction in November itself. Growth in bank credit fell to 6.6% in November 2016 with food credit contracting sharply by 15.7%. Although year-on-year growth in the Index of Industrial Production (IIP) at 5.7% in November 2016 shows an upturn, this was driven by a favourable base effect. Month-on-month IIP growth shows contraction in October at (-) 0.7% and November at (-) 1.3%. The International Monetary Fund has reassessed India's post-demonetization GDP growth for FY17 at 6.6%, 1.4 percentage points below the potential growth of 8%.

Financing fiscal stimulus

A substantive fiscal stimulus is needed and feasible. First, the government can access a one-time fiscal windfall linked to currency extinguishment supplemented by additional tax revenues through Income Disclosure Scheme (IDS) 1 and IDS 2. Together, the extent of this gain could be as much as 0.75% of GDP. Second, given the economic slowdown, the government may relax the Fiscal Responsibility and Budget Management Act norms. Cyclical adjustment is desirable in a slowdown. Borrowing 0.5% points above the FY18 target of 3% of GDP would be justifiable, noting that the consolidated government's debt-GDP ratio has fallen to 69% in 2015 from its peak of 84% in 2003. Many states asking for relaxation of their borrowing norms due to revenue erosion can together be allowed additional borrowing up to 0.5% of GDP. But cyclically adjusted targets call for strict discipline to ensure that borrowing is driven below the mean target in the expansionary phase.

Further, departmental enterprises such as posts and railways and non-departmental public enterprises can take up expansion plans given the prevailing low prices of investment goods. Their borrowing, largely off-budget, can add another 0.75% of GDP to the fiscal stimulus, which together may amount to 2.5% of GDP. The surge in bank deposits implying augmented financial savings would enable the government to borrow the extra amount without putting pressure on the interest rate. Most of this stimulus should be directed towards augmenting infrastructure. Qualitatively, some push to construction, housing and manufacturing particularly for the automobile sector through sector specific incentives should help these demonetization-afflicted sectors. Investment demand would pick up only after existing inventories are exhausted. At that point, monetary stimulus would become effective.

Uplifting tax-GDP ratio

Due to demonetization, people who have deposited unaccounted money in banks would remain in the tax net for the current as well as subsequent years. With Goods and Services Tax and greater coverage of transactions through digitized means, the tax buoyancy should significantly go up on a sustained basis. We estimate that with a buoyancy of 1.3, the tax-GDP ratio can increase by a margin of 2 percentage points by 2020-21 under feasible growth assumptions. The country needs to augment the tax-GDP ratio by about 4 percentage points to give due attention to education and health.

Expenditure side reforms

Significant efficiency gains can also be obtained on the expenditure side. With the abolition of Plan and non-Plan distinction, and the merger of a large part of Plan grants in the regular fiscal transfers under the Finance Commission, the central government should scale down many of the ministries that have been dealing with state subjects and administration of Plan grants. Together, these initiatives can provide the means to uplift India's growth close to its long-term potential. Expenditure restructuring is crucial for the much-needed increase in expenditure on health and education. Spread of education would lead to a sustained increase in digitization.

D.K. Srivastava is chief policy adviser at EY India.

http://www.livemint.com/Opinion/XQruNfpixftLjUSQ7TSkNJ/Budget-2017-A-Case-for-aggressive-fiscal-stimulus.html

4.2   Budget 2017: Government should stick to fiscal targets

The best policy defense for a country like India in an uncertain global environment is to keep its own house in order

In about two weeks, Union finance minister Arun Jaitley will present his fourth, and possibly most important, budget so far. The presentation of the budget has been advanced by about a month so that the government is in a position to start spending from the beginning of the financial year. Apart from the changing global economic order, Jaitley will have to account for domestic factors such as the impact of the currency swap on economic output and the implementation of the goods and services tax (GST). Given this context, Reserve Bank of India governor Urjit Patel's remark last week that good policy housekeeping should be the cornerstone for India gains importance.

It must be considered against the backdrop of global developments. For one, significant policy changes are expected in the US as the incoming Donald Trump administration is likely to opt for an expansionary fiscal policy which can lead to higher interest rates and tightening of financial conditions in global markets. Bond yields have gone up in the US after the November election and the Federal Reserve is now expected to tighten rates at a faster pace this year. These changes will affect capital flows as money managers may get more selective in deciding fund allocation.

Second, financial conditions can also be affected by the ongoing rebalancing in China. Chinese policymakers are now dealing with capital outflows more aggressively, though the falling foreign exchange reserves suggest that the pressure on the renminbi is likely to continue.

The best policy defense for a country like India in this uncertain global environment is to keep its own house in order to minimize the impact. However, economic uncertainty in the Indian economy has risen after the government's decision to withdraw high-denomination currency notes. While the first advance estimate by the Central Statistics Office (CSO) showed that the economy is expected to grow at 7.1% in the current fiscal, it did not account for the possible impact of the currency swap on economic activity. Incoming forecasts, including that by the International Monetary Fund, suggest that growth could be considerably lower in the current year and output might suffer in the next year as well.

As a result, a view is emerging that the government should give a demand push to the economy by delaying fiscal consolidation. According to a report published in *Mint* on Wednesday, unlike last year, there is near unanimity in the government over the need for fiscal stimulus. The government would be well advised to avoid taking such a decision for several reasons.

First, the initial assumption was that the impact of the currency swap would be temporary, so fiscal intervention would not be warranted. Second, as economist Sajjid Z. Chinoy of JP Morgan argued in these pages earlier this week, a positive demand shock is not the perfect response to a negative supply shock and could lead to price pressures. Also, a monetary stimulus is already under way as lending rates have come down significantly after the currency ban, which will help output to recover. Third, postponing consolidation on the fiscal front will affect the government's credibility and keep the combined fiscal deficit at higher levels. As Patel noted in his above-mentioned speech, and this paper has highlighted on several occasions in the past, India's consolidated budget deficit is one of the highest among its peers. This affects credit ratings and capital flows. According to the fiscal consolidation road map, the government will need to bring down the fiscal deficit to 3% of gross domestic product (GDP) in the next financial year from the current year's target of 3.5% of GDP.

Furthermore, since the revised estimates and the budget estimates are likely to be prepared on the basis of the CSO's advance estimate, it would be prudent on the part of the government to plan more conservatively, which will help keep the fiscal deficit close to the target even if actual output deviates from current estimates. Put differently, the government will have to work carefully to avoid any divergence from the fiscal consolidation road map as it will not only affect credibility but will also add to economic uncertainty after the currency swap.

To be sure, this will complicate the budget exercise as the government needs to push capital expenditure since private-sector investment continues to remain weak. But higher allocation for capital expenditure should not come at the cost of fiscal prudence. The government will also have to move forward on bank recapitalization. Although the fall in bond yields due to policy accommodation and liquidity gush will boost profits in the banking sector, it is unlikely to significantly reduce the need for capital infusion.

The 2017 budget should be a part of the ongoing process of creating the necessary conditions for sustainable growth while maintaining fiscal discipline. Last year, Jaitley took a prudent decision to adhere to the fiscal target. There is no compelling reason why he should not be moving forward on the same path.

http://www.livemint.com/Opinion/d5kH45JJOAEKGunqtOtmPK/ Government-should-stick-to-fiscal-targets.html

4.3   Growth Deficit and the Fiscal Deficit

The budget is likely to overestimate the expected revenue and the absolute level of the permissible fiscal deficit.

Growth forecasts are more important than is commonly understood. Firms use them for planning sales. Financial institutions use them in their investment allocation templates. Multilateral agencies use them for global outlook assessments and governments use them for annual budgeting. The advance estimate of national income for 2016-17, released by the Central Statistics Office (CSO) on 6 January, provides the basis for computing the revised estimate of the fiscal deficit and other key fiscal ratios realized in 2016-17 in the forthcoming budget. More importantly, the advanced estimate also provides the basis for setting fiscal targets for 2017-18. Incorrect forecasts can mess up the government's fiscal planning.

Like all forecasts, economic growth forecasts are also by their very nature probabilistic statements. Actual outcomes often turn out to be different from the forecast. The aim of the forecaster is to minimize the probability of getting it wrong. In a recent exercise undertaken at the National Institute of Public Finance and Policy, my colleague Parma Devi Adhikari and I have used an automatic leading indicator (ALI) model to forecast the growth rate of the Indian economy for 2016-17. This approach has come to be recognized globally as being possibly the most effective for accurately forecasting gross domestic product (GDP). Without getting into technicalities, let me just say that in this approach the forecaster starts with a whole set of collateral variables which she considers most linked to growth and uses them in running the ALI model to derive a growth forecast. The skill of the forecaster lies in selecting the appropriate set of initial collateral variables.

In using this model to forecast GDP, we faced a major hurdle, as would any macro econometric research requiring time-series GDP data for India. There is a break in the GDP time series in 2011-12. In that year, the CSO launched a new series of national accounts, which has generated a great deal of controversy. New series need to be issued from time to time to reflect changes in the structure of the economy, new sources of data, new concepts. It is standard practice that when a new series is issued, it is also extrapolated backwards for earlier years to have a continuous, comparable time series. The CSO used to do this in the past. However, till date it has not produced the back numbers of GDP for earlier years consistent with the new 2011-12 series. This has compromised any econometric exercise that requires a reasonably long GDP time series.

Analysts have had no option but to use a time series with an abrupt non-comparability of data before and after 2011-12. Fortunately, the CSO has provided GDP estimates based on both the old series and the new series for three overlapping years—2011-12 to 2013-14. The GDP growth rate for these overlapping years is significantly higher with the new series compared to the old series. This shift requires a correction factor to be applied to any forecast that is perforce mostly based on the old GDP time series. With this adjustment we arrived at a preliminary forecast of 6.8% real GDP growth for 2016-17, which is slightly lower than the CSO's advance estimate of 7.1%.

However, neither our preliminary forecast nor the CSO's advance estimate take into account the impact of demonetization since November 2016. There is plenty of evidence, not all of it anecdotal, of a sharp decline in economic activity. The Society of Indian Automobile Manufacturers, for instance, reported that automobile sales in December declined the most in 16 years. Housing sales in the October-December quarter fell by a massive 44% in the largest eight cities, again the lowest in 16 years. The All India Manufacturers' Organization, which largely represents small and medium enterprises, undertook a sample survey 34 days after demonetization. It indicated that revenue had dropped by 50% and jobs by 35% among its member enterprises.

Reflecting this decline in productive employment, the labour ministry has reported an increase of around 20% in demand for relief employment under the Mahatma Gandhi National Rural Employment Guarantee Act (MGNREGA).

Such data are clearly indicative of a significant decline in economic activity post demonetization. However, they do not provide a basis for estimating the impact of demonetization on aggregate GDP. One source of data usable for this purpose is the Reserve Bank of India's fortnightly data on the outstanding credit of scheduled commercial banks. There is a strong statistical relationship between outstanding non-food credit, a good proxy for bank credit to the private sector, and GDP (technically, it is statistically significant at the 1% level). There is no such statistically significant relationship between GDP and food credit, which mainly goes to the public sector to maintain food grain stocks.

This relationship between non-food credit and GDP can be exploited, without asserting any direction of causality, to infer movements in one from the other. Between 30 October and 25 December of 2015, outstanding non-food credit increased by Rs1.85 trillion. In contrast, between 28 October and 23 December of 2016, outstanding non-food credit declined by Rs. 39,200 crores, a massive negative change in the last two months of 2016 compared to the same period in 2015. This change is reflected in a decline in the annual growth of outstanding non-food credit in December from 10.7% in 2015 to only 5.4% in 2016. Factoring this into our growth forecast via the statistical relationship cited earlier, our growth forecast would have to be adjusted down to 6.5% to take account of demonetization up to the end of December.

However, the process of remonetization is not over. The squeeze on economic activity driven by the rationing of cash withdrawals is expected to continue till end-February, if not later, hence also the deceleration in credit growth. This requires a further downward adjustment of our forecast. Our ALI model-based forecast, after taking into account the adverse impact of demonetization, comes to 6.1% as compared to the official advance estimate of 7.1%.

This growth deficit, if our forecast turns out to be correct, can undermine ongoing fiscal calculations. The budget for FY 2016-17 was prepared based on a projected nominal GDP of Rs150.76 trillion, which assumed an 11% nominal growth. However, adding the CSO's implicit GDP deflator of 2.5% to our real GDP growth forecast of 6.1% would imply a nominal GDP growth of only 8.6%.

This 2.4 percentage point growth deficit would translate to a lower nominal GDP in 2016-17, lower revenue, and a larger deficit. The government will find it hard to meet its 3.5% fiscal deficit target under these conditions. However, this will not be revealed in the 2016-17 revised estimates in the forthcoming budget. That is because the budget will be presented two months before the end of the financial year, so the revised estimate will be based on assumed GDP and revenue-growth rates. And these will be made consistent with the 3.5% fiscal deficit target. The actual size of the fiscal deficit will be known only two or three months later.

There is a further problem with fiscal planning for 2017-18. The ongoing budget calculations are being based on the official nominal GDP baseline of Rs151.9 trillion. However, if the actual nominal GDP baseline for 2017-18 is lower at Rs147.4 trillion as per our forecast, this would bias the fiscal projections for 2017-18 as well. Specifically, the budget is likely to overestimate the expected revenue and the absolute level of the permissible fiscal deficit within the fiscal responsibility and budget management (FRBM) target of 3% of GDP for 2017-18.

To summarize, there is likely to be a deficit in actual growth compared to the official projection for 2016-17. As a consequence, the actual fiscal deficit is likely to overshoot the target in both 2016-17 and 2017-18. What is the implication of breaching these targets from a fiscal policy perspective?

In answering that question, it is important to recognize that macroeconomic stability requires a counter-cyclical fiscal policy stance, i.e., allow the deficit to go up when growth dips below the desired norm and compress it when growth spikes above the norm.

Most advanced economies and several emerging market economies now target a structural deficit, which serves as an automatic counter-cyclical stabilizer. The structural deficit is the deficit consistent with sustainable public debt under conditions of normal growth. The actual deficit is allowed to exceed or fall below this target when growth is too low or too high.

The FRBM targets which have been set from the outset as a fixed percentage of GDP do just the opposite. The deficit shrinks when growth dips and balloons when growth rises. This pro-cyclical target setting has forced successive finance ministers to look for creative ways of getting around a dysfunctional FRBM straitjacket. In extreme situations, it has even been abandoned, as during the financial crisis of 2008. The report of the FRBM committee will hopefully set this right. Meanwhile, if the fiscal deficit target of 3.5% for 2016-17 is breached and the 3% FRBM target or 2017-18 is eased in the forthcoming budget, this would not be a bad thing. Given the benign inflation outlook, such pump priming would be a welcome corrective after the adverse growth shock of demonetization.

Sudipto Mundle is emeritus professor at the National Institute of Public Finance and Policy, and was a member of the 14th Finance Commission.

http://www.livemint.com/Opinion/6WDgd5KZdRhlKLrqjMXfWP/Growth -deficit-and-the-fiscal-deficit.html?li_source=LI&li_medium=news_rec

4.4 Budget 2017: N.K. Singh Committee Favours New Fiscal Rules

N.K. Singh panel prescribes fiscal path for governments, but with escape clauses that have been 'quantified', desists from specifying range for fiscal deficit.

Former revenue secretary N.K. Singh, who heads the Fiscal Responsibility and Budget Management (FRBM) Committee - Photo: Hindustan Times

The Union government is likely to announce new fiscal rules which will provide it with more flexibility in spending.

This assumes the government accepts the recommendations of the expert panel headed by former revenue secretary N.K. Singh, which has prescribed a fiscal path—for both the centre and states—but with escape clauses that have been "quantified". The panel, said a person familiar with the report, also desisted from specifying a range for the fiscal deficit. The panel submitted its report on Monday.

"The Government will examine the FRBM (Fiscal Responsibility and Budget Management) Committee Report and take appropriate action," a finance ministry statement said. The key recommendations are likely to be announced in the budget, while the full report will be released later, said a government official.

The panel had been mandated to explore the option of moving to a flexible fiscal deficit target instead of targeting a fixed number every year. It is not clear whether the panel has used the fiscal deficit or the revenue deficit as the metric to define the path. After deciding to stick to the fiscal deficit target of 3.5% of gross domestic product for 2016-17, finance minister Arun Jaitley in last year's budget proposed an expert group to amend the FRBM Act.

"Given the kind of volatility that is prevailing all around, I think the world over governments need some political headroom to move the goalpost either way," economic affairs secretary Shaktikanta Das said **in an interview to Mint after last year's budget**. "The government should have some policy space and at the same time the band for policy adjustment should not be so large that it defeats the purpose of fiscal consolidation."

Madan Sabnavis, chief economist at Care Ratings Ltd, said the government suggestion of putting in place a fiscal deficit band was pragmatic. "Government needs to maintain growth momentum for which it should have a flexible fiscal deficit target. However, this year, with enough revenue gains, it need not deviate from the current fiscal consolidation roadmap," he added.

http://www.livemint.com/Politics/3gEQytUeuNNl1B7r6tnGvN/NK-Singh-committee-favours-new-fiscal-rules.html?li_source=LI&li_medium=news_rec

4.5   Government expenditure as a share of GDP shrinks

The centre's expenditure as a share of GDP has fallen from 14.9% of GDP at market prices in 2011-12 to 13.4% in 2016-17.

The central government's expenditure as a proportion of gross domestic product (GDP) has been shrinking. Central government spending, as seen from Union budgets, has fallen from 14.9% of GDP at market prices in 2011-12 to 13.4% in 2016-17, according to the revised estimates, while total expenditure is budgeted to shrink further to 12.7% of GDP in 2017-18, quite a fall. *Chart 1* has the details.

The expenditure / GDP ratio has come down since the current government took over, but as the chart shows, the process started during the last years of the United Progressive Alliance (UPA) government. To be sure, the metric went up a bit during the current financial year due to the increase in pay of central government employees, but even so, the jump has been contained and the process of pruning expenditure is expected to continue to 2017-18.

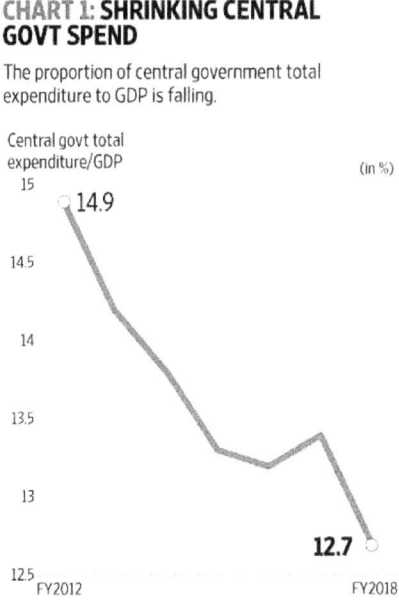

CHART 1: SHRINKING CENTRAL GOVT SPEND

The proportion of central government total expenditure to GDP is falling.

Central govt total expenditure/GDP (in %)

Is this shrinking due to lower expenditure on subsidies, particularly the petroleum subsidy? *Chart 2* shows that the central government's expenditure, less subsidies, as a proportion of GDP has also been falling, albeit not so dramatically. This percentage moved up this year on account of the pay commission outgo, but it's expected to fall next fiscal. So even apart from subsidies, expenditure as a proportion of GDP has been coming down.

Did lower interest rates, leading to lower interest outgo on government debt; have a hand in reducing expenditure? The key is to find out whether government expenditure less subsidies and interest payments has been declining as a proportion of GDP.

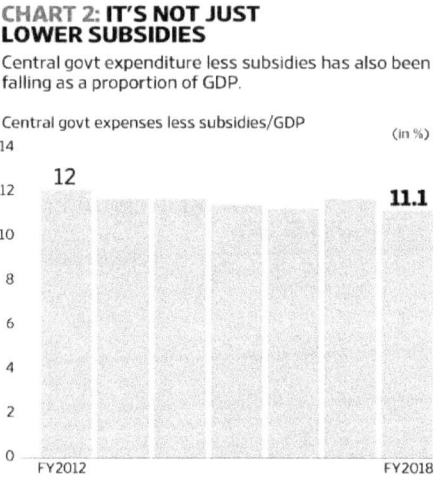

CHART 2: IT'S NOT JUST LOWER SUBSIDIES

Central govt expenditure less subsidies has also been falling as a proportion of GDP.

Central govt expenses less subsidies/GDP (in %)

Chart 3 shows that this yardstick fell rapidly in FY13 and was further pruned during the first year of the National Democratic Alliance (NDA) government. But note that this has been budgeted to remain at 8% in FY18, the same level as in FY15, indicating the government is in no mood to shrink its expenditure further, with elections ahead. However, this metric was at 8.8% in FY07, at the height of the last boom, so there really has been some compression in central government expenditure, apart from interest payments and subsidies.

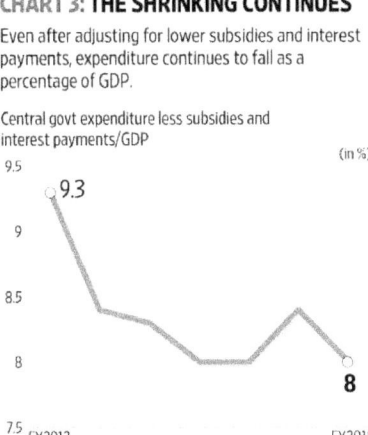

CHART 3: THE SHRINKING CONTINUES

Even after adjusting for lower subsidies and interest payments, expenditure continues to fall as a percentage of GDP.

Central govt expenditure less subsidies and interest payments/GDP

Has the quality of government expenditure improved? ***Chart 4*** shows an uptick in the central government's capital expenditure (capex) / GDP ratio, but it has been marginal. Note also that budgeted capex for FY18, as a proportion of GDP, is at the same level as in FY12. The much vaunted rise in capital expenditure is no big deal.

CHART 4: NO BIG CHANGE IN CAPEX

Central govt capital expenditure as a proportion of GDP has risen, but marginally.

Central govt capex/GDP

Chart 5 shows, however, that the NDA government has done really well in increasing the tax / GDP ratio, in large part due to higher excise duties on petroleum products and higher collections from service taxes.

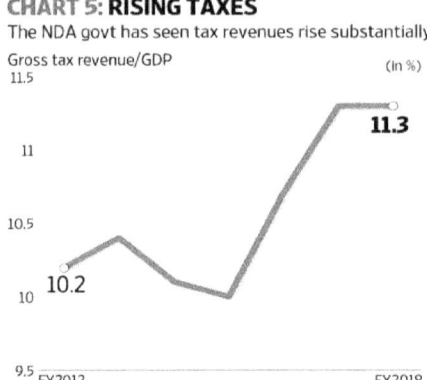

CHART 5: RISING TAXES

The NDA govt has seen tax revenues rise substantially.

Gross tax revenue/GDP (In %)

Nevertheless, after sharing with the states, the centre's net tax revenue as a percentage of GDP has remained at 7.2% in the current fiscal year, the same percentage as in FY12. That is shown in ***Chart 6***. In spite of a higher gross tax / GDP ratio, more of those taxes are going to the states, thanks to the finance commission recommendations.

It is important to recall that, during 2006-07, at the height of the last boom, the central government's total expenditure / GDP ratio was 13.6%. The fiscal consolidation achieved during the boom years was frittered away as a result of the stimulus given immediately after the financial crisis. You could argue that the central government has been slowly and steadily shrinking its way towards that lost fiscal rectitude.

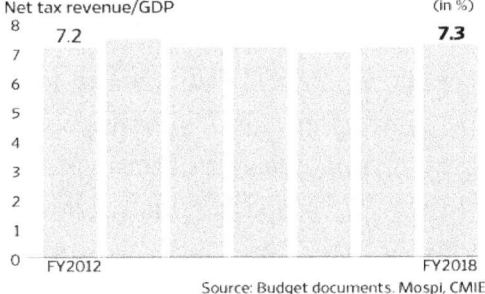

CHART 6: NET TAX REVENUE TO THE CENTRE HASN'T GONE UP

As a result of sharing more revenues with states, the centre's share hasn't risen.

Net tax revenue/GDP   (in %)

Source: Budget documents. Mospi, CMIE

http://www.livemint.com/Opinion/FBYsARzVn7u3DcHrlO5d0H/ Government-expenditure-as-a-share-of-GDP-shrinks.html?li_source=LI&li_ medium=news_rec

4.6 The Right Processes for a Good Budget

A transparent policymaking process is necessary for taking the right decision and obtaining a buy-in from stakeholders.

Post demonetization, the challenge that finance minister Arun Jaitley faces this time is far greater than any of the earlier occasions.

Decision making is a difficult ask, especially when the decision is going to affect millions. Politicians are in this profession, and are expected to make difficult choices almost every day. The presentation of the annual budget is one such important occasion wherein the Union finance minister is expected to lay out difficult choices while explaining the rationale in a manner which soothes those likely to be hurt.

The challenges that finance minister Arun Jaitley faces this time is far greater than any of the earlier occasions. Our economy is still grappling with the impact of demonetization, while simultaneously being force-fed digital payments despite inadequate infrastructure. As if this double whammy on the domestic front was not enough, protectionist voices are globally gaining political mileage and threatening to disrupt the movement of people, capital, goods and services that we have grown accustomed to.

So what choices should Jaitley make to ensure India remains on the inclusive growth trajectory? A lot has been written pertaining to this, including by myself. Whatever decisions are taken in the budget, there will always be supporters and critics, both with strong hypotheses in favour of their arguments. Post-mortems of decisions are always easier than ex-ante assessments of the potential impacts that the decisions are likely to have. This is despite the fact that an ex-ante assessment is much more important than a post-facto assessment for an economy.

Good processes lead to good outcomes

To tackle the twin challenges of taking the right decision (which is often unpopular), and obtaining a buy-in from stakeholders, a transparent policymaking process is recommended. It involves publishing the different policy options and related costs and benefits in the public domain, and involving the stakeholders in decision making.

This is not just theory but has been put into practice by several governments. For instance, the UK publishes Tax Information and Impact Notes on proposed tax policy changes to provide a clear explanation of the policy objective together with the details of the tax impact on the exchequer, economy, individuals, businesses, civil society organizations—as well as any other specific area of impact. In addition, at least three months prior to the introduction of the Finance Bill, it publishes consolidated draft clauses for inclusion in the Finance Bill, for public comments. This provides taxpayers with more certainty, and a window for pre-legislative scrutiny. Details of public consultation along with government responses to suggestions are available for review in the public domain.

With every budget, the UK also publishes a comprehensive document on "Policy Costs" which sets out the assumptions and methodologies underlying costing for tax and annual expenditure of policy decisions having a fiscally significant impact on public finances. The document also explains the general methodology used to calculate the cost or yield of each government policy. A comprehensive document on "Data Sources" is also published to facilitate transparency, public scrutiny and accountability. Taking into account the concerns of the common man, another dedicated document the UK publishes relates to distributional analysis of the "Impact on Households" of the government's tax, welfare and spending decisions.

The UK has also introduced several organization-level reforms to complement its process reforms. It has set up an Office of Tax Simplification (OTS) to provide advice on simplifying the UK tax system with the objective of reducing the compliance burden on both businesses and individual taxpayers. In addition, it has in place an Office for Budget Responsibility (OBR) to examine and report on the sustainability of public finances. While the OTS aids in the assessment of impact of policy proposals on households, the policy costs estimated by the government are reviewed and certified by the OBR.

Make a beginning

While adopting reforms as comprehensive as the UK will require significant preparation and resources, it is time the Indian government at least made a beginning. In almost all the pre-budget consultations with the finance minister over the past few years, I have argued for competition reforms, which includes the adoption of a Regulatory Impact Assessment (RIA)—similar to one of the ex-ante impact assessment process reforms adopted by the UK. Unfortunately, I have met with limited success.

I am not alone in calling for the adoption of RIA in India. Since 2011, almost every other high-level expert committee has made this suggestion. These include the Planning Commission's working group on business regulatory framework, the Financial Sector Legislative Reforms Commission, the Damodaran committee and the Ajay Shankar committee, among others. Even the recently executed memorandum of understanding (MoU) between the UK and India on ease of doing business includes cooperation on RIA. I hope this MoU can be a catalyst for the government to take concrete steps for the adoption of RIA in the policymaking process.

It is time that a structured ex-ante assessment framework is integrated in the government decision-making process to ensure that right policy choices are made, to the extent possible. This will go a long way in ensuring that policy decisions are well-thought-out and impose minimum costs on the economy to achieve the desired policy objectives. We will be able to avoid knee-jerk reactions originating from the sub-optimal wisdom of a close coterie of government advisers. The country deserves this. Make the right choice, finance minister!

Pradeep S. Mehta is secretary general of CUTS International.

Amol Kulkarni of CUTS International contributed to this article.

http://www.livemint.com/Opinion/WjGcW2lfMxo44mWTV4TQlM/The-right-processes-for-a-good-budget.html?li_source=LI&li_medium=news_rec

4.7   Union Budget and the Need for Structural Reforms

The budget has done some things right but there is a limit to what can be achieved through stroke-of-the-pen reforms.

The immediate audience for the Union budget presentation on 1 February was Parliament, but the targeted audience was rating agencies—and of course, the electorate in the five state elections looming up. The first audience ensured that the fiscal consolidation path was broadly adhered to, with the message that India has the kind of responsible government deserving of a reward through a ratings upgrade. For the electorate in the large and important states going to the polls, details were provided of non-compliance in the upper income-tax brackets, with a promise of follow-up action. The message here was that demonetization was somehow a needed starting point for elimination of *kala dhan* (black money), although, of course, it was not. The tax base could and should have been expanded 25 years ago, or last year, or the year before.

The link made by the finance minister between tax-base expansion and demonetization was the promise that data from the pattern of cash deposits in bank accounts between 8 November and 31 December 2016 would be mined for information on individuals outside the tax net. He reported that deposits of an average size of Rs.3.31 crores were made in 148,000 bank accounts. As information, it is startlingly revelatory of the mammoth size of cash that was being held outside the banking system, and of the scale of tax evasion in past years, but it does not necessarily map on to an easy expansion of the tax base. Those large deposits most likely came from charitable organizations and religious trusts, and if stories are to be believed, folded in contributions from individuals who did not want to be tracked through their individual bank accounts. Whatever the case, the finance minister has certainly marked a date from which his own performance can be tracked, in terms of adding to the number of taxpayers, particularly at the high end, and he is to be commended for having designed his own report card.

The most promising tax-revenue enhancement measure is the limit on deductibles from taxable income in the form of cash expenditure—a maximum of Rs.10,000. This will not raise the number of people in the tax net, but will curtail the most commonly used avenue for reducing tax liability by business and trader assesses. An even more important curtailment is the reduced limit on cash donations to charitable trusts, from Rs.10, 000 to Rs.2, 000, although I see no way this can be enforced. The Income-Tax Act is proposed to be amended to rule out cash settlement of any transaction over the value of Rs3 lakh. In the normal course, the goods and services tax (GST) would have eliminated cash payment even for much lower-value transactions—in product markets, that is. But how such a ruling is to be enforced in the urban house rental market, or in contractual payments in the informal sector, is not clear at all. In urban real estate sale transactions, where cash plays (or has hitherto played) a major supplementary role to a formal component routed through banks, it cannot be enforced at all. These are the more intractable segments of the black economy where reform can be achieved only at a measured and carefully sequenced pace over a long period of time.

Another measure that will defy enforcement is the Rs 2,000 limit on the cash donation any single individual can make to a political party (is that per year?). Larger amounts have to be made through formal cashless channels. There is no explicit reference to corporate contributions, but by implication they are denied the option of donations in cash. There is no mention of how this can be enforced.

I found the idea of electoral bonds bought by a donor, redeemable in the account of a registered political party, very innovative, perhaps the most interesting budget idea in a long time. This could, however, lead to a further proliferation of fake political parties, an issue the Election Commission is already grappling with. Also, unless electoral bonds are given an income-tax deduction of the kind currently available for political contributions under sections

80GGB and 80GGC of the Income-Tax Act, they might not prove very popular. As for political parties having to file income-tax returns, this will actually happen only if it is made a legal precondition for a political party to contest an election at any level.

Meanwhile, cashless India is party time for foreign manufacturers of point-of-sale (POS) card readers and fingerprint and iris readers/scanners, especially after the elimination in the budget of basic and additional customs duty on such machines. Why did no domestic entrepreneur see this market coming when Aadhaar kicked off as long ago as 2009? What was the department of industrial policy and promotion (DIPP) doing?

DIPP's failure to project the market for POS gadgetry is only a small instance of the larger failure of the government in its growth-enabling and regulatory roles. Government disabling of economic activity through delays and misuse of its role as regulator is the principal cause of stalled private sector investment in the Indian economy.

A whole section of the finance minister's speech was indeed devoted to measures by which to improve the ease of doing business in India, but the proposals merely nibble at the fringes of what is a much larger problem. They include raising the threshold beyond which compliance with audit or bookkeeping requirements apply, relaxing income-tax monitoring of domestic transfer pricing between related parties, and reducing the time taken by income-tax authorities for scrutiny and refund claims.

All very welcome, of course, but by definition applicable to ongoing businesses. What of aspiring businesses which have achieved financial closure, and cannot commence commercial operations because of a hold-up in one or the other government clearance?

The prospect of these indefinite delays is what retards private investment, and makes potential entrepreneurs shift their sights to overseas locations. For investors who despite everything want to persist with projects in India, delayed government permissions add hugely to the stress on banks. The state of the Indian banking system is a major reason why rating agencies are unwilling to grant an upgrade. In terms just of that limited objective, if no other, structural reform of the functioning of government is no longer just a preferable option. It is an imperative. Structural reform, in turn, is about the recognition and correction of government as it functions at the ground level, a process which calls for deep immersion and follow-through. There is a limit to what can be achieved through stroke-of-the-pen reforms, although there was enough opportunity even there that the budget has very usefully exploited.

These were listed by the finance minister right at the beginning of his speech. The most major was the advancement of the date of the budget announcement to the start rather than the end of February. It gives enough time for the Finance Bill to be actually passed before the start of the next fiscal year, and therefore prevents the kind of delayed start to implementation that is a major cause of poor outcomes. The merger of Plan and non-Plan expenditure, another welcome departure from the past, became naturally possible at this juncture since March marks the end of the 12th (and last) Plan. It gets us on to a new platform where the expenditure under a budget head gets unified, instead of being splintered by source of funding. It will be a great relief for those who have to prepare and oversee the printing of budget documents in finance departments all over the country.

Finally, the merger of the railway budget with the overall budget is another welcome change, enabling as it does integrated transport planning across modes. If, as announced, the railways will design integrated end-to-end transportation solutions specific to commodities and destinations, with a particular focus on perishable agricultural commodities, we might begin to see a reduction in the post-harvest losses that are such a notorious feature of the agricultural supply chain in India.

But the neglect of any mention of the horrendous rail accidents that have happened over the last year was an egregious omission. What we needed was a listing of these, the cause as ascertained through the inquiry into each, and what is proposed to be done in respect of each cause in the rail segment where it happened. What we have instead is a generalized Rashtriya Rail Sanraksha Kosh, which will develop a corpus of Rs. 1 trillion over five years, and will harness "expert international assistance" to improve rail safety. My sense is that several reviews of railway safety have already identified the courses of action needed. This is a problem too immediate and too damaging in its past and future consequences to be fobbed off with a corpus.

As for cleanliness, the SMS-based "Clean My Coach" service is very welcome, provided the service is equipped to catch mice. Bio toilets are most welcome too, but more immediately, there is a need to ensure water supply in the toilets of every train for the full duration of its run. Here again. There is that futile sense the citizen gets, of grand talk about cleanliness way up there in the stratosphere, while the most elementary basics are lost sight of.

Finally, to end on a positive note, the performance since 2014 on road construction, both highways and the Pradhan Mantri Gram Sadak Yojana for village connectivity, has been most impressive. It could have been even better had the problems with public-private partnership contracts been sorted out, along the lines suggested in the report of the Kelkar committee. Road construction on the scale required cannot possibly rely on public funds alone.

Indira Rajaraman is an economist.

http://www.livemint.com/Opinion/HEGu14oatDOYNqGkgEEJQO/The-Union-budget-and-the-need-for-structural-reforms.html?li_source=LI&li_medium=news_rec

Chapter-5: Union Budget 2017

5.1   How the Union Budget is made?

On 1 February, finance minister Arun Jaitley will present to most significant budget of the Narendra Modi government. Here's a behind the scenes look at the budget process.

Photo: PTI

Finance minister Arun Jaitley is going to present the most significant budget of the Narendra Modi government that comes in the immediate backdrop of demonetization meant to wipe out black money and counterfeit notes that has caused significant disruptions in the economy.

The 2017-18 budgets will also see many departures from the past. It will be presented a month in advance on 1 February as against the traditional practice of presenting it on the last day of February. The rail budget will be merged with the Union budget and the finance minister will present a single comprehensive budget. This budget will also do away with the distinction of plan and non-plan expenditure replacing it by capital expenditure and revenue expenditure classification. This will provide a clear distinction between productive and recurrent spending trends.

Here is a low-down of what goes behind the scene in making the budget.

HOW THE BUDGET IS MADE

The 2017-18 budget will be presented on 1 February rather than the customary practice of presenting it on 28 February. It will also see the rail budget being merged with the Union budget.

The cabinet gave its nod to merge the rail budget with the Union budget and advancing the budget dates in September. However, the finance ministry started the preparatory work much before, anticipating the advancement of the Union budget. The finance ministry collects information about receipts and expenditure from various departments to prepare the revised estimates for the budget.

The pre-budget discussions with industry bodies, economists, trade unions, agriculturists and state finance ministers also started in November this year as against December-January. The budget is made in close consultation with the Prime Minister's Office.

This year, Jaitley is expected to increase public spending significantly to boost the economy adversely impacted by the government's decision to invalidate high-value currency and lagging private investment.

The budget-making process is shrouded in complete secrecy, replete with closed-circuit cameras and scrutiny by Intelligence Bureau officials to prevent any breaches. North Block, which headquarters the finance ministry, was made off-limits to the media in December. Budget documents are printed at a printing press located in North block's basement.

A week before the budget, officials involved in the process of preparing it are not allowed any contact with the outside world to ensure there are no leaks.

Two days before the budget speech, officers of the Press Information Bureau, the government's public relations wing, enter the picture. A team of around 20 officials are tasked with preparing press releases in three languages-English, Hindi and Urdu. They are not allowed to leave the premises till the time the speech is delivered by the finance minister. The cabinet is shown a gist of the budget 10 minutes before Parliament meets on budget day.

BUDGET GLOSSARY

○ **Gross domestic product (GDP):** The added value of output of all productive sectors in the Indian economy as measured by the Central Statistics Office.

○ **Fiscal deficit:** The total additional borrowings made by the government every year to bridge the gap between its income and expenditure. Thus, the fiscal deficit is the gross addition to the government's domestic debt burden.

○ **Capital and revenue expenditure:** Expenditure that does not create any asset, such as subsidies and interest payments, is classified as revenue expenditure. Conversely, spending to create assets such as highways, buildings and dams as well as loans given by the centre to the states come under capital expenditure.

○ **Subsidies:** Economic benefits given by the government in the form of cash or kind to individuals to ameliorate income inequality. Companies also receive subsidies in the form of tax rebates to encourage industrialization and employment generation.

○ **Tax revenue:** It is the primary source of income for the government. The government funds its expenditure by either directly taxing income of individuals/companies or by taxing goods and services consumed by people.

○ **Non-tax revenue:** The additional source of revenue for the government other than from direct and indirect taxes. This includes revenues from interest receipts, spectrum auction and disinvestment among other things.

○ **Debt servicing:** Like individuals, who serve existing loans through periodic repayment of the principal and interest amount, government also repays borrowings made from outside the country from multilateral agencies and those made from within the country through bond issue.

○ **Market borrowing:** Government sells sovereign bonds to borrow from the market to meet its additional expenditure or to service existing debts.

http://www.livemint.com/Politics/09ASwzxIEuA5K7XNJTZS0O/How-the-Union-budget-is-made.html?li_source=LI&li_medium=news_rec

5.2   India   Unveils   Budget   for   Recovery   after   Cash   Crunch

Wednesday, 1 Feb 2017 | 1:07 AM   ET Reuters

Dhiraj Singh | Bloomberg | Getty Images

India is a "bright spot" in the world economy, Finance Minister Arun Jaitley said as he unveiled his annual budget on Wednesday, adding that the impact on growth from the government's cash crackdown would wear off soon.

"We are seen as an engine of global growth," Jaitley said as he delivered the opening remarks of his fourth budget.

Prime Minister Narendra Modi's surprise decision last November to scrap high-value banknotes worth 86 percent of India's cash in circulation has hit consumer demand, disrupted supply chains and hurt capital investments.

The worst of the cash crunch is now over and the government expects it to be fully cleared by the end of April. A private manufacturing survey on Wednesday showed business is slowly returning to normal.

Still, the finance ministry forecasts that growth could dip to as low as 6.5 percent in the current fiscal year to March, before picking up slightly in the coming fiscal year to between 6.75 and 7.5 percent.

The Indian economy, post-demonetization

That is below the target rate of 8 percent or more that Modi needs to create enough jobs for the 1 million young Indians who enter the workforce in India - a nation of 1.3 billion where half the population is below the age of 25.

While opinions vary on how long the disruptions caused by Modi's crackdown on untaxed and illicit wealth will last, there is near unanimity among economists that Asia's third-largest economy needs a helping hand.

Arvind Subramanian, Jaitley's chief economic adviser, on Tuesday advocated slashing personal income tax and accelerating cuts in corporate tax rates. He cautioned, however, against pursuing debt-fuelled fiscal expansion.

Still, economists are penciling in a federal fiscal deficit of 3.3 percent of GDP for 2017/18. That would be higher than the 3 percent pledged earlier but lower than 3.5 percent that the government has budgeted for the year soon to end.

The rollout of a nationwide Goods and Services tax (GST) expected in July after years of delays and could also weigh on economic growth.

Countries that have introduced GST in the past have often faced a relative economic slowdown before the benefits of a unified tax regime feed through.

http://www.cnbc.com/2017/02/01/india-budget-2017-demonetisation-to-weaken-growth-but-modis-government-expects-impact-to-wear-off-soon.html

Markets cheer Arun Jaitley's budget speech, Rahul slams it

Finance minister Arun Jaitley has presented the Union Budget 2017 in Parliament. Here are the live updates following his budget speech

Union finance minister Arun Jaitley on Wednesday presented the Union Budget 2017, proposing revised income tax limits for individual assesses, higher spending in the infrastructure sector, and measures to push India towards a digital economy. Here are the live updates following his budget speech:

Union Budget 2017 shows Modi has fulfilled promise on black money, says Amit Shah

BJP president Amit Shah on Wednesday said that Union Budget 2017 shows that Prime Minister Narendra Modi has fulfilled the promise made in 2014 to curb black money and bring transparency in political funding. "We had promised in 2014 to root out influence of black money in political funding and bring in transparency. Prime Minister Narendra Modi has today fulfilled that promise. By reducing the limit of cash funding to political parties to Rs. 2,000 from Rs. 20,000, he has ushered in a new era," Shah said.

Well-being of the Indian economy guiding light of Union Budget 2017: Arun Jaitley

In an interview to DD News on Wednesday, finance minister Arun Jaitley said the guiding philosophy behind Union Budget 2017 was the well-being of the Indian economy, with a focus on strengthening sectors that will boost the overall economic performance. The Union finance minister also said that his measure are aimed at going hard on tax evaders while providing tax payers relief and with additional spending power.

Sensex closes 486 points up after Union Budget 2017 cheers investors

BSE Sensex on Wednesday rose 485.68 points, or 1.76%, to 28,141.64 while the Nifty 50 rises 155.10 points, or 1.81%, to 8,716.40 after finance minister Arun Jaitley's budget speech. Read more

Union Budget 2017 a damp squib, lacks vision: Rahul Gandhi

Slamming the Union Budget presented by finance minister Arun Jaitley, Congress vice-president Rahul Gandhi on Wednesday said it lacked a clear vision and had nothing for farmers, youths and job creation. "We were expecting fireworks; instead it was a damp squib. It is just 'sher-o shayari' in the budget. There is nothing for farmers and youth and nothing for job creation. There is no clear vision," the Congress vice-president said soon Jaitley's budget speech in the Lok Sabha. Read more

Budget 2017 futuristic, says Narendra Modi

Prime Minister Narendra Modi on Wednesday described Union Budget 2017 as "futuristic", with an aim on fulfilling the "dreams" of every section, including the poor, the farmers and the under-privileged while focusing on job creation, transparency, urban rejuvenation and rural development.

"This is a budget for the future—for farmers, underprivileged, transparency, urban rejuvenation, rural development, enterprise," Modi said while commenting on the document presented by finance minister Arun Jaitley in the Lok Sabha. Read more

5.3   Reactions to Union Budget 2017

Union finance minister Arun Jaitley's Union Budget 2017 has evoked diverse reactions from politicians, industry leaders, experts and the Twittered.

Here are some of the reactions:

■ Prime Minister Narendra Modi: "The FM has presented an 'Uttam' Budget, devoted to strengthening the hands of the poor," tweets PMO.

■ Power minister Piyush Goyal: "Congratulate @arunjaitley ji on reform oriented budget with concessions to middle class & SMEs while maintaining taxes through compliance," tweeted.

■ Yogendra Yadav: "The bullish tone of FM and rosy picture of economy is not borne out by the modest picture painted by economic survey yesterday. Reducing cash limit for political funding from Rs. 20K to Rs. 2K is meaningless; because there is no limit in number of persons," tweeted. Read more

Budget 2017: Jaitley reduces income tax rates

Union finance minister Arun Jaitley during his budget speech on Wednesday proposed revised tax limits for individual assesses in his presentation of the Union Budget 2017.

Here is what the finance minister proposed:

—Tax liability for those with annual income between Rs2.5 and 5 lakh at 5% instead of the existing 10%.

—Surcharge of 10% for those individuals whose annual income is Rs.50 lakh and Rs.1 crores.

—Surcharge on individual annual income of Rs.1 crores or more remains unchanged at 15%.

—A single-page income tax return filing form for taxable income under Rs. 5 lakh.

Here are the live updates on Arun Jaitley's budget speech:

- **12.50 pm:** Income tax rate for individuals earning between Rs.2.5 lakh and Rs.5 lakh reduced to 5% from 10%; 10% surcharge on those individuals who have an income between Rs. 50 lakh and Rs.1 crores; A single one-page form for filing income tax returns for taxable income up to Rs.5 lakh.

- Maximum amount of cash donation to any political party will be Rs. 2,000 from one individual.

- **12.47 pm:** Political parties will be entitled to receive donation, by cheque or in digital mode, from their donors.

- **12.41pm:** Arun Jaitley limits cash transactions for individuals at Rs. 3 lakh.

- **12.39 pm:** Basic customs duty on LNG to be reduced from 5% to 2.5%.

- **12.37 pm:** To make MSMEs (micro, small and medium enterprises) more viable, income tax for smaller firms to be reduced. Tax rate for companies with an annual turnover up to Rs.50 crores is to be reduced to 25%.

- Rate of growth in advance tax in personal income tax in last three quarters of this financial year is as high as 34.8%.

- **12.33 pm:** 24 lakh people show income above Rs.10 lakh in 2016. 1.7 crores people file income tax returns out of 4.2 crores salaried people.

- **12.32pm:** Due to demonetization, advance tax on personal Income tax increased by 34.8%

- **12.28 pm:** We are committed to make taxation rates reasonable. This approach will change the colour of money.

- **12.27pm:** From 8 November to 30 December (demonetization period), deposits between Rs. 2 lakh and Rs. 80 lakh were made in 1.09 crores bank accounts.

- **12.25pm:** Arun Jaitley says India largely a tax non-compliant country.

- **12.24pm:** Trade Infrastructure Export Scheme to be launched in 2017-18; total allocation for infrastructure at record Rs 3.96 lakh crores (Rs. 3.96 trillion).

- **12.22pm:** Digi Gaon will be launched to promote tele-medicine and education. Dedicated micro-irrigation fund is to be set up by Nabard to achieve mission of Per Drop, More Crop. (PTI)

- Second phase of solar power development is to be taken up with an aim of generating 20,000 MW. Trade Infrastructure Export Scheme is to be launched in 2017-18. The total allocation for infrastructure at record Rs. 3.96 trillion. (PTI)

- **12.20pm:** Budget allocation for highways stepped up to Rs.64,000 crores in FY18 from Rs.57,676 crores. For transport sector, including railways, road and shipping, government provides Rs. 2.41 lakh crores. (PTI)

- Allocation of Rs.10,000 crores for Bharat Net project for providing high-speed broadband in FY18. (PTI)

- **12.12pm:** Service charge on e-tickets booked through IRCTC will be withdrawn; railway tariffs to be fixed on the basis of cost, social obligation and competition; new metro rail policy to be unveiled. (PTI)

- Delhi and Jaipur is to have solid waste management plants and five more to be set up later. (PTI)

- **12.11pm:** Government proposes Coach Mitra facility to redress grievances related to rail coaches. (PTI)

- **12.08pm:** Capital and development expenditure pegged at Rs. 1.31 lakh crores for railways in 2017-18 from the budget. Rs.1 lakh crores (Rs.1 trillion) will be corpus for railway safety fund over five years. Five hundred stations will be differently able by providing lifts and escalators. (PTI)

- **12.04pm:** FIPB (Foreign Investment Promotion Board) to be abolished in 2017-18 to liberalize FDI policy. Over 90% of FDI proposals are now processed through automatic route. (PTI)

- **12.03pm:** 35% increase in allocation for Scheduled Castes to Rs. 52,393 crores.

- **12.02pm:** Model Shops and Establishment Bill to open up additional opportunities for employment of women. For senior citizens, Aadhaar-based health cards will be issued.

- **12.00pm:** The government to set up dairy processing fund of Rs. 8,000 crores over three years with initial corpus of Rs.2,000 crores.

- **11.55am:** In higher education, we will undertake reforms in UGC (University Grants Commission), give autonomy to colleges and institutions. The allocation for rural agro and allied sector in 2017-18 is record Rs. 181,223 crores. (PTI)

- Pradhan Mantri Kaushal Kendra will be extended to 600 districts; 100 international skill centers to be opened to help people get jobs abroad (PTI)

- **11.52am:** Cabinet extends tenure of loans under Credit Linked Subsidy Scheme of Pradhan Mantri Awas Yojana from 15 to 20 years.

- Coverage of Fasal Bima Yojana to go up from 30% of cropped area, to 40% in 2017-18 & 50% in 2018-19: FM #Budget2017 https://youtu.be/TYJsH_y8ytI

- A system of annual learning outcome in schools to be a system of annual learning outcome in schools to be introduced; innovation fund for secondary education to be set up.

- **11.50am:** We propose to provide safe drinking water to 28,000 arsenic and fluoride affected habitations. Sanitation coverage in villages has increased from 42% in October 2016 to 60%, a rise of 18%. (PTI)

- **11.48am:** Rs. 27,000 crores on to be spend on Pradhan Mantri Gram Sadak Yojana; one crores houses to be completed by 2017-18 for the homeless. (PTI)

- **11.47am:** The merger of the railway budget with the general budget brings focus on a multi-modal approach for development of railways, highways and inland water transport. Functional autonomy of the railways will be maintained. (PTI)

- **11.46am:** Demonetization was a continuation of series of measures taken by the government in two years it is bold and decisive measure. It will have only transient impact on economy and bring in long-term benefits including higher GDP growth and tax revenue. Demonetization will help in transfer of resources from tax evaders to government. (PTI)

  - **Farmers:** for whom we have committed to double income in five years.

  - **Rural population:** providing employment and basic infrastructure.

  - **Youth:** Energizing them through education, skills and jobs.

  - **Poor and under-privileged:** strengthening the system of social security, health care and affordable housing.

  - **Infrastructure:** for efficiency, productivity and quality of life.

- **Financial sector:** growth and stability through stronger institutions.

- **Digital Economy:** for speedy accountability and transparency.

- **Public Service:** effective Governance and efficiency of service delivery through people's participation.

- **Prudent Fiscal Management:** to ensure optimal deployment of resources and preserve financial stability.

- **Tax Administration:** Honouring the Honest.

- **11.45 am:** The government took two tectonic policy initiatives in 2016-17: the passage of Goods and Services Tax (GST) Bill and demonetization. Pace of remonetization has picked up; demonetization effects will not spill over to next year. (PTI)

- **11.43 am:** We are seen as engine of global growth. The International Monetary Fund (IMF) sees India to grow fastest in major economies. Effects of demonetization not expected to spill over to the next year.

- **11.41 am:** Agricultural sector is expected to grow at 4.1% this fiscal. Target of agriculture credit fixed at Rs10 trillion in 2017-18. Rs.9,000 crores higher allocation for payment of sugarcane arrears.

- Allocation under MGNREGA increased to 48,000 crores from Rs. 38,500 crores in Union Budget 2017. This is highest-ever allocation. Space technology will be used for monitoring MGNREGA implementation.

- **11.38 am:** Arun Jaitley says committed to double farm income in five years.

- **11.35 am:** The government's agenda for next year is to transform, energize and clean India. World Bank expects India GDP growth rate at 7.6% in FY18 and 7.8% in FY19.

- Mini labs by qualified local entrepreneurs to be set up for soil testing in all 648 *krishi vigyan kendras* in the country. Plan, non-plan classification of expenditure is done away with in Union Budget 2017-18 to give a holistic picture.

- **11.33 am:** The government will spend more in rural areas, infrastructure, poverty alleviation, while maintaining fiscal prudence as guiding principle of the budget. Budget presentation advanced to help begin implementation of schemes before the onset of monsoon.

- **11.31 am:** The merger of railway budget with the Union budget is a historic step, does away with a colonial practice, and will allow for an integrated plan.

- **11.19 am:** Demonetization was a bold and decisive strike in a series of measures to arrive at a new normal of bigger, cleaner and real GDP. Double-digit inflation has been controlled, sluggish growth replaced by high growth. There are positive signs that point to a positive outlook for the next year.

- **11.18 am:** We are moving from informal to formal economy, and the government is now seen as a trusted custodian of public money.

- **11.16 am:** India stands out as a bright spot in world economic landscape. Growth in a number of emerging economies is expected to recover in 2017.

India stands out as a bright spot in world economic landscape. Growth in a number of emerging economies is expected to recover in 2017. Photo: Mint

- **11.15 am:** Arun Jaitley says have moved from a discretionary-based administration to a policy and system-based administration, A massive war on black money has been launched.

- **11.10 am:** Finance minister Arun Jaitley starts presenting the Union Budget in the parliament amid ruckus from the opposition benches.

- **11.05 am:** Mahajan says it is an exceptional situation as the budget session has been called by President Pranab Mukherjee. The House will not sit on Thursday as a mark of respect for the dead parliamentarian. Congress's Mallikarjun Kharge demands the adjournment of House today; he says the Union budget can be presented tomorrow.

- **11.00 am:** Lok Sabha speaker Sumitra Mahajan reads out an obituary reference to late MP E. Ahamed.

Lok Sabha speaker Sumitra Mahajan - Photo: AFP

- **11.00 am:** Opposition opposes budget presentation, calling for the parliament to be adjourned following the death of MP E. Ahamed.

- **10.46 am:** PM Narendra Modi arriving in Parliament House for the cabinet meeting.

- **10.44 am:** Lok Sabha speaker Sumitra Mahajan says "budget will be there as it is a constitutional obligation".

- **10.22 am:** The finance minister is expected to present the annual federal budget on schedule later on Wednesday despite the death of a sitting member of parliament, a spokesman for the prime minister's office said.

Parliament typically adjourns for a day after the death of a member, although Indian TV channels cited a precedent where the budget presentation had still gone ahead in a previous year.

A final decision on the timing of the budget will be taken when political parties and the speaker of the house meet early on Wednesday, officials said.

Finance minister Arun Jaitley is expected to boost spending and ease back on cutting the deficit when he presents his fourth budget, as he seeks to lift growth hit by the government's drive to purge the economy of "black money".

http://www.livemint.com/Politics/FC3OLQnhteJm6qUz6GfEsI/Union-Budget-2017-Live-Budget-presentation-on-schedule-desp.html?li_source=LI&li_medium=news_rec

5.4   Union Budget 2017: Key highlights and themes

Key highlights and themes of Arun Jaitley's budget speech including new income tax rules, actions on black money and push towards a digital economy:

Finance minister Arun Jaitley presented the Union Budget 2017 in Parliament on Wednesday. Here are the key highlights of his budget speech:

Jaitley divided his budget proposal into 10 distinct themes: Farmers; rural population; energizing youth; poor and underprivileged; infrastructure; financial sector; digital economy; public service; prudent fiscal management; and tax administration.

*Finance minister delivering the budget speech in the
Parliament on Wednesday - Photo: PTI*

OPENING REMARKS:

- Our government was elected amidst huge expectations; the underlying theme was good governance: Arun Jaitley

- Massive war against black money has been launched

- Government now seen as a trusted custodian of public money: FM

- We will focus on energizing youth to reap benefits of growth

- World economy faces considerable uncertainty: FM

- Three major challenges for emerging economies: US Federal Reserve's stance, uncertainty over commodity prices, especially crude prices and signs of increasing retreat from globalization as protectionist fears build up

- India stands out as a bright spot

- Govt. has continued with steady path of fiscal consolidation: FM

- We are seen as an engine of global growth: FM

- There are two tectonic policy initiatives: GST implementation and demonetization

- Demonetization was the continuation of series of measures taken in last two years and was a bold and decisive measure

- Demonetization seeks to create a new normal where GDP would be cleaner and bigger

- Drop in economic activity due to remonetization is expected to have only a transient effect

- Demonetization has strong potential to generate long-term benefits

- Demonetization helps to transfer resources from tax evaders to govt.

- Firmly believe demonetization and GST will have epoch-making impact

- Pace of remonetization will soon reach comfortable levels; effect of demonetization not expected to spill over into next year

- Surplus liquidity in banking system will raise access to credit, leading to multiplier effect on economic activity: FM

- Overall approach in budget to spend more in rural areas

- Budget 2017-18 contains 3 major reforms: advancement of date of presentation, merger of railway budget with general budget, abolition of Plan and non-Plan expenditure

FARMERS:

- Farmer credit fixed at record level of Rs. 10 trillion; will ensure adequate flow to underserved areas

- Soil health cards: Govt. to set up mini-labs in Krishi Vigyan Kendras

- Long-term irrigation fund in Nabard—corpus at Rs. 40,000 crores

- Model law on contract farming to be circulated

- Dairy processing infra fund with corpus of Rs. 8,000 crores

- Dedicated micro-irrigation fund with Rs. 5,000 crores corpus

RURAL POPULATION:

- Mission Antyodaya to bring 1 crores households of poverty

- MGNREGA: Rs. 48,000 crores has been allocated; participation of women now at 55%; using space technology in a big way

- Prime Minister Gram Sadak Yojana: Rs. 19,000 crores allocated; along with states, Rs. 27,000 crores will be spent in FY18

- Pradhan Mantri Awas Yojana: Rs. 23,000 crores allocated

- 100% village electrification by May 2018

- Rural livelihood mission: Rs. 4,500 crores allocated

- Mason training to be provided for 5 lakh people

- Panchayat Raj: Human resource reform programme to be launched

- Rs. 1,87,223 crores allocated for rural programmes

YOUTH:

- Education: System of measuring annual learning outcomes, emphasis on science

- Innovation fund for secondary education

- Reforms in UGC: Colleges to be identified based on ranking and given more autonomy

- Propose to leverage information technology with launch of SWAYAM platform for virtual learning

- National testing agency to be established for all entrance exams, freeing up CBSE, AICTE and other bodies

- 100 Indian international skill centers to be established with courses in foreign languages

- Rs. 4,000 crores allocated to launch skill acquisition and knowledge awareness

- Special scheme for creating employment in leather/footwear sector

- Tourism: Five special zones to be set up

POOR AND UNPRIVILEGED:

- Women: Mahila Shakti Kendra with Rs. 500 crores corpus

- Stepped up allocation to Rs. 1.84 trillion for various schemes for women and children

- Affordable housing to be given infrastructure status

- Action plan to eliminate leprosy by 2018, TB by 2025, reduce IMR to 29 in 2019

- To create additional PG medical seats per annum

- Two new AIIMS in Jharkhand and Gujarat

- New rules to be introduced for medical devices

- Labour rights: Legislative reforms to simplify and amalgamate existing labour laws

- Allocation to SCs increased to Rs. 52,393 crores; STs given Rs. 31,920 crores, minority affairs allocated Rs. 4,195 crores

- Senior citizens: Aadhaar-based smart cards with health details to be provided

INFRASTRUCTURE:

- Total capex and development expenditure of railways pegged at Rs. 1.31 trillion

- Railways: Passenger safety—Safety fund corpus set up; unmanned level crossings to be eliminated by 2020

- Railway lines of 3,500 km to be commissioned

- To launch dedicated tourism/pilgrimage trains
- 500 stations to be made differently-able friendly
- Cleanliness in railways: To introduce Coach Mitra facility; By 2019, bio-toilets for all coaches
- Railways to offer competitive ticket-booking facility; service charge withdrawn for tickets booked on IRCTC
- New metro rail policy to be announced
- Roads sector: Allocation for national highways at Rs. 64,000 crores
- Airports Authority of India Act to be amended to enable monetization of land resources
- Total allocation to transport sector at Rs. 2 trillion
- Telecom sector: Allocation to Bharat Net programme at Rs.10,000 crores
- Digi-gau initiative to be launched
- To make India global hub for electronics manufacture
- Export infra: New restructured central scheme to be launched
- Total allocation for infrastructure: Rs. 3.96 trillion

FINANCIAL SECTOR:

- Foreign Investment Promotion Board (FIPB) to be abolished
- Commodities market: panel to study legal framework for spot and derivative markets
- Resolution mechanism for financial firms
- Cyber-security: Computer emergency response team to be set up

- Listing of PSEs will foster public accountability; revised mechanism for time-bound listing

- To create integrated public sector oil major

- New ETF to be launched

- Pradhan Mantri Mudra Yojana: Lending target at Rs. 2.44 trillion

- Stand-up India scheme: over 16,000 new enterprises have been set up

DIGITAL ECONOMY:

- India at cusp of massive digital revolution

- Govt. to launch two new schemes to promote BHIM app, including cash back scheme for merchants

- Aadhaar Pay to be launched for people who don't have mobile phones

- Focus on rural and semi-urban areas

- To strengthen financial inclusion fund

- Panel on digital payments has recommended structural reforms

- To create payment regulatory board at RBI

PUBLIC SERVICES:

- To use head post-office for passport services

- Defense: centralized defense travel system developed

- Defense: Centralized pension distribution system to be established

- Govt. recruitment: To introduce two-tier exam system

- Govt. looks to introduce laws to confiscate assets of economic defaulters

- High-level panel chaired by PM to commemorate Mahatma Gandhi's 150th birth anniversary

FISCAL MANAGEMENT:

- Total budget expenditure: Rs21 trillion

- Rs. 3,000 crores to implement various budget announcements

- Defense expenditure excluding pensions: Rs. 2.74 trillion

- Consolidated outcome budget for all ministries being created

- Fiscal deficit for FY18 pegged at 3.2% of GDP

- Revenue deficit for FY18 at 1.9%

TAX ADMINISTRATION:

- Direct tax collection not commensurate with income/expenditure pattern of India

- We are largely a tax non-compliant society; predominance of cash in society enables tax evasion

- After demonetization, data received will increase tax net

- Black money: No cash transactions above Rs. 3 lakh

- Transparency in political funding: Parties continue to receive anonymous donations; propose system of cleaning up

- Political funding: Maximum amount of cash donation that can be received is Rs. 2,000; political parties can receive donations by cheques or digitally; amendment proposed to RBI Act to issue electoral bonds; every party has to file returns within specified time

- Personal income tax: Rate reduced to 5% for income bracket of Rs2.5-5 lakh; All other categories to get uniform benefit of Rs12,500 per person; to levy surcharge on income bracket Rs.50 lakh - Rs.1 crores

- Personal income tax: To have simple one-page form for taxable income up to Rs. 5 lakh

- GST: preparedness of IT system on schedule

- Not many changes to excise duties since GST will be implemented soon

- FPI category 1 and 2 investors exempted from indirect transfer provisions

- Time period of revising tax returns reduced to 12 months

- Real estate: to make changes in capital gains tax

- Concessional withholding rate will be extended to 30 June 2020, rupee-denominated masala bonds to be included

- MAT not to be abolished at present; to allow carry-forward for 15 years

- Corporate tax rate: MSMEs' rate (annual turnover less than Rs50 crores) reduced to 25%

- LNG: Reduce customs duty to 2.5%

- Limit of cash donation for charitable trusts cut to Rs. 2,000.

CLOSING REMARKS:

- It is said when my goal is in sight, the winds favour me and I fly. There is no other day more appropriate than this: FM Jaitley

http://www.livemint.com/Politics/HIabhPn5ApPsL8Na879uEO/Highlights-of-Union-Budget-201718.html

5.5 Budget 2017: Cash transactions above Rs 3 lakh banned from 1 April

The proposed cash transaction limit at Rs3 lakh, as proposed by Arun Jaitley in his budget speech, is another step towards curbing black money

New Delhi: Finance minister Arun Jaitley on Wednesday proposed a cash transaction limit at Rs. 3 lakh, in line with the recommendations of the special investigative team (SIT) on black money.

The government will make the necessary amendments to the income tax act to facilitate this, the finance minister said.

Curbing black money has been one of the major electoral promises of the National Democratic Alliance government. It has announced a number of steps over the last couple of years to check black money, including the recent demonetization move.

The Supreme-constituted SIT in its report last year had proposed banning cash transactions above Rs. 3 lakh and capped the cash holdings of individuals and companies at Rs. 15 lakh.

These measures can check cash transactions, ensure a paper trail for every high-value transaction and prevent tax evasion. High-value transactions in cash are a common feature, especially in the real estate sector where buyers try to get away with paying lower stamp duty.

http://www.livemint.com/Politics/xyQuQ8XRxQ5Pwnr2cqHgbJ/
Budget-2017-Cash-dealings-above-Rs3-lakh-banned-from-1April.html?
li_source=LI&li_medium=news_rec

5.6   Union Budget 2017: Here are the winners and losers

The rural sector came away as undisputed winner in Arun Jaitley's Union Budget 2017

Mumbai: India's annual budget is one of the nation's most closely watched events—not just for the numbers, but for the political message during a speech that runs for about 90 minutes.

The thrust of Wednesday's speech by finance minister Arun Jaitley for the fiscal year starting 1 April was on rural and infrastructure spending after advisers warned of a steep slowdown triggered by Prime Minister Narendra Modi's cash ban. Here are the winners and losers.

Winners

Farmers: Pledges a record **agricultural credit** of Rs10 trillion by the fiscal year through March 2018; Rs. 48,000 crores **allocated** for its rural job guarantee program; electrification of villages. Companies that may benefit include tractor makers such as Mahindra & Mahindra Ltd.

Real estate: Proposes extension of affordable housing program to five years; gives the sector infrastructure status. **Plans to** also lower holding period for taxing capital gains on sale of immovable property to two years from three. Shares of DLF Ltd, Godrej Properties Ltd and Oberoi Realty Ltd could be affected.

Consumer goods and automakers: Jaitley proposed **cutting the tax rate** for people with income of between Rs. 2,50,000 and

Rs.5,00,000 to 5% from 10%, leaving more cash in the hands of consumers to spend more on toiletries, household goods, cars and two-wheelers. Shares that may be affected are ITC Ltd, Hindustan Unilever Ltd, Marico Ltd, Maruti Suzuki Ltd and Hero MotoCorp Ltd.

Banks: Government proposes to inject at least Rs.10,000 crores of capital into state-owned lenders and provide additional capital; also proposed increasing allowable provisions for bad loans. Stocks involved include State Bank of India, Bank of India, Bank of Baroda.

Fiber optics: The budget allocated Rs.10,000 crores to lay fiber optic network covering 150,000 villages stocks benefiting including Sterlite Technologies Ltd.

Infrastructure: The outlays here may aid stocks such as Larsen & Toubro Ltd., Hindustan Construction Co., and IRB Infrastructure Developers, as well as Electro steel Steels Ltd. and Aegis Logistics Ltd.

Also read: <u>Budget 2017: Arun Jaitley unveils series of post-demonetisation digital reforms</u>

Losers

Drug makers: As part of the rural focus, government proposes to **<u>amend rules</u>** governing pharmaceuticals to help lower prices, make healthcare affordable and encourage generics. Stocks affected include Dr. Reddy's Laboratories Ltd and Sun Pharmaceutical Industries Ltd.

Cigarette makers: An increase in the excise duty on **<u>cigarettes</u>** by 6%, as well as boost in the levy on cigarettes made with tobacco substitutes, may affect companies including ITC and Godfrey Phillips India Ltd. **Bloomberg**

5.7 Budget 2017: Arun Jaitley unveils series of post-demonetization digital reforms

These include Rs. 3 lakh cap of cash transactions, proposal to set up a payment regulatory board and withdrawing service charges on e-tickets booked via IRCTC

Finance minister Arun Jaitley said digital transformation was a crucial pillar of efforts to transform, energize and clean India. Photo: PTI

Mumbai: Finance minister Arun Jaitley on Wednesday set out the vision of a Digital India as he unveiled a series of post-demonetization digital reforms—including a Rs3 lakh cap on cash transactions—that he said were aimed at fetching the government Rs.2,500 crores in revenue.

"India is at the cusp of a massive digital transformation," said Jaitley as he listed 'Digital' as one of the 10 key themes in the Union Budget 2017.

Digital transformation, he said, was a crucial pillar of efforts to Transform, Energize and Clean (TEC) India.

Claiming that demonetization will have long-term benefits—one of them being greater digitization that could lead to higher and cleaner GDP growth—Jaitley announced a host of reforms to promote a digital payments ecosystem.

These include a proposal to set up a payment regulatory board, encouraging digital payments at petrol pumps and hospitals, withdrawing service charges on railway e-tickets booked via Indian

Railway Catering and Tourism Corporation (IRCTC), launch of two new schemes to promote the Bharat Interface for Money (BHIM) cashless app and a soon-to-be-unveiled biometric Aadhaar payment system.

All these steps, said Jaitley, are aimed at garnering Rs. 2,500 crores through digital transactions across platforms including the united payment interface (UPI).

Simultaneously, in a bid to promote cashless transactions, Jaitley announced a host of measures including exempting miniature point of sale (POS) and micro-POS machines from countervailing duty (CVD) and special additional duty (SAD). Besides, no transaction over Rs3 lakh will be permitted in cash, Jaitley said even as he move to cut the presumptive turnover threshold for companies with a turnover up to Rs. 2 crores to 6%.

He did not spare politicians either, announcing that the maximum cash donation receivable by a political party from any one source was capped at Rs. 2,000— down from Rs. 20,000 earlier.

To be sure, the launch of the mobile app Bhim has already seen over 11 million downloads by mid-January. As many as 14 banks have already come on board for Aadhaar Pay, which will enable people to make and receive payments using their Aadhaar number and biometrics. Besides, Digidhan Abhiyaan and 200,000 Common Service Centers are providing employment to over 500,000 youth, and spreading digital literacy, as President Pranab Mukherjee noted in his speech on Tuesday.

To take the banking system to the doorstep of the poor and the unbanked, the government has already launched the Indian Postal Payment Bank. The postal network has over 150,000 post offices.

Besides, the over 100,000 'bank mitras' appointed by banks, over 250,00 'Gram Dak Sewaks' will also function as banking correspondents.

In a bid to bridge the digital divide through online education, Jaitley on Wednesday also announced that the government's **Swayam** platform, which has been developed by the ministry of human resource development and All India Council for Technical Education with the help of Microsoft Corp., will start offering 350 online courses.

Swayam "would be ultimately capable of hosting 2,000 courses and 80,000 hours of learning, covering school, under-graduate, post-graduate, engineering, law and other professional courses", according to its website.

Jaitley said the government has received over 250 proposals for electronics manufacturing in the last two years, entailing investment of Rs1.26 trillion. This will help the electronics ecosystem as the country will need thousands of sensors and chips to build Digital India.

The FM said the financial allocation for Bharat Net, conceived as the world's largest rural broadband connectivity project, was being increased to Rs.10,000 crores. Under Bharat Net, the government has laid 155,000 km of optic fiber cable till date, Jaitley said, adding that high-speed fiber optic broadband will be available in over 150,000 gram panchayets (village councils) with hotspots and access to digital services at low tariffs.

A 'Digi Gaon' initiative, said Jaitely, will also be launched to provide telemedicine, education and skills through digital technology. Jaitley believes that these moves will "give a major fillip to mobilizing broadband and Digital India, for the benefit of people living in rural areas".

To be sure, technology has been the government's fulcrum for growth in the last two years.

Jaitley's budget speech also underscored how technology will be used across sectors—be it to increase tax compliance and accountability with the help of data analytics, increase digital literacy, strengthen rural markets, improve agriculture, modernize ports and airports or to store digital documents.

This year's budget was a continuation of the government's earlier budget policy announcements. In the 2016 budget, Jaitley had announced two schemes to improve digital literacy—-the *national digital literacy mission* and *digital saksharta abhiyan*—-both aimed at enabling more Indians to get connected to, and benefit from, the Internet while simultaneously helping rural employment generation and skill development in colleges and Industrial Training Institutes (ITIs).

Similarly, the government had announced plans to cover about 60 million houses in rural areas in the next three years and provide digital devices like computers, tablet PCs and smart phones. According to Jaitley's 2016 budget speech, of the 168 million rural households, as many as 120 million households did not have computers and are unlikely to have digitally literate persons.

Jaitley had then proposed a Digital Depository for school leaving certificates, as a part of its Digital India initiative, to be a one-stop house for storing all education-related certificates of schools and colleges.

Given that most people, especially in rural areas do not have proper storage facilities for important documents, the tablet PCs along with an Internet connection and cloud storage can help in keeping these documents secure.

In July, 2015, the government had introduced the Digital Locker facility and linked it with the Aadhaar card, permitting users to store scanned copied of their documents such as passports, PAN cards and driving licenses. The site is secured and allows users to access their documents using the cloud.

http://www.livemint.com/Politics/jTqfpNYhVv2QEOFuXp8axO/Budget-2017-Arun-Jaitley-unveils-series-of-postdemonetisat.html

5.8   Budget 2017: Jaitley raises allocation for electronics makers to Rs. 745 crores

An ecosystem is being created to make India a global hub for electronics manufacturers, says Arun Jaitley.

New Delhi: Aimed at positioning India as a global manufacturing hub, Finance Minister Arun Jaitley on Wednesday announced increase in allocations towards schemes like Modified Special Incentive Package Scheme (M-SIPS) and Electronic Development Fund (EDF) to Rs. 745 crores in 2017-18. "We are also creating an ecosystem to make India a global hub for electronics manufacturers. Over 250 investment proposals for electronics manufacturing has been received in the last 2 years, totaling an investment of Rs. 1.26 lakh crores," Jaitley said while presenting Union budget 2017-18 in the Lok Sabha.

A number of global leaders and mobile manufacturers have set up production facilities in India, he added. "I have therefore exponentially increased the allocation and incentives of schemes like

M-SIPS and EDF to Rs. 745 crores in 2017-18, this is an all-time high," he said.

http://www.livemint.com/Politics/DHGKcZX0lG0BWMu86RecLI/
Budget-2017-Jaitley-raises-allocation-for-electronics-maker.html

5.9 Union Budget: more hits than misses

The government has taken several reform measures in the budget that will help the economy. Arun Jaitley's fourth budget had many firsts. The presentation of the budget was advanced by almost a month so that the government could start spending from the beginning of the financial year. For the first time in the history of independent India, the railway budget was included in the general budget. This will help in better transport planning, which is likely to improve outcomes. It was also the budget that marked the end of the planning era in the country. As a result, the classification of expenditure has ***changed to revenue and capital expenditure from Plan and non-Plan expenditure***. And it was the budget that was presented after the unprecedented exogenous shock of the currency swap—intended to attack black money—to the economy. Given the backdrop of the currency swap initiative, weakness in economic growth and continued sluggishness in private sector investment, there are at least three broad issues worth noting in the budget.

First is the impact of the currency swap on black money and the economy in general. As Jaitley highlighted in his speech, the government now has an enormous amount of data on bank deposits made after the currency reform was announced. The challenge now for the tax department will be to ***mine the data*** and be able to check tax evasion in a meaningful way. As has been noted in this space before, it will have to be done with care so that honest taxpayers don't face any hardship. Reduction in evasion and improvement in compliance will, over time, reduce the burden on honest taxpayers.

The drive to push digital transactions will also lead to greater formalization of economic activity, which will help the economy in a number of ways in the medium to long term. The pain of the currency swap was always expected to be transient and will wane entirely in the coming weeks and months. The government will now have to focus on maximizing the gains. The finance minister also announced tax incentives for equipment used in *cashless transactions*. This could have been avoided as movement on this front is happening at a satisfactory pace. Personal income-tax relief for individual taxpayers needs to be welcomed, but the imposition of a surcharge on large taxpayers goes against the desire of simplifying the tax structure.

Second, the government has taken several reform measures in the budget that will help the economy. It has also not lost sight of the fact that private investment continues to remain weak and the state needs to fill the gap. Consequently, it has increased capital expenditure by over 25%, which will help push growth in the coming year. The special focus on agriculture and rural India will also benefit the economy. Renewed efforts will be made to list public sector undertakings. Movement on this front has been slow—one of the reasons why the government normally falls short of the disinvestment target. The government is also taking steps that will help increase foreign investment, which is already buoyant. The commitment to abolish the Foreign Investment Promotion Board in 2017-18 is a positive.

However, there is one big disappointment on the reforms front. While the finance minister lowered the rate of tax for smaller companies, the corporate tax rate has not been reduced, as was widely expected by the market. At the least, a clear road map for reduction in the corporate tax rate would have lifted sentiment among investors. The government has also done well by initiating reforms in political finance which will help reduce the role of cash and lead to greater transparency and accountability. Currently, about 70% of the donations that political parties receive come in cash. It can be argued that parties can still show donations in cash even with the reduced limits. But the fact that steps have been taken in this direction is a positive. Outcomes can always be reviewed and rules can be adjusted.

Third, while the tone of the budget was positive and encouraging, the decision to target the fiscal deficit at 3.2% of the gross domestic product (GDP) is a disappointment even as market borrowing has been pegged at a lower level. In the given circumstances, there was a strong case for adhering to the 3% target. It would have enhanced government credibility a great deal and placed it in a much better position to implement the new fiscal rules.

Overall, the budget has moved in the right direction and should help augment growth. A clear road map on rationalization of corporate tax and adherence to the fiscal deficit target of 3% of GDP would have given the government some bonus points.

http://www.livemint.com/Opinion/HzJXlkTzUKmxLR7wRwITdJ/Union-Budget-more-hits-than-misses.html?li_source=LI&li_medium=news_rec

5.10 Budget 2017: An Opportunity Lost for Renewable Energy

The budget's real test lay in its approach to mitigating financial risk in the renewable energy, where capital costs are high, payback periods are long and off-taker, construction and foreign exchange risks raise cost of debt.

India has an ambitious target of 175 gigawatts (GW) of solar, wind and other renewable energy by 2022. The financial needs are mammoth and India needs to look beyond fiscal allocations if the signals for clean energy have to be bold and consistent. Solar, alone, would require $100 billion in debt to reach 100 GW. International debt markets, estimated at $95 trillion, are the world's largest pool of capital and need to be made accessible to Indian developers at affordable cost. The budget must be evaluated against this scale of need and opportunity. The role of public funds should be to catalyze action, attract investment, or underwrite risk.

Solar, alone, would require $100 billion in debt to reach 100 GW.
Photo: Bloomberg

Let us first examine fiscal priorities to catalyze action. Compared to last year (Rs. 5,036 crores), this year the allocation to the Ministry of New and Renewable Energy stands at Rs. 5,473 crores. As much as 74% of the outlay is directed to grid-interactive renewable, specifically mentioning the second phase of solar park development for 20 GW of capacity. The total budget is further split between Rs.3,361 crores for solar and only Rs. 408 crores for wind, a clear indication that the government will continue to prioritize solar. Additionally, the budget extends support to power 2,000 railway stations through solar, under the Indian Railways 1GW solar mission. Smaller sums of Rs. 135 crores and Rs. 76 crores have been earmarked for small hydro and bio-power respectively. Despite recent suggestions, large hydro remains outside the purview of renewable energy.

One continuing area of uncertainty is the role of the National Environment Fund (NEF). The cess on coal remained unchanged at Rs. 400 / tons. While the total cess collected (projected up to 31 March 2017) was a mammoth Rs. 54,336 crores, only Rs. 25,810 crores have been transferred to NEF. Of this, under half (Rs. 12,427 crores) has been spent on renewable energy projects. While nearly all of the budgetary allocation to renewable in 2017-18 will be from NEF, the budget could have clarified the proportion of the cess that would be transferred to NEF.

Another uncertainty is how the goods and services tax (GST) will impact renewable. Researchers at the Council on Energy, Environment and Water (CEEW) find that if solar components were categorized based on current levied tax rates (including exemptions and subsidies), GST would impact solar tariffs minimally. However, if preferential tax benefits to renewable energy were not accounted, then GST could raise utility scale solar tariffs by as much as 9.5%, hampering progress.

How has the budget performed in attracting new investment? Two market opportunities stood to gain significantly from strategic budgetary support. First, residential rooftop projects could create 15

GW of renewable energy capacity in India by 2022. While budgetary support was extended for housing infrastructure, no direct support was announced for rooftop solar.

Secondly, replacing 15% of India's irrigation pumps with solar pumps could build 20 GW of capacity. Aiming to double farmer incomes within four years, the budget discusses mainstreaming and interlinking Primary Agriculture Credit Societies with District Central Cooperative Banks. If this increases access to low-cost loans, the incentive to invest in the upfront capital expense for solar pumps could increase.

The budget's real test lay in its approach to mitigating financial risk in the renewable energy, where capital costs are high, payback periods are long and off-taker, construction and foreign exchange risks raise cost of debt significantly. CEEW research shows that 70% of the costs embedded in already low solar tariffs owe to return on equity and debt servicing. But no budgetary support was extended to any agency to address risks. Moreover, financial support to the Solar Energy Corporation of India, the nodal agency for commissioning many solar and wind projects has been halved to Rs. 50 crores.

Nor has the budget given any impetus to technology development. Only Rs. 144 crores has been budgeted for research and development, nearly half of last year's allocation. A recent CEEW study showed that energy storage has a number of current commercial applications for telecom towers, petrol pumps, commercial establishments, rural ATMs, and academic institutions. Yet, funding remains constrained. In 2016-17 Rs. 20 crores was allocated for developing, testing and deploying energy storage technologies. In 2017-18 there is no allocation for energy storage, which could exacerbate challenges with integrating renewable energy into the grid.

Again, despite some focus on transport infrastructure, no allowances have been made for electric vehicles or biofuels. While total budgetary outlay to renewable energy marginally increased, there is little to celebrate. This budget is unlikely to catalyse action, attract private investment or underwrite risks. An opportunity was lost.

Dr. Arunabha Ghosh is CEO and Kanika Chawla is Senior Programme Lead at the Council on Energy, Environment and Water (http://ceew.in), *one of South Asia's leading independent think-tanks. Dr. Ghosh is co-author of Energizing India: Towards a Resilient and Equitable Energy System (SAGE, 2016).*

http://www.livemint.com/Opinion/5A1IxEWKobkHUz1Ku7x6gO/
Budget-2017-An-opportunity-lost-for-renewable-energy.html?li_source=
LI&li_medium=news_rec

5.11 Prudent budget that emphasizes investment while attempting fiscal consolidation

The most significant aspect of the budget is its commitment to curtail the fiscal deficit to 3.2% of GDP, despite the FRBM committee providing leeway to relax it to 3.5% of GDP.

With GST to be implemented next year, there has been no major change in indirect taxes, except some tinkering with customs duty.

The expectations from this year's budget were unusually high, and so were the challenges. The need to 'stimulate' the economy had created wide expectations of a cut in tax rates, an increase in allocations to the social sectors and enhanced infrastructure spending. At the same time, fiscal prudence had to be maintained, amidst considerable uncertainties about the impact of the note ban on nominal GDP (gross domestic product) growth, the gains that could be expected on account of voluntary disclosures of untaxed income and penalty schemes, and the manner in which tax revenues would evolve after the implementation of GST (goods and services tax).

The most significant aspect of the budget is its commitment to curtail the fiscal deficit to 3.2% of GDP, despite the FRBM (Fiscal Responsibility and Budget Management) committee providing leeway to relax it to 3.5% of GDP. On expected lines, there has been an increase in budgetary allocations to the infrastructure sector and the rural sector and a mild consumption stimulus through reduction in personal tax rates in the lowest slab. Attempts to clean up electoral funding, abolition of FIPB approvals from next year and some innovative proposals like time-bound listing of identified CPSEs and creation of integrated public sector oil major are other highlights of the budget.

However, the inadequate allocation for bank capitalization is disappointing.

Given the twin balance sheet stress, which has resulted in a decline in gross fixed capital formation, the budget focused on reviving public investments. Accordingly, capital investment for roads, railways and other infrastructure sectors is projected to increase by 25%, including borrowing through extra budgetary sources. There are also some announcements with regard to using the PPP route for undertaking O&M at airports owned by Airports Authority of India (AAI), expansion of broadband connectivity in rural areas as also modifications in the Metro Railway Act. There is also mention of strengthening the dispute resolution mechanism for contracts in the infrastructure sector, which has been a long-pending demand of players in this sector.

Apart from transport, affordable housing has been a major focus in this budget, given the multiplier effect it has in terms of employment generation and increased demand for products like cement and steel. Other areas that received focus are tourism and skill development. The significant expansion of agriculture credit, setting up funds for micro irrigation and dairy processing and increased coverage of e-NAM are in line with the government's emphasis on improving social/rural infrastructure.

With GST to be implemented next year, there has been no major change in indirect taxes, except some tinkering with customs duty. The reduction in tax rates for MSMEs with turnover up to Rs. 50 crores, apart from providing relief to such companies, may also aid the process of formalization of the economy. There are also some steps designed to increase the ease of doing business with respect to areas like transfer pricing and increase in threshold limit for levy of presumptive taxes.

The higher 10.7% expansion of capital expenditure compared to the 5.9% rise in revenue expenditure in FY18 budget estimates (BE) relative to FY17 revised estimates (RE) would augment the quality of spending. The budget has incorporated lower dividends (partly because of railways) and non-tax revenues from communication services in FY18 budget estimates relative to FY17 revised estimates. The forecasts for growth of nominal GDP (11.75%) and gross tax revenues (12.2%) may prove somewhat optimistic, in light of initial hiccups in the transition to GST. Moreover, the disinvestment and strategic divestment target of Rs. 72,500 crores also appears high.

Overall, the tone of the budget appears prudent, with an emphasis on public investments, incremental steps to promote schemes like Digital India and Skill India, and the absence of populist giveaways and negative shocks pertaining to capital gains tax on equity investments. Nevertheless, the achievement of the revenue and disinvestment targets would be crucial to ensure the budgeted reduction in the fiscal deficit to GDP ratio, and the lower than expected gross borrowing figure. Also the government has factored in a pickup in inflows from small savings schemes and if the latter doesn't materialize, the market borrowing figure may need to be revised upward.

Anjan Ghosh is chief ratings officer, ICRA Limited.

http://www.livemint.com/Opinion/DVlCIo9LZctt6hKwoMpqLL/Prudent-budget-that-emphasizes-investment-while-attempting-f.html?li_source=LI&li_medium=news_rec

5.12 Budget 2017: Arun Jaitley pegs fiscal deficit at 3.2% of GDP for 2017-18

Finance minister Arun Jaitley targets to achieve revenue deficit of 1.9% of GDP in 2017-18 from the earlier target of 2% of GDP.

Finance minister Arun Jaitley signaled a reset of India's fiscal policy by focusing more on the parameter of debt-to-GDP ratio than fiscal deficit in coming years as recommended by an expert panel.

The panel on reviewing India's performance on fiscal discipline and suggesting a future road map headed by former revenue secretary N.K. Singh has suggested a sustainable debt path must be the principal macroeconomic anchor of India's fiscal policy. The committee has favoured combined debt-to-GDP of 60% by 2023, 40% for the central government and 20% for state governments.

Arun Jaitley said an expert panel formed to set a new fiscal framework has recommended maintaining a fiscal deficit of 3% of GDP for the next three fiscal years.   Photo: Pradeep Gaur / Mint

The committee has also recommended 3% fiscal deficit for the next three years and has also provided for 'escape clauses', for deviations up to 0.5% of GDP, from the stipulated fiscal deficit target.

Among the triggers for taking recourse to these escape clauses, the panel has included "far-reaching structural reforms in the economy with unanticipated fiscal implications". Demonetization, for instance, would fit that description. "Although there is a strong case to invoke this escape clause, I am refraining from doing so. The report of the committee will be carefully examined and appropriate decisions taken in due course," Jaitley said.

Jaitley marginally deviated from his earlier fiscal consolidation road map by pegging fiscal deficit at 3.2% of gross domestic product (GDP) for 2017-18, deferring the 3% of GDP target by a year. In the medium-term fiscal policy statement presented along with the budget, the finance ministry said the government on a reassessment of the macroeconomic needs of higher public expenditure in a scenario when private investment is not picking up has tilted in favour of the gradual reduction of fiscal deficit. The government has also reduced revenue deficit to 2.1% of GDP in 2016-17 from the budget estimate of 2.3% of GDP and has pegged it at 1.9% of GDP for 2017-18 from 2% of GDP as mandated by the Fiscal Responsibility and Budget Management Act.

"It will be our endeavour to improve upon these fiscal numbers, especially the fiscal deficit, in the next year, through greater focus on quality of expenditure and higher tax realization from the huge cash deposits in banks, triggered by demonetization," Jaitley said in his budget speech.

William Foster, vice-president, Sovereign Risk Group, Moody's Investors Service, in a statement said this year's budget marks a continuation of the government's fiscal objectives and policies.

"The budget speech's emphasis on fiscal prudence indicates continued commitment to gradual fiscal consolidation remains. This is consistent with the target of a deficit at 3.2% of GDP this fiscal, followed by 3%. These targets are not materially different from the previous road map and our projections," he said.

Foster said the FRBM committee's recommendation of targeting a debt-to-GDP ratio to 60% by 2023 is achievable as long as nominal GDP growth is sustained at robust levels. "It will imply gradual fiscal consolidation, largely through higher nominal GDP growth feeding in the government's revenue," he said.

At the core of the fiscal arithmetic is the assumption regarding nominal GDP growth of 11.75% which economists say may be too ambitious. N.R. Bhanumurthy, professor at the National Institute of Public Finance and Policy, said the nominal growth projection which comes on the back of an 11.9% growth estimate by the statistics department for 2016-17 may be difficult to achieve. "The 2016-17 GDP number is likely to see a huge revision as it has not taken into account the demonetization impact. The upward revision of 2015-16 GDP growth figure will also put downward pressure on 2016-17 GDP numbers due to a higher base in the previous year," he said.

The statistics department raised its real GDP growth estimate for 2015-16 to 7.9% from 7.6% earlier.

Bhanumurthy said the tax revenue buoyancy assumed for 2017-18 also looks over-optimistic. Government has assumed 12.7% growth in net tax revenue in 2017-18 which may be difficult with rising oil prices and uncertainty surrounding impact of goods and services tax on tax receipts in the first year.

Government has also set an ambitious Rs. 72,500 crores target for disinvestment for 2017-18 against the revised estimate of Rs.45,500 crores for 2016-17. The government has so far collected Rs.27,917 crores through stake sales in public sector units in 2016-17, implying government targets aims to sell stakes (in state-owned companies) worth around Rs. 17,583 crores in the next two months.

Jaitley said in his budget speech that the government will put in place a revised mechanism and procedure to ensure time-bound listing of identified state-owned companies on stock exchanges.

The finance minister identified Railways-owned state-owned firms and general insurance firms as probable candidates for listing in the stock market along with a second PSU exchange traded fun.

http://www.livemint.com/Politics/rkh0BNb6dWpRJyyolGj2oK/Budget-2017-Arun-Jaitley-pegs-fiscal-deficit-at-32-of-GDP.html

5.13 Budget generally positive for infrastructure sectors

Indian investors should be happy with newer projects that will come to the market on the back of higher outlay for all infrastructure subsectors.

Apart from giving a boost to all construction and cement companies, hopefully the budget announcement on affordable housing will be complemented by lots of other policies, institutional and process changes to make real progress.
Photo: Mint

It is commendable that the finance minister stuck to the script and gave no surprises. International investors should be happy with the progress on the fiscal responsibility roadmap—which is always critical from their perspective—and a small relief of abolition of Foreign Investment Promotion Board.

Indian investors should be happy with newer projects that will come to the market on the back of higher outlay for all infrastructure subsectors and a clear indication that the government believes that private sector can be a good partner. It is great to hear that a large amount of money is being put aside for a safety fund in railways. The enhanced allocation across the board for capex for roads, railways and other infrastructure such as irrigation (including water-efficient micro-irrigation) is a great boost to the sector. The finance minister's confidence in making states a joint partner and work cooperatively in boosting infrastructure project investments is in the right direction. While we don't yet have many successful progress to show in such models, hopefully, successes will come.

The budget also confirms that public-private partnerships in all infrastructure sectors will be encouraged. Tier-II city airport operations and management will hopefully now take off, improving services and connectivity, aided by the recent regional air connectivity program. End-to-end service by the railways will also clearly give rise to private sector participation in more railway activities. The new coastal connectivity projects will also give rise to new opportunities to the private sector. Of course, listing of some of the public sector enterprises from the railways will also bring in private investment though of a different kind.

Mainstreaming the affordable housing sector by giving it infrastructure status, increasing allocations and redefining what is affordable housing will hopefully move that sector a step closer to making it a reality.

Budget has also clearly given some good concessions to land pooling in Andhra Pradesh but hopefully this is just the beginning and land pooling as a concept for any public purpose/infrastructure will also get similar benefits in future. And that would really help the affordable housing sector too.

Apart from giving a boost to all construction and cement companies, hopefully the budget announcement on affordable housing will be complemented by lots of other policies, institutional and process changes to make real progress. Let us hope that some of the bigger housing developers will enter this market seriously.

The finance managers of infrastructure companies will be happy to see some welcome changes. Domestic transfer pricing regulations have been liberalized and their scope reduced to only the transactions involving an entity availing of profit-linked tax incentives.

Minimum alternate tax credit extension from 10 years to 15 years partially offsets the impact of phasing out of incentives to infrastructure sector. Reduced tax of 5% on interest income of foreign currency borrowings and masala bonds has been extended to 2020, which will hopefully make foreign financiers look at investments in energy and infrastructure sector more positively.

Amendment to the Arbitration and Conciliation Act 1996 has been proposed, which will be a positive for the significant impact it would have on the amounts stuck due to dispute issues in the infrastructure sectors—particularly in PPP and EPC projects.

Where the budget disappoints a bit is the near-absence of anything very concrete or new for sectors such as urban infrastructure (or at least how to galvanize existing schemes like AMRUT and smart cities), renewable sector, drinking water and rural infrastructure relating to essential services. While lots of attention has been given to the rural sector (rural roads, irrigation, loan related concessions, doubling farmers income in five years etc.), essential rural infrastructure for improving quality of living (power in real sense of availability, reliable and good quality water) also needs attention in a bigger way.

What also appears missing in the budget is the indication of the progress made on the big or critical announcements made in the previous budgets such as NIIF (National Investment and Infrastructure Fund), 3P India Institute, resolution of stuck infrastructure PPP projects, etc. Overall, the budget is positive particularly because there were no surprises and fiscal responsibility has been demonstrated.

Amrit Pandurangi is partner at Deloitte Touche Tohmatsu India LLP. The views expressed are personal.

http://www.livemint.com/Opinion/lgEzkeQcFozswHcFGblNjM/Union-Budget-2017-Generally-sounds-positive-for-infrastruct.html?li_source=LI&li_medium=news_rec

5.14 Budget presents 'future', aim to fulfill dreams of all: Narendra Modi

Budget will create new employment opportunities, help in overall economic growth and help in raising the income of the farmers, says Narendra Modi.

New Delhi: The budget presents the "future", Prime Minister Narendra Modi said on Wednesday, while asserting that it is an important step towards overall development of the nation with focus on fulfilling the "dreams" of every section, including the poor, the farmers and the under-privileged.

Prime Minister Narendra Modi during presentation of the Union Budget 2017-18 in Lok Sabha in New Delhi   Photo: PTI

He said the budget will create new employment opportunities, help in overall economic growth and help in raising the income of the farmers. Modi, whose government presented the third budget, said it is a reflection of the development measures, undertaken over the past two-and-a-half years, and the vision to carry forward the momentum in this direction.

"In a way, it is a reflection of our ongoing efforts to see to it that the speed with which our country is changing, gathers momentum," the prime minister said, while describing it as an "excellent" and a "historic" budget.

"It is my belief that the budget will carry forward the development agenda of the government, generate a new climate of confidence and help the nation to scale new heights," he said. Contending that this budget was "associated with our aspirations, our dreams and in a way depicts our future", he said, "This is the future of our new generation, the future of our farmers."

Explaining about the "future", he said it has a meaning in each of its letters. "In FUTURE, the letter 'F' stands for the farmer, 'U' stands for underprivileged which includes dalit, oppressed, women etc., 'T' stands for transparency, technology up gradation—the dream of a modern India, 'U' stands for urban rejuvenation – the urban development, 'R' stands for rural development and 'E' stands for employment for youth, entrepreneurship, enhancement to give a push to new employment and boost to young entrepreneurs," Modi said.

Underlining that the budget will empower the poor and live up to the expectations of all, he said "It will provide an impetus to infrastructure, strength to the financial system and a big boost to the development." Modi said the budget has provisions to "fulfil the expectations of everyone—from construction of highways to expansion of I-ways, from the cost of pulses to the data speed, from the modernization of railways to simple economic constructions, from education to health, from entrepreneurs to industry, from textile manufacturers to tax deduction."

http://www.livemint.com/Politics/zOuZRVmvR56wqnueVOnzAI/Budget-presents-future-aim-to-fulfil-dreams-of-all-Naren.html

5.15 Budget 2017: A Three-Pronged Mission

Within rural development, improving the long-term sustainability of agriculture seems to be a key mission.

The proposal to enhance the coverage of the National Agriculture Market (e-NAM) will, in the long run, help farmers secure better prices for their produce.   Photo: Mint

Rural development, housing, and infrastructure are the standout themes of the budget for next fiscal. The think-through seems to be increased spending in these areas would hopefully provide some kicker to consumption in the medium-term.

Indirect taxes haven't been tinkered with, and that's understandable given the imminent implementation of the goods and services tax (GST) in the second quarter of next fiscal.

Within rural development, improving the long-term sustainability of agriculture seems to be a key mission. To wit, there is a substantial 25% increase in MNREGA spending and a Rs. 8,000 crores jump in allocation for rural housing to Rs. 23,000 crores. Then spending under the Pradhan Mantri Krishi Sinchai Yojana will increase 40%, the corpus of the long-term irrigation fund set up in NABARD will double to Rs. 40,000 crores, and a separate Rs. 5,000 crores fund focused on micro-irrigation is being set up.

Additionally, the proposal to enhance the coverage of the National Agriculture Market (e-NAM) will, in the long run, help farmers secure better prices for their produce. Also, the increase in coverage of the Pradhan Mantri Fasal Bima Yojana from 30% of cropped area this fiscal to 50% by fiscal 2019 would help make farm incomes more predictable.

The granting of infrastructure status to affordable housing, change in the definition of area from built-up to carpet area, relaxation in the area limit for regions in the peripheral areas of metros, and extension of period for claiming tax deduction for affordable housing projects from 3 years to 5 years should make affordable housing projects more attractive to developers. That, in turn, would increase supply and work towards the objective of achieving the vision of 'Housing for All' by 2022.

On the downside, investment demand for houses would be hit further by the move to restrict set-off of loss under income from house property to Rs2 lakh for any assessment year.

On the infrastructure side, overall budgetary spending is proposed to be increase by 10% to Rs. 3.96 lakh crores. The budgetary support towards highways has been significantly hiked to Rs. 64,900 crores compared with the revised estimate of close to Rs. 52,500 crores for the current year. This step-up in spending would improve award of road project and their execution.

The 22% rise in budgetary allocation will drive investments in railway infrastructure projects. The creation of a new fund to augment rail safety also tackles a much-neglected area. The proposed move to take up select airports in tier-2 cities for operation and maintenance under the PPP mode is also directionally positive.

MSMEs also had something to cheer from the budget, as the corporate tax rate for units with a turnover below Rs. 50 crores in fiscal 2016 was reduced by 5% to 25%.

On the downside, the budget lacked big ideas to boost consumption, which would be a disappointment for consumption-oriented sectors. The reduction in tax rates for tax payers in the lowest tax bracket should put an additional Rs. 15,500 crores in the hands of consumers, but this, by itself, is unlikely to give a material boost to consumption. Larger corporate would be aggrieved as they have not been granted any tax relief. The lack of announcement of specific steps to tackle the twin balance sheet problem (banks saddled with bad assets and firms struggling with high leverage) was also bit of a letdown. The reduced allocation to key schemes focused on urban rejuvenation – AMRUT and Smart Cities – was surprising, considering the imperative to develop cities.

All in all, the budget does a good job of further driving the inclusion and sustainability agenda of the government with the limited fiscal leeway available. The policy focus on affordable housing, roads, and MSMEs, should also help in boosting employment as these sectors have a high labour intensity. Creating jobs is a key worry for the government, as ~1.5 million people are entering the labour force every month, with most of them seeking jobs.

One would watch out for further steps over the next few months to fix critical issues constraining the economy – such as the twin balance sheet problem – and develop mechanisms for tracking outcomes from schemes announced in the past 2-3 years.

Nagarajan Narasimhan is Senior Director at CRISIL Research. CRISIL is a global analytical company providing ratings, research, and risk and policy advisory services

http://www.livemint.com/Opinion/TcB3VunTFJBvOWZPrjcn6M/Budget-2017-A-threepronged-mission.html?li_source=LI&li_medium=news_rec

5.16 Budget 2017: Indian Railways in a New Avatar

Indian Railways will need to shore up its spending capabilities as this year's performance in fund utilization has not been too encouraging.

The budget has allocated Rs. 1.31 trillion to Indian Railways in 2017-18—an increase of Rs. 14,000 crores over the current fiscal year.   Photo: Mint

For the first time in 93 years, India has dispensed with a separate railway budget, which has now become an important and integral part of the general budget. The budget for 2017-18 mandates Indian Railways to provide end-to-end solutions for commodities transport.

What it means is that Indian Railways will need to provide both first-mile and last-mile connectivity for transport of freight. This will open up new logistic opportunities.

For the entity booking a consignment for transport, a single-window interface will do away with many hassles. Transport integration is a win-win for both the national transporter and its customers.

The budget has allocated Rs. 1.31 trillion to Indian Railways in 2017-18—an increase of Rs. 14,000 crores over the current fiscal year. Gross budgetary support is now Rs. 55,000 crores. Indian Railways will need to shore up its spending capabilities as this year's performance in fund utilization has not been too encouraging.

A recent spate of accidents leaving to heavy casualties has highlighted the need for the creation of a separate safety fund for the national carrier. The finance minister has announced the formation of a fund with Rs1 trillion to be spent over five years. The government will contribute the seed capital.

Projects to improve safety will be identified in advance and utilization of money from the fund will be governed by clear guidelines. This is a fund for which the time has come. Ancient railway tracks and bridges, train coaches and outdated signaling systems should be on their way out. The government is already committed to eliminating by 2019 all unmanned level crossings to reduce accidents.

Another welcome feature of the budget is the elimination of service charge on railway e-tickets. The finance minister has found an innovative way of promoting digital transactions and addressing queues at railway reservation offices. This would be welcomed by passengers who may have been concerned at the possibility of travel becoming more expensive.

To make travel a little more comfortable, the concept of 'clean my coach' services has been widened. One can expect a coach *mitra* (friend) to assist travelers on matters not limited to cleaning alone.

The redevelopment of 25 railway stations shall commence soon with the objective of turning them into multi-modal transport hubs that will also house shopping malls, hotels and entertainment outlets. Indian Railways has been talking about the concept for some time.

A roadmap for generating internal resources has not been presented in the budget speech, but what the budget highlights is that tariffs would be based on costs, quality of services and competition from other forms of transport.

The budget outlines other passenger-friendly measures and green initiatives. Five hundred stations shall be made disabled-friendly with lifts and escalators being installed. Seven thousand stations will be powered using solar energy. And cleaner tracks will become a reality as there will be no toilet discharge on tracks once all train coaches have been fitted with bio-toilets by 2019.

To improve mobility, it is proposed to increase throughput by 10%. It is a challenge as the existing capacity is already overstretched. It is proposed to seek expert international assistance for maintenance. This is welcome as it will bring in much-needed new technology.

The separate railway budget that had been the norm until last year gave us a detailed account of railway finances and plans to improve freight and passenger services. Having been merged in the general budget, it still finds a very prominent place in the speech of the finance minister.

And the icing on the cake is that the transporter's autonomy remains untouched. The railway budget's merger with the regular budget is off to a sound start.

Arunendra Kumar: *Arunendra Kumar is a former chairman of the railway board.*

http://www.livemint.com/Opinion/XX1gUXUwbHrb7aMmoozJzH/Budget-2017-Indian-Railways-in-a-new-avatar.html?li_source=LI&li_medium=news_rec

5.17 Budget 2017: Railways Gets Largest-Ever Allocation at Rs. 1.31 Trillion

Arun Jaitley said in his budget speech Railways would focus on passenger safety, 'swachch' railways, accounting reforms and finances.

Arun Jaitley also increased the railway line construction target from 2,800 km in 2016-17 to 3,500 km in 2017-18.   Photo: Hemant Mishra / Mint

Apprehensions that the first railway budget in 93 years to be announced as part of the Union budget will lead to a loss of focus for the national transporter were laid to rest on Wednesday, with finance minister Arun Jaitley announcing the largest ever allocation of Rs1.3 trillion to Indian Railways, with a gross budgetary support of Rs.55,000 crores.

Jaitley also said the national carrier will focus on four major areas of passenger safety, capital and development works, cleanliness and finance and accounting reforms—matters traditionally announced by the Union railway minister.

Among the highlights: A corpus of Rs1 trillion for a rail safety fund to be spent over five years; solar power for 7,000 railway stations; redevelopment of 25 railway stations; 70 projects for construction and development through joint ventures with nine state governments; and commissioning of 3,500km railway lines in 2017-18, up from 2,800 km in 2016-17.

The budget also proposed stock market listing of railway enterprises like Indian Railways Catering and Tourism Corporation (IRCTC), Ircon International Ltd and Indian Railways Finance Corporation (IRFC), and end-to-end transport solutions by Indian Railways in selected commodities by partnering logistics companies.

The budget also waived service charges on railway e-tickets to encourage cashless transactions and made AC class tickets cheaper by Rs40 and sleeper class by Rs. 20.

Hinting at a passenger fare hike, the finance minister said that railway tariffs would be fixed taking into consideration costs, quality of service, social obligations and competition from rival transport forms.

Biswanath Bhattacharya, Partner, Infrastructure and Government Services of KPMG, says the initiatives seem to acknowledge the fact that railways is losing share in both freight and premium passenger services to alternative modes of transport, necessitating an integrated approach to greater safety, cleanliness and passenger comfort, and higher service levels to freight customers through end-to-end services. Accounting reforms will also facilitate better management control systems to track performance improvement, Bhattacharya said.

Welcoming the budget, railway minister Suresh Prabhu said it's a good and supportive budget as it focuses on making railways a better mode of transport. He said it will help synergize the investments in railways, roads, waterways and civil aviation.

"One of our major demands was a railway safety fund which would help to eliminate a lot of barriers which impact train speeds. The fund would be used for several purposes like building railway over bridges, ending unmanned crossings, etc," Prabhu said.

Prabhu said one of the focuses would be solar power which will help Indian Railways accomplish its Mission 41K, a plan to save Rs. 41,000 crores in next 10 years by electrifying 90% of railway lines, and also reduce expenditure on power.

"Railways' plans to develop 1,000 mega-watt (MW) solar (power) at 7,000 stations will help in developing a distributed solar ecosystem across India and also 100% electrification of rural areas should also integrate solar distributed generation as part of the scheme for better reliability," said Sanjeev Aggarwal, managing director and chief executive of Amplus Energy.

Freight loading is expected at 1,165 million tons (MT) in 2017-18, which is 71.50MT over revised estimates 2016-17 and earnings at Rs. 1,18,998 crores. Railways is expected to earn Rs. 50,125 crores in passenger traffic, taking total receipts to Rs.1,89,498.37 crores.

http://www.livemint.com/Politics/1HkSvH6JIaZLuXoVt5ccGI/Budget-2017-Railways-gets-largestever-allocation-at-Rs131.html

5.18 Budget 2017: Push for BHIM app, Railway e-tickets

The government will launch two new schemes to promote the usage of BHIM; service charges scrapped on railway e-tickets.

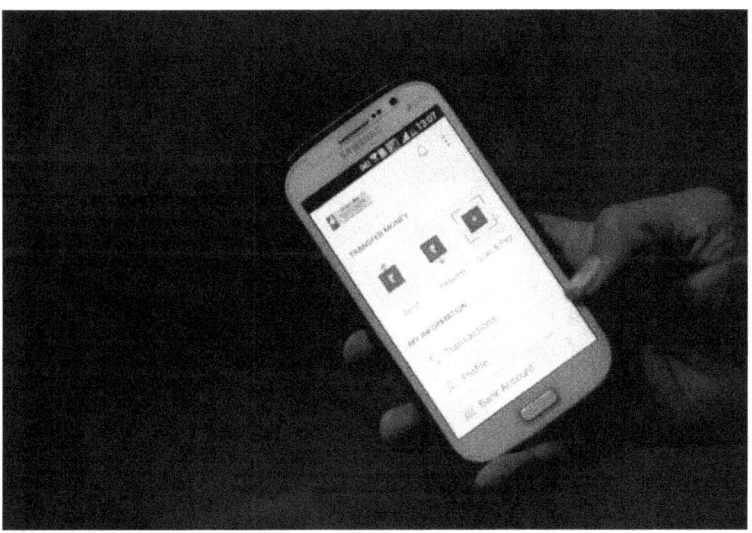

Abhijit Bhatlekar/Mint

Just a month after the launch of the Unified Payments Interface (UPI) based Bharat Interface for Money (BHIM) app, finance minister Arun Jaitley announced more steps to strengthen the digital payments ecosystem and two more schemes to incentivize users of the BHIM platform.

The minister said that the BHIM app will unleash the power of mobile phones for digital payments and financial inclusion. As many as 12.5 million people have downloaded the BHIM app so far. "The government will launch two new schemes to promote the usage of BHIM; these are a referral bonus scheme for individuals and cash back scheme for merchants," the minister said in his Budget speech for financial year (FY) 2017-18.

The details of the schemes announced were not available immediately. A referral bonus scheme for individuals means that if you refer anyone on BHIM, you are likely to get an incentive—like schemes that some e-commerce companies offer to their customers for referring friends.

This app allows you to send and receive money over the Unified Payments Interface (UPI) platform. UPI allows customers with bank accounts to send money, like they would a text message. As UPI runs on the Immediate Payment Service (IMPS) platform, the transaction is instant. To use the BHIM app, you need to have a bank account with a UPI member bank, a registered mobile number, internet access and an Android smart phone. To use the app, you need to download it from the Google Play store. Remember that you can use this facility only if you are a customer of a UPI member bank. You can create your virtual payment address (VPA) on the app—name@upi.

Besides sending and receiving money using VPA, you can also scan a QR code and pay. There are no charges for making payments through the BHIM app. But your bank may levy a nominal charge: as UPI or IMPS transfer fee. All payments through UPI go directly to a bank account.

The government also plans to take steps to promote and possibly mandate petrol pumps, fertilizer depots, municipalities, block offices, road transport offices, universities, colleges, hospitals and other institutions to have facilities for digital payments, including from the BHIM app.

According to data released by the Reserve Bank of India (RBI), UPI transactions between 1 January and 30 January doubled from over

2 million in December to over 4 million. The volume of transactions also more than doubled, from Rs.700 crores to Rs.1,590 crores. The UPI-based BHIM app was launched on 30 December.

The government has also scrapped service charges levied on e-tickets by the Indian Railway Catering and Tourism Corporation (IRCTC), a public sector company under the Ministry of Railways. IRCTC currently levies a service charge on each ticket booked. It levies a service charge of Rs. 20 (plus service tax) per ticket for second class and sleeper tickets, and Rs. 40 in case of all other classes for e-tickets. A maximum of six passengers can be booked on a single ticket. Cashless reservations have gone up from 58% to 68%, the finance minister said. IRCTC books over 1 million tickets each day.

However, the service charge will continue to be applicable on i-tickets booked through IRCTC. For this category of tickets, the service charge is Rs.80 for second class and sleeper tickets and Rs.120 for all other upper classes. The finance minister also said that digital payment infrastructure and grievance handling mechanisms in the country shall be strengthened.

http://www.livemint.com/Money/F5dO6ST0xKANl8ngKs5q4L/BHIM-app-gets-a-new-incentive-push-in-Budget.html

5.19 Budget 2017: Jaitley Gives Infrastructure a Massive Push

Government to invest almost Rs. 4 trillion in the next fiscal in creating and upgrading infrastructure; railways gets got largest-ever allocation at Rs. 1.31 trillion.

India will invest as much as Rs. 3,96,135 crores in creating and upgrading infrastructure in the next financial year, finance minister Arun Jaitley said in his fourth budget speech on Wednesday.

As part of the new integrated infrastructure planning paradigm comprising roads, railways, waterways and civil aviation, the National Democratic Alliance government unveiled the largest-ever rail budget of Rs1.31 trillion, an 8.26% increase over the Rs1.21 trillion allocated to the national carrier in 2016-17.

This is for the first time in 92 years that a combined budget has been presented on 1 February after the merger of the railway budget with the Union budget.   Photo: Ramesh Pathania / Mint

Jaitley said an effective multi-modal transportation system was important for a competitive economy and stressed upon 'synergic investments.'

Of the Rs. 1.31 trillion, the highest-ever capital outlay for the Indian Railways, a gross budgetary support (GBS) of Rs. 55,000 crores will be provided by the finance ministry, as reported by *Mint* on 19 January.

As part of the radical rethinking on improving the country's transportation architecture, this is for the first time in 92 years that a combined budget has been presented on 1 February after the merger of the railway budget with the Union budget. This is a break from the colonial legacy of having a separate railway budget which was recommended by British politician William Ackworth in 1924.

Given the abysmal safety record of the national carrier, the finance minister also announced the creation of Rs1 trillion railway safety fund which will be given seed capital by the finance ministry, with the balance to be raised by the railways from other sources.

Indian Railways will also list its subsidiaries—Indian Railway Catering and Tourism Corporation, Indian Railway Finance Corporation and Ircon International Ltd.

Jaitley said the railways will increase its throughput by 10% by upgrading dedicated corridors which have high traffic volumes. The national carrier will lay down 3,500 km of tracks in 2017-18 as compared with 2,800 km in 2016-17.

Conscious of the falling freight revenues of the Indian Railways, Jaitley announced that the national carrier will offer end-to-end transportation solutions for commodities. Indian Railways registered a 2.15% dip in December revenue earning to Rs. 9,240 crores, compared with Rs. 9,442.32 crores in December 2015.

"The set of initiatives announced seem to acknowledge the challenge that Railways is losing share in both freight and premium passenger services to alternate modes of transport, and hence an integrated approach to improving safety, cleanliness and passenger comfort, and higher levels of service to freight customers through end to end services have been introduced in this budget," said Biswanath Bhattacharya, partner, infrastructure and government Services, KPMG in India.

"The introduction of accounting reforms will also facilitate better management control systems, to track performance improvement of the Railways," added Bhattacharya.

For the road sector, finance minister has allocated Rs. 67,000 crores for the national highways in 2017-18 as compared to Rs. 57,676 crores in 2016-17. Also, 2,000 km of coastal connectivity roads will be constructed.

In addition, an allocation of Rs.19,000 crores has been made towards the Pradhan Mantri Gram Sadak Yojana (PMGSY) to connect far flung habitats, which, along with the spending by the state governments, may result in a total capital expenditure of Rs. 27,000 crores.

Jaitley said the pace of road construction was 133km per day under PMGSY in 2016-17 as compared to 73 km during 2011-14. The country has a road network of 3.3 million, the second largest globally. India has been constructing highways at a rate of 27-28 km per day, with the aim of speeding up the construction rate to 41 km per day.

The government has made an allocation of Rs. 2,41,387 crores for roads, railways and ports in 2017-18. The finance minister also announced a proposed amendment in the Airports Authority of India Act to monetize surplus land for the development of airports.

"The focus on investment in infrastructure was expected and in line with previous policy direction. An infrastructure gap in India has likely hampered growth and contributed to economic volatility. Higher government spending in that area may partly address the infrastructure constraints," said William Foster, vice president, Sovereign Risk Group, Moody's Investors Service, in an emailed statement.

http://www.livemint.com/Politics/L5RaFY18KaRmxPpI0GGDUN/Budget-2017-Arun-Jaitley-unveils-largestever-rail-budget-i.html?li_source=LI&li_medium=news_rec

5.20 The Budget and Your Income Tax

The tax rate for individuals earning between Rs. 2.5 lakh and Rs. 5 lakh was cut to 5%, and the tax obligation for everyone was brought down by Rs. 12,500.   - <u>**Deepti Bhaskaran**</u>

Photo by: Pradeep Gaur / Mint

Acting along expectations of the common man, especially after demonetization, the government has reduced the personal income tax rate for those in the tax slab of Rs. 2.5 lakh to Rs. 5 lakh to 5% from 10% earlier.

The Union Budget 2017-18 aims to reduce the tax liability for those earning up to Rs. 5 lakh to either zero or by half.

Currently, the basic exemption limit for individuals below 60 years of age is Rs. 2.5 lakh. The first slab rate, of 10%, applies to taxable income between Rs. 2.5 lakh and Rs. 5 lakh.

This translates into a tax liability of Rs. 25,000. But in financial year (FY) 2017-18, this rate will be 5%, thus reducing the tax liability by Rs. 12,500 for everyone.

A cess of 3% will continue to apply. The tax rate for individuals with income between Rs. 2.5 lakh and Rs. 5 lakh will be 5%.

For individuals with income between Rs. 5 lakh and Rs. 10 lakh, the rate of taxation continues to be 20% and it will be 30% for individuals earning more than Rs. 10 lakh.

"There was a lot of expectation around increasing the deduction limits, but nothing significant happened. For individuals with lower income reducing the tax rate is good, but after a tax rate of 5% there is a straight jump to 20% for the next slab", said Homi B. Mistry, partner, Deloitte Haskins & Sells LLP.

Rebate

But if your taxable income is up to Rs. 3.5 lakh, you also need to factor in the benefit of the rebate. A rebate is a relief given on the tax liability of an individual. Currently, the rebate is Rs. 5,000 and is for those with taxable income of up to Rs. 5 lakh.

The rebate has now been reduced to Rs. 2,500 and it would apply only if your taxable income is up to Rs. 3.5 lakh. Within this income limit, if someone has a tax liability of Rs. 2,500, she will not have to pay income tax. And, even if the tax liability in this case is more than Rs. 2,500, the amount will get reduced by Rs. 2,500. According to the finance minister, those with income of up to Rs. 3 lakh will be exempt from paying taxes, as their tax liability will come up to Rs. 2,500 and those who earn up to Rs. 3.5 lakh will pay a tax of only up to Rs. 2,500. Also, those who earn up to Rs. 4.5 lakh will not have to pay tax if they use up the entire deduction of Rs. 1.5 lakh, which is available under section 80C of the income-tax Act.

Surcharge

What the finance minster gave with one hand, he took away from the other. If you are part of the mass affluent Indian population with your annual taxable income at Rs. 50 lakh or more, get ready to pay a surcharge. Until now a surcharge was applicable for individuals earning more than Rs. 1 crores. The surcharge was levied at a rate of 15% taking the effective income tax rate on the super-rich to 35.54%.

But now individuals with income levels between Rs. 50 lakh and Rs. 1 crores will pay a surcharge at 10%. "The intention of the government is to reduce the tax burden on the lower income category and pass it to the high-income category," said Mistry. Accordingly the marginal rate of income tax for this income category will be 33.99%. For instance, if your annual income is Rs. 75 lakh, after factoring in the section 80C deduction your taxable income will come to Rs. 73.50 lakh. Your tax liability on this will come to about Rs. 20.17 lakh. A 10% surcharge on this will come to about Rs. 2.02 lakh taking your total tax liability to about Rs. 22.19 lakh. So you will pay a total tax of Rs. 22.86 lakh, including a cess of 3%.

However, you continue to be subject to marginal relief. Marginal relief provides relaxation to taxpayers whose income marginally exceeds the threshold limit of income (Rs. 50 lakh in this case) such that the net amount payable as income-tax and surcharge does not exceed the total amount payable as income-tax on total income of Rs. 50 lakh by more than the amount of income that exceeds Rs. 50 lakh.

For instance, suppose an individual earns a taxable income of Rs. 50.50 lakh. The total tax payable in this case will be about Rs.14.60 lakh including the surcharge of 10%. Now, the total tax on Rs. 50 lakh is about Rs. 13.13 lakh and given that the income exceeds Rs. 50 lakh by only Rs. 50,000, the actual tax payable will be Rs.13.28 lakh (calculated on Rs. 50.50 lakh without the surcharge) plus

Rs.35,000 (after reducing 30% tax from Rs. 50,000), which is about Rs.13.63 lakh."The maximum income for which marginal relief will be available is about Rs. 51,95,900," said Rahul Garg, leader, direct tax, PwC India.

It is hard to argue for lower taxes for those who earn over Rs.50 lakh a year in a poor country like India.

http://www.livemint.com/Money/P7X9bn3dQQjeVWOADqJUBL/Tax-liability-reduced-by-Rs12500.html?li_source=LI&li_medium=news_rec

5.21 Union Budget 2017 and Income Tax Slabs: Who Gains, Who Loses

Arun Jaitley has reduced the income tax rate for those earning between Rs2.5 lakh and Rs5 lakh, but for the rich, there is some pain in the form of a surcharge

Arun Jaitley's Union Budget 2017 has provided some relief to those whose income fall in the Rs.2.5 lakh to Rs.5 lakh tax slab. Photo: Mint

Finance minister Arun Jaitley's Union Budget 2017, which was presented on Wednesday, may not have met the high expectations set especially in the backdrop of demonetization, but it did bring some relief for everyone. The government has reduced the personal income tax rate for those in the tax slab of Rs.2.5 lakh to Rs.5 lakh to 5% from 10% earlier, which translates into a saving of Rs.12,500 (without including cess) for everyone. For those who earn up to Rs.5 lakh, the savings are a lot more. The reduction in the first tax slab along with a rebate of Rs. 2,500 for income up to Rs3.5 lakh means that if your annual income is Rs.3 lakh, you don't pay any taxes. Even those who earn up to Rs.4.5 lakh a year don't pay taxes if you factor in the section 80C deduction of Rs1.5 lakh and the rebate.

BUDGET 2017: WHO GAINED, WHO LOST

The budget 2017 may not have met the high expecations set especially in the backdrop of demonetization, but it did bring some relief
for everyone. The government has reduced the personal income tax
rate for those in the tax slab of Rs2.5 lakh to Rs5 lakh to 5% from 10%
earlier, which translates into a saving of Rs12,500 (without including
cess) for everyone. For those who earn up to Rs5 lakh, the savings
are a lot more. The reduction in the first tax slab along with a rebate
of Rs2,500 for income up to Rs3.5 lakh means that if your annual
income is Rs3 lakh, you don't pay any taxes. Even those who earn up
to Rs4.5 lakh a year don't pay taxes if you factor in the section 80C
deduction of Rs1.5 lakh and the rebate. But for the rich there is some
pain in the form of a surcharge. This budget levied a surcharge of 10%
for those with incomes Rs50 lakh-Rs1 crore. Those above Rs1 crore
already pay a surcharge of 15%. This table tells you how much extra
you pay or save. This is for individuals below 60 years of age and the
calculation includes a cess of 3%.

Income	Individual tax (in Rs)		
Gross total income (in Rs lakh)	Tax you will pay in financial year 2016-17	Tax you will pay in financial year 2017-18	Your benefit or loss
3	-	-	-
5	5,150	2,575	2,575
10	97,850	84,975	12,875
15	236,900	224,025	12,875
20	391,400	378,525	12,875
25	545,900	533,025	12,875
30	700,400	687,525	12,875
35	854,900	842,025	12,875
40	1,009,400	996,525	12,875
45	1,163,900	1,151,025	12,875
50	1,318,400	1,305,525	12,875
55	1,472,900	1,606,028	-133,128
60	1,627,400	1,775,978	-148,578
65	1,781,900	1,945,928	-164,028
70	1,936,400	2,115,878	-179,478
75	2,090,900	2,285,828	-194,928
80	2,245,400	2,455,778	-210,378
85	2,399,900	2,625,728	-225,828
90	2,554,400	2,795,678	-241,278
95	2,708,900	2,965,628	-256,728
100	2,863,400	3,135,578	-272,178
105	3,270,250	3,455,779	-185,529
110	3,648,260	3,633,454	14,806
115	3,825,935	3,811,129	14,806
120	4,003,610	3,988,804	14,806
125	4,181,285	4,166,479	14,806
130	4,358,960	4,344,154	14,806
135	4,536,635	4,521,829	14,806
140	4,714,310	4,699,504	14,806
145	4,891,985	4,877,179	14,806
150	5,069,660	5,054,854	14,806

Assumes a deduction of Rs1.5 lakh　　　　　　　　　　　　　　　　　　　　　　Source:EY

But for the rich there is some pain in the form of a surcharge. This budget levied a surcharge of 10% for those with incomes Rs.50 lakh-Rs.1 crores. Those above Rs.1 crores already pay a surcharge of 15%. This table tells you how much extra you pay or save. This is for individuals below 60 years of age and the calculation includes a cess of 3%.

To check your income tax for 2017-18, click here.

http://www.livemint.com/Money/JFmiV3R5nrTu1QpX6jEPvM/Union-Budget-2017-and-income-tax-slabs-Who-gains-who-loses.html?li_source=LI&li_medium=news_rec

5.22 RBI Seen Cutting Rates By 25 bps As Inflation Slows

Fiscally prudent budget also opens up space for RBI to reduce the repo rate at its February monetary policy meeting.

*RBI has already surprised the market twice, when it cut rates in October
2016 and when it held fire in December, both contrary to expectations.
Photo: Aniruddha Chowdhury / Mint*

Slowing inflation and a fiscally responsible budget may sway
the Reserve Bank of India (RBI) to cut interest rates on Wednesday,
according to a *Mint* survey of economists from 10 banks.

Seven out of 10 bank economists expect RBI to cut its repo rate
by 25 basis points to 6% when the central bank's monetary policy
committee meets on 7-8 February for the bimonthly credit policy. The
other three expect the repo rate to remain unchanged. A basis point is
one-hundredth of a percentage point.

RBI has already surprised the market twice: in October 2016
Governor Urjit Patel announced a 25 basis point reduction when the
market was widely expecting a status quo. And in December, the
banking regulator kept interest rates unchanged against a popular
expectation of a rate cut.

"It could be a close call this time as the inflation situation looks
good and the government has made it clear that it wants to push
growth. But the benefit due to deposits that came in during the 50 days
of demonetization has already helped the interest rates in the markets
to come down. We have factored in a 25bps rate cut," said Soumya
Kanti Ghosh, chief economic adviser, State Bank of India.

Retail inflation decelerated to a two-year low of 3.41% in
December from 3.63% the previous month as vegetable prices
continued to fall.

RBI is aiming to keep retail inflation under 5% in the fourth
quarter and 4% within a band of 2 percentage points on either side in
the medium term.

Announcing the last monetary policy on 7 December, the central bank said that a drop in vegetable prices might bring down overall retail inflation. Any inflexibility in the downward movement of inflation components other than food and fuel, however, may cause some resistance in the future softening of the headline inflation number.

Following the announcement of demonetization on 8 November, most banks saw a surge in deposits held in savings account, giving a boost to their current account, savings account (CASA) ratio and reducing their cost of funds. Most banks pay only 4% interest on savings bank accounts.

According to Rajib Sahoo, chief economist at state-run Canara Bank, interest rates may drop since the US Federal Reserve has hit the pause button on interest rates, while inflation has been softening.

"The latest PMI (purchasing managers' index) numbers for services was 48.7 in January as against 46.8 in December and PMI manufacturing has slightly improved to 50.4 in January from 49.6 in December, but is still very modest," Sahoo said.

The low PMI numbers and slow credit growth indicate that India's private sector has been struggling with growth. In this situation, a lower interest rate may actually spur growth.

However, some specialists say that given the way banks have cut interest rates in the last few weeks, a rate reduction by RBI may not be necessary. In the last month alone, several banks have reduced their marginal cost-based lending rates by up to 90bps, ushering in a low interest rate regime for new borrowers across the board. This was due to the low-cost deposits coming in after demonetization.

Apart from this, the regulator may want to wait for some more macroeconomic data.

"Given that economic conditions still remain very uncertain, it is likely that the central bank will defer a decision on a rate cut till April. Although the budget was conservative, global risks are still evolving, commodity prices remain high, core inflation remains sticky, and the first forecasts of monsoon will be released among other things," said Saugata Bhattacharya, chief economist, Axis Bank Ltd.

http://www.livemint.com/Politics/fkaP3EZIhrSZJafoyfozxI/RBI-seen-cutting-rates-by-25bps-as-inflation-slows.html?li_source=LI&li_medium=news_rec

5.23 What the Four Big Changes in Real Estate Mean for You

A strong push has been given to the affordable housing sector by giving it the status of 'infrastructure'.

Indranil Bhoumik / Mint

Union Budget 2017-18 has focused a good deal on real estate. Homebuyers, developers and investors, all stand to benefit from it.

Some categories of investors may have lost out though. Here are four major changes in real estate, which emanate from this budget.

Affordable housing gets a boost

A strong push has been given to the affordable housing sector by giving it the status of 'infrastructure'. This will attract more investments and funding to the sector and may result in bringing down the cost of capital for developers.

In addition, the criteria of qualifying for affordable housing have been changed from a built-up area of 30 sq. m. in metro areas and 60 sq. m. in non-metro areas, to a carpet area of 30 sq. m. and 60 sq. m. respectively. This would make the affordable housing units more attractive for the buyers, as they will be able to get bigger houses.

"This should amplify the interest of developers further, to build more affordable projects, thereby increasing supply," said Sunil Mishra, chief strategy officer, PropTiger.com.

Further, the permission to complete affordable housing projects in 5 years instead of existing requirement of 3 years—to qualify for tax exemption under section 80IB of the income tax Act—is a big relief for developers.

Developers are now also allowed to keep their unsold inventory without attracting any income tax liability, for up to 1 year after receiving the completion certificate for their housing projects.

Redefinition of long term

The reduction of holding period—from 3 years to 2 years—to qualify for a long-term capital gains (LTCG) status, will benefit investors in real estate.

Currently, the short-term capital gains (STCG) from property investments are taxed at the slab rate which is applicable to the individual. On the other hand, LTCG is taxed at 20%—this excludes cess but comes with the big advantage of indexation.

In addition, the base year for indexation will be shifted from 1 April 1981 to 1 April 2001, for all classes of assets including immovable property. "It will help property owners to ascertain the fair market value of a property bought much before 1981, as it will be relatively easier to ascertain the fair market value of a property as on 1 April 2001," said Amit Maheshwari, managing partner, Ashok Maheshwary & Associates LLP. This may result in further bringing down the capital gains and subsequently the taxes on the capital gain.

The government will also introduce more financial instruments for parking the capital gains to save tax.

According to prevailing tax rules, Rs50 lakh of the long-term gains from sale of property can become tax free, if invested in specified bonds under section 54EC of the Income-tax Act, 1961.

Currently, these specified bonds include only those from the National Highways Authority of India and the Rural Electrification Corporation Ltd. The new products will make it easier for investors to park their capital gains.

Loan-bought rented properties

At present, a home loan borrower can claim tax deductions under section 24(b) against interest paid on home loan. The current limit allows a deduction of up to Rs2 lakh for payment of interest in case of a self-occupied house. If the house is let-out, then the entire interest paid on home loan can be claimed as a deduction.

To remove this anomaly, the tax deduction due to interest paid on rented-out properties, which are bought on loan, will be restricted to Rs2 lakh.

However, the additional interest that is above Rs2 lakh paid during the year can now be set-off in next eight assessment years.

Tax deduction at source on rent

If you are living in a rented accommodation and paying a rent of above Rs. 50,000 per month, then there is some more work ahead for you.

You will be required to make tax deduction at source (TDS) at the rate of 5% while making the payment to your landlord. For instance, if your monthly rent is Rs. 60,000, you will need to deduct Rs. 3,000 (5% of Rs. 60,000) and pay Rs. 57,000 to your landlord.

Giving some respite to the tenants, the TDS collected by the tenant can be deposited once a year, for the whole year.

Besides that, the tenants are neither required to obtain tax deduction and collection account numbers (TAN) nor to file a TDS return to do this.

http://www.livemint.com/Money/VRdUNRnnWFjNCUSM0ApmIP/What-the-four-big-changes-in-real-estate-mean-for-you.html?li_source=LI&li_medium=news_rec

5.24 Four Takeaways from this Budget, for the Householder

The Union Budget 2017-18 will impact the lives of common people in significant ways. Read on to know how

Finance minister Arun Jaitley focused on TEC—Transform, Energize and Clean—as the theme of the Union Budget 2017-18. The integration of the railway budget into the general budget, the collapsing of the 'plan' and 'non-plan' parts of the expenditure and bringing forward the date of the budget to 1 February; are all obvious pointers to winds of change in the way the government thinks about the future.

The macro pieces of an economy translate into our micro lives, as they work themselves out through the system. The fact that Jaitley has kept the fiscal deficit number at 3.5% of GDP for this year, and promised to bring it down to 3.2% next year—while keeping the revenue deficit number pinned down to 2.1% this year and down to 1.9% next year—is good for us. A financially prudent government will not unleash inflation and will keep government borrowing in check.

Photo by: Hemant Mishra/Mint

Four things in the budget affect us.

One, it looks as if this is the first time that the honest taxpayer has got a mention and sympathy in the budget speech. Apart from greater scrutiny of the money found in banks post-demonetization, there will now be a limit on how much you can spend in cash. No payments of over Rs. 3 lakh per transaction, per day, will be allowed in cash. Yes, people will split their bills into Rs. 2.99 lakh and get multiple bills in the name of multiple family members or employees, but the cost of using cash goes up another notch.

Also heartening is the push to make political funding legit: no cash contribution of over Rs. 2,000 will be allowed to a political party, and the launch of electoral bonds by the Reserve Bank of India will facilitate legitimate donations.

Two, there is a redistribution from the rich to the not-so-well-off. People in the tax slabs of Rs. 2.5 lakh to Rs. 5 lakh will now see their tax rates halved—from 10% to 5%. Those in the tax slabs above this will also see a gain, of Rs. 12,500, and their average tax rate will fall. But if you earn between Rs50 lakh and Rs. 1 crores, get ready for a 10% surcharge on the tax paid. Your marginal tax rate, post-surcharge and cess, is now 33.99%, up from 30.9%. Those who earn over Rs. 1 crores will continue with the existing surcharge and cess, and their marginal tax rate remains at 35.54%.

Three, the fear of equity losing its long-term capital gain tax benefits turned out to be unfounded. In fact, real estate has benefitted with the 'long term' now being defined as 2 years instead of 3 years. Long-term capital gains taxes are lower than the taxes on short term capital gains.

Now, you will also have more avenues to park your capital gains. As of now, you can invest up to Rs50 lakh of your capital gains in bonds of National Highways Authority of India (NHAI) or Rural Electrification Corporation Ltd (REC) to mitigate the long-term capital gains tax on real estate.

Of course, in the current real estate market only somebody who bought more than 10 years ago would be booking a profit. The budget has removed the anomaly of those who let out loan-bought houses being able to charge the entire interest as cost. Now, the limit of Rs2 lakh will apply.

Four, as a balm after the shock of demonetization that hurt the small businessmen hard, the tax rate is down to 25% for firms with a turnover of Rs. 50 crores or less. There is also a promise that the first-time taxpayer would not be subjected to tax scrutiny. Expect your neighbourhood grocer and baker to come into the tax net.

Finally, if you want to understand why the insurance agents were singled out to get an exemption from the 5% tax deducted at source (TDS)—if their income is below the taxable limit—we need to circle back and look at the macro picture. Insurance agents bring low-cost household funds to the government via insurance companies, to fund the deficit, hence the star treatment. Once the tax-to-GDP ratio goes up, we will see this change.

Monika Halan works in the area of consumer protection in finance. She is consulting editor Mint, consultant NIPFP, and on the board of FPSB India. She can be reached at monika.h@livemint.com.

http://www.livemint.com/Money/z5L8r5s0F12Xk8N0JZlBdJ/4-takeaways-from-this-budget-for-the-householder.html?li_source=LI&li_medium=news_rec

5.25 ESOPs' Exempt from Budget Proposals on Long-Term Capital Gains Tax

Budget 2017 proposed to deny LTCG tax exemption on sale of listed securities, if securities transaction tax was not paid at the time of acquiring them.

Under current norms, any capital gains from shares held for more than a year are fully tax-exempt if securities transaction tax of 0.1% is paid at the time of selling them. Photo: Mint

All genuine transactions, including employee stock options, will be exempt from the budget proposals on long-term capital gains tax (LTCG), finance ministry officials said on Monday, seeking to assure investors worried about the implications of this provision.

The budget proposed to deny LTCG tax exemption on the sale of listed securities if securities transaction tax (STT) had not been paid at the time of acquiring them.

This was introduced as a provision to prevent misuse. The tax department estimates that people and firms have shown bogus long-term capital gains amounting to more than Rs. 80,000 crores over several years; that has prompted it to tighten norms. Under current norms, any capital gain from shares held for more than a year is tax-exempt if STT of 0.1% is paid when they are sold.

Currently, STT is not paid when shares are acquired in off-market transactions such as gifting, issuing employee stock options and selling shares to private equity firms. This has resulted in concerns that such transactions could come under the tax department's scanner.

The memorandum explaining the tax proposals did mention specific instances where tax would be exempt by government notification. But it was silent on employee stock options. Speaking at a post-budget event organized by the Confederation of Indian Industry, Sushil Chandra, chairman of the Central Board of Direct Taxes, said employee stock options would be a part of the exemption list.

He stressed that the provision was only aimed at clamping down on fake transactions.

To be sure, the list notifying transactions that will be exempt will be put out by the tax department after the finance bill receives Parliament's nod.

Expressing concern at the implications of the budget provisions, the Indian Private Equity and Venture Capital Association had said that it would take up the matter with the government, especially on the question of venture capitalists exiting after an initial public offering. The association had said it would urge the government to exclude all transactions related to funds registered with the Securities and Exchange Board of India, including domestic venture capital funds and alternative investment funds.

A senior tax department official, requesting anonymity, said the government was aware that genuine transactions would have been impacted by the proposal. "This is the reason we have empowered the tax department in the finance bill to exempt all genuine transactions," he said.

"Shares acquired in amalgamations and demergers and gift of shares from one person to the other also need to be exempted from these provisions," said Amit Singhania, partner at law firm Shardul Amarchand Mangaldas and Co.

http://www.livemint.com/Money/9Tld4hOkJkP39RdmhyIdpK/ESOPs -will-be-exempt-from-budget-provisions-on-longterm-cap.html?li_source= LI&li_medium=news_rec

5.26 Are NDA and UPA Budgets Radically Different?

Whether the present Modi-led NDA government can live up the legacy of high capital expenditure by the Vajpayee government is the big question

Arun Jaitley presented his fourth budget on 1 February 2017. This budget would be remembered for historical breaks from its predecessors due to dropping of plan versus non-plan expenditure categories, merging of railway budget into Union budget and advancing of budget date by a month etc.

While these are important changes, a more fundamental question is whether the BJP-led NDA government's budgets are radically different from Congress-led UPA's budgets. Both these political formations have ruled the country since 1999.

Simply speaking budget is an exercise where the government announces its spending plans for the forthcoming year on the basis of projected earnings and gives an account of the same announcements it made in the previous two years. Therefore, budgets should fundamentally be judged by how spending is allocated and whether the government is able to honour these commitments.

Has the overall spending pattern changed?

To be sure, a large part of budgetary spending is pre-destined on account of interest payments, salaries and pensions, defense spending and subsidies; as was pointed out in an earlier **Plainfacts column**. The latest budget has allocated 61% of the total union budget spending on these four counts for 2017-18, same as previous year and actually slightly higher than the average value of 59% during the decade when UPA was in power. Given this similarity, it is not surprising that broad trends in spending pattern of UPA and NDA budgets have not undergone much change.

One major difference which can be seen in the UPA and present NDA government's spending patterns is the drop in share of social services spending in the overall budgetary expenditure. From a peak value of 10.2% in 2009, it has come down to 5.3% as per 2016-17 revised estimates (RE).

However, it would be unfair to put the blame for this reduction on the NDA government alone for two reasons. One, the decline had started under UPA II itself. And, two, after the 14th finance commission's recommendations, increase in tax devolutions to states has been compensated by cutback on Centrally sponsored schemes, which might have led to reduction in social sector spending in Union budgets.

Having said that, the fact remains that welfare programmes such as Sarva Shiksha Abhiyan, Integrated Child Development Scheme and Mid-day Meal Scheme have seen a decline in their proportional share in budget allocations.

Which coalition has adhered to fiscal consolidation better?

The latest budget has been lauded by **ratings agencies** for broadly sticking to the fiscal consolidation roadmap. However, part of the credit is also due to the later years of UPA-II, which saw a steady decline in the fiscal deficit (as percentage of GDP) from 5.9% in 2011-12 to 4.5% in 2013-14, the last year of UPA.

Thus, the current round of fiscal consolidation, which began in 2012-13 appears similar to the period between 2001-02 and 2007-08, which saw a reduction in the deficit from 6% to 2.5% in a span of six years, divided between the later years of Vajpayee government (NDA-I) and the initial years of Manmohan Singh government (UPA-I). The onset of the financial crisis in 2008 led to the government's abandoning of its fiscal consolidation framework, which led to a large increase in the size of fiscal deficit.

What distinguishes the NDA's latest fiscal consolidation attempts from UPA II's course correction is the fact that the Jaitley has done this by managing to realize (actually exceed) its tax collection targets unlike its predecessor.

Historically, actual tax revenue collections have often lagged budget estimates, while actual revenue spending has often exceeded initial estimates, thereby necessitating cuts in capital expenditure. An important reason for this success under Modi government has been low oil prices, which has brought in large amounts in excise duty collections on petroleum products, as was pointed out in an **earlier Plain facts** column. With oil prices likely to increase, and government's ability to raise additional revenue coming under squeeze, it remains to be seen whether this trend would continue.

Prioritizing investment

One thing which differentiates NDA budgets from UPA is the former's attempts to increase the share of capital expenditure in overall budgetary spending. NDA-I government left it at an all-time high in recent past, and the figure has been slowly climbing up under NDA II's tenure. This year's budget has also predicted an increase in this figure.

However, as was pointed out in **article published** in *Mint*, two things could compromise this promise from materializing: assumption of a low growth in revenue expenditure (half of what it was in previous year), and little focus on the need to recapitalize and deal with bad debt. It is on this count that the NDA government faces its most important challenge, in terms of providing stimulus to the economy as well as matching the record of Atal Bihari Vajpayee government as driver of large scale public investments in the country.

5.27 Union Budget 2017: The Hits and Misses, According to Montek Singh Ahluwalia

A Union Budget should be judged on four criteria—macroeconomic balance, tax changes, pattern of expenditure and policy initiatives. A look at how Arun Jaitley's fourth budget fares on these parameters.

There are four criteria by which a budget should be judged. (i) Does it ensure macroeconomic balance given the circumstances? (ii) Are the tax changes consistent with the overall objectives? (iii) Does the pattern of expenditure and the design of programmes appropriate? (iv) Does it announce significant new policy initiatives in other areas? Here is my take on each of these for the Union Budget 2017:

Macroeconomic Balance

The finance minister has achieved the fiscal deficit target of 3.5% of gross domestic product (GDP) that was set for 2016-17. He had targeted reducing it to 3% in 2017-18, but in the aftermath of demonetization, which had a larger negative effect than anticipated, many had recommended a larger deficit to offset the shrinkage of demand created by demonetization. Against this, there were legitimate concerns about how markets would react, given uncertainties in the global economy, weaker exports, and the possibility of capital outflows. The FRBM Committee reportedly recommended flexibility of up to 0.5 %. The finance minister has wisely opted to use only some of the space provided and revised the earlier target to 3.2 %.

The finance minister has wisely opted to use only some of the space provided and revised the earlier target to 3.2 %. Photo: Pradeep Gaur / Mint

Fiscal purists may regret the relaxation, but the expansion is small and the process of fiscal consolidation continues. Markets are unlikely to react negatively as long as the economy looks like returning to 7.5% GDP growth in 2017-18. The question to ask is, are we really on track for a 7.5 % growth? The Economic Survey estimated that the demonetization would reduce growth in the current year to between 6.5 and 6.75%. Many feel it may be significantly lower, at about 6%. If so, the projected recovery to 7.5 % is unrealistic. Without it, revenues will fall short of what is projected, jeopardizing the fiscal target. We need to do whatever we can to ensure quick revival and it is not clear that the budget does that.

Tax Policy Reform

The most important development in tax policy is the implementation of the Goods and Services Tax (GST). Decisions on this issue lie with the GST Council, but the finance minister reported that progress is being made, and we may well have a GST in place by

1 September. Unfortunately, what the Council has agreed to is a flawed structure, with too many rates. There will be a zero rate that will apply to half the items, and other items will be distributed across five tax slabs—5%, 12%, 18% and 28% for luxury goods, with additional cesses on some luxury goods for compensating the states and also financing clean energy, the latter effectively constituting a fifth slab . The states have not agreed to include alcohol and real estate.

Fiscal purists may regret the relaxation, but the expansion is small and the process of fiscal consolidation continues. Markets are unlikely to react negatively as long as the economy looks like returning to 7.5% GDP growth in 2017-18. The question to ask is, are we really on track for a 7.5 % growth? The Economic Survey estimated that the demonetization would reduce growth in the current year to between 6.5 and 6.75%. Many feel it may be significantly lower, at about 6%. If so, the projected recovery to 7.5 % is unrealistic. Without it, revenues will fall short of what is projected, jeopardizing the fiscal target. We need to do whatever we can to ensure quick revival and it is not clear that the budget does that.

The Union budget has proposed to apply the 25% corporate tax rate to all MSMEs—a good move which will support the employment creating end of industry and thus encourage job creation.   Photo: HT

The ideal structure would have had only one or at most two rates, other than a zero rate, and real estate at least should have been included, since it is a large part of the capital cost of setting up new factories. The flawed GST will still be an improvement on the existing structure of central and state taxes, but it will contribute much less to growth than a GST with far fewer slabs. There is probably no room at this stage to reopen the issue, but we should keep an open mind about raising it as soon as possible.

The promise to lower the corporate tax rate to 25% and abolish exemptions is receding into the future. It is now proposed to apply the 25% rate to all MSMEs (micro, small and medium enterprises with a turnover up to Rs. 50 crores). This will cover 90% of all companies currently paying tax, but they will account for a relatively small percentage of the total tax paid. However, despite its limitations, it is a good move which will support the employment creating end of industry and thus encourage job creation.

The reduction in income tax rates in the first slab from 10% to 5% has been widely welcomed, but I regret to say that it is not well conceived. We now have a much distorted rate structure, with the first slab, from 2.5 lakh to 5 lakh, taxed at 5% followed by a sudden jump to 20% for incomes from Rs. 5 lakh to Rs. 10 lakh and 30% for incomes above this limit. However, all this is complicated by a new surcharge of 10% for those with taxable income between Rs50 lakh and Rs. 1 crores, and a continuation of the old surcharge of 15 % for incomes above Rs. 1 crores. If the idea was to start with a lower tax slab to encourage tax payers to get into the net, the entire rate structure should have been rejigged to allow a more gradual transition from 5%

to the highest rate, avoiding sharp increases as at present, from 5% to 20 %. The surcharges should simply have been abolished since they violate the spirit of cooperative federalism as they are not shared with the states.

In the absence of reforms in tax administration that encourage tax payers to comply, it will be difficult to shield them from what is often called "tax terrorism".   Photo: Pradeep Gaur / Mint

A missing element on the tax side is modernization of tax administration to improve compliance. The finance minister rightly pointed out that there are too few people declaring reasonable amounts of income. The budget takes credit for a 25% increase in revenue from personal income tax, which is entirely reasonable if we look at the potential. But in the absence of reforms in tax administration that encourage tax payers to comply, it will be difficult to shield them from what is often called "tax terrorism". The Parthasarathi Shome committee had made a number of recommendations in this regard two years ago, but hardly any of them have been acted upon. Setting high revenue targets without modernization of tax administration will only lead to more complaints from harassed tax payers.

Expenditure programmes

A positive feature on the expenditure side is the absence of new populist schemes. The Economic Survey seemed to be pushing for an unconditional Universal Basic Income, which could be financed by abolition of other subsidies. There was a real danger that the scheme, if introduced, would have been applauded, without the subsidies being abolished! It is best to make progress in this area gradually, by substituting existing subsidies with cash transfers. The ongoing experiment with the public distribution system in Puducherry and Chandigarh needs to be carefully studied to see if it can be expanded.

There is wide support for the idea that there should be a focus on infrastructure development, and more generally towards capital expenditure. The infrastructure emphasis is not evident in the budget because expenditure on infrastructure schemes has increased by 13.5% (budget estimates to budget estimates) whereas the total expenditure on all "developmental schemes" has increased by 17.8 %. The picture may well look better if "off budget" expenditure in the railways, ports, highways etc. is included.

Capital expenditure in the budget has increased by 25.4%, which is impressive. However, this is certainly not enough to compensate for the slowdown in private investment. A revival of investment in the economy cannot be achieved simply through the budget, or even the private sector. The constraints holding up private sector investment need to be directly addressed.

Revival of bank lending

A disappointing feature of the budget is the absence of a credible plan to ensure a revival of bank lending. Commercial credit expansion by banks has slowed down considerably, and if personal loans are excluded, lending to industry is actually contracting! There is no way the economy can get back to 7.5% growth without a robust revival in bank lending.

There is no way the economy can get back to 7.5% growth without a robust revival in bank lending   Photo: Bloomberg

A mistaken notion commonly expressed is that because bank deposits have increased following demonetization, the banks will now be able to expand lending. In the first place, much of the increased deposits are likely to flow back into the system when the existing restrictions on withdrawals are removed. The budget could have given a clear road map for when these restrictions will go. Even if the decision is to be taken by the Reserve Bank of India (RBI), that could have been done in parallel and announced in the budget as a signal of impending return to normalcy.

The real problem constraining bank lending is that state-owned banks do not have enough capital to support higher lending. A credible scheme for recapitalization should therefore have had top priority, but the budget only provides Rs. 10,000 crores, which is hopelessly inadequate, based on the estimate of need made two years ago. Since then, RBI's asset quality review showed that non-performing assets (NPAs) are much larger than expected. This will force the banks to make larger provisions, shrinking their capital base considerably. The government could use this opportunity to reduce its shareholding below 51%, and there is much to recommend this course of action, but if this is not possible, then much larger amounts would be needed from the budget.

The problem of cleaning up the balance sheets of the banks is intimately linked with the weaknesses in the balance sheets of corporate borrowers. The problem has been comprehensively analyzed in Chapter 4 of the Economic Survey and it is, therefore, all the more disappointing that no corrective steps are proposed. Unless it is believed that a sudden return to high growth will reduce stress on corporate balance sheets, we need to take hard decisions to clean up the existing NPAs relatively quickly.

Cases where there is clear malfeasance on the part of defaulting borrowers obviously call for punitive action, but cases where defaults reflect adverse commercial outcomes, including over-optimism on the part of the borrowers, call for a different approach.

What is needed in such cases is that both the borrowers and the banks take a haircut. This will be necessary even if it is decided to hand over the companies to new owners, since these investors will only take up a project if it is felt to be viable.

Public sector bank managers are understandably reluctant to agree to their bank taking a haircut for fear of being accused of collusion to benefit the private party. This is the real reason why we may need a "bad bank" type of solution, in which the bad bank takes the asset off the books of the bank, with some haircut to the bank.

Public sector bank managers will be more willing to take a haircut demanded by another government entity, which then deals with the defaulting borrowers to seek a resolution. This problem has been pushed under the carpet for too long, and it is not going to go away.

There are many other initiatives in the budget that are well intentioned, including initiatives to roll out the digital infrastructure, new initiatives for skill development, reforming the University Grants Commission, etc. How effective these are will depend on the detailed design and the manner of implementation, but I do not have the space to deal with these issues.

The big picture is that there is much that is sensible in the budget, and nothing that does any harm. But there is a great deal more that needs to be done if we want to get back to 7.5% growth.

Montek Singh Ahluwalia was the deputy chairman of the erstwhile Planning Commission.

http://www.livemint.com/Opinion/NbenUh6dQvFOXMH8Q9bLCJ/
Union-Budget-2017-The-hits-and-misses-according-to-Montek.html?li_
source=LI&li_medium=news_rec

5.28 Note Ban Dividend Hasn't Been Factored in Union Budget 2017: Shaktikanta Das

Economic affairs secretary Shaktikanta Das calls Arun Jaitley's Union Budget 2017 fiscally prudent and hopes economic growth will pick up next year.

New Delhi: Economic affairs secretary Shaktikanta Das, who recently got a three-month extension until 31 May, is an old hand in the finance ministry. He defends the budget as fiscally prudent and hopes growth will pick up next fiscal year. Edited excerpts from an interview:

Some experts have pointed out that the increase in public expenditure may not be enough to boost economic growth at a time when private investment is contracting.

If by merely increasing government expenditure growth were to happen, then every country will record double-digit growth. We have to keep in mind our high level of interest payments; it's about 24% of our total expenditure. So we have to ensure our debt is sustainable. After five years, 10 years, all the money will go to interest payments. So we have to remain fiscally prudent. We cannot sacrifice the interest of our future generations for the benefit of today's generation. So a sustainable debt is very important. At the same time, sectors of the economy which need funding, adequate funds have been provided. But by merely stepping up allocation, it is not necessary that you will attain higher growth. There is no one-to-one correlation. You need to spend on critical sectors and spend well.

I would expect growth to be upwards of 7% in 2017-18. The remonetization process is near complete; the budget has been well received. I am sure the economy will bounce and will record 7%-plus growth rate.

Are we inclined to accept the N.K. Singh Committee's suggestion of debt to GDP ratio as a benchmark for a new fiscal discipline road map?

Debt to GDP is an important fiscal parameter, there is no denying that. Let's study the report as I don't want to take a guess at this point.

Have the fiscal gains from demonetization that the finance minister spoke about, through a one-time dividend from the Reserve Bank of India (RBI), been factored into the budget?

We have not factored that in. Whatever we get as a one-time dividend from RBI, whatever higher tax collection we get from Garib Kalyan Yojana, will come as a bonus. It is difficult to make an assessment about how many people will take the benefit of Garib Kalyan Yojana. We will know only on 31 March. In all such schemes, the response comes in the last 10 days. We have assumed dividend from RBI this year almost at last year's level of around Rs. 66,000 crores. Let's see.

By when do you think RBI will be able to release more data on demonetization?

The window technically is now open till June. RBI is engaged in counting notes. Let that be complete. We will get a clearer picture. The bigger thing to keep in mind is that the process of remonetization is almost complete. I don't know how much time they will take.

How soon can the electoral bonds be issued? Will the government pay interest on the bonds?

The bonds will be issued as soon as the finance bill is passed by Parliament. There will be no interest rate on electoral bonds. Why should interest be paid? We are only enabling donors to maintain their anonymity.

How will inter-ministerial consultations be carried out once the Foreign Investment Promotion Board is abolished?

Either the sectoral regulator will be in charge of the government approver or the concerned ministry or department. It should also fit in under the regulator's responsibility under individual laws. You cannot give responsibility to a regulator beyond what the law permits. For certain cases, you can authorize RBI which is in charge of FEMA (Foreign Exchange Management Act). Anything to do with stock markets, you can ask SEBI (Securities and Exchange Board of India) to be in charge of it. There will be less of inter-ministerial consultation. Wherever security clearance is involved, they will take it (from home ministry). The announcement is more to provide a signal to foreign and domestic investors that we want to create a hassle-free environment for investment.

What were the issues before the finance ministry while preparing the budget and have you addressed them in the budget?

First factor which was to be kept in mind was to remain fiscally prudent. Second factor was to step up public investment in critical sectors of infrastructure and certain select social sectors such as agriculture and rural development. The third factor was to continue with the process of economic reforms. The budget addresses all the three aspects. With regard to fiscal prudence, the fiscal deficit has been kept at 3.2% of GDP which is well within the range given by the N.K. Singh committee. With regard to stepping up public expenditure, infrastructure spending has increased, agriculture spending has increased, allocation for road, railway, ports, irrigation, have been stepped up which in turn will generate a lot of economic activity. On reforms, we have announced a contract farming law; perishables have been removed from APMC market requirements. It also talks of UGC reforms. It talks of amendment to the Airports Authority of India Act. Then in the financial sector, FIPB was done away with, oil major is being created, and there is the amendment to arbitration and conciliation act to deal with PPP disputes.

Almost under similar circumstances when growth was slowing down and private investment was yet to pick up, finance minister decided to stick to the fiscal consolidation road map. So what has changed this year?

You cannot say that the finance minister has deviated from the fiscal path. He has basically remained within the number which was given by the N.K Singh committee. Even this year, the finance minister has said that it would be our effort to improve upon the fiscal number. The following year, fiscal deficit will be at 3% of GDP.

So basically we have partially used the escape route provided by the N.K Singh committee?

No, we have not used the escape route. We have not yet studied the report in detail. But what we are saying is that given the current requirement of the economy, fiscal deficit of 3.2% of GDP is very appropriate and can be considered as fiscally prudent; because you cannot also choke growth because if you choke growth, your tax revenue will be adversely affected. In that sense, there is no deviation.

Private investment has started contracting from this year. Is that a cause of concern?

So far as the government is concerned, it is providing an enabling environment—where there is no hassle to making an investment, there is ease of doing business, there is less of government interference, no inspector raj, a friendly tax environment. Government is also stepping up public expenditure which in turn will give a spurt to private sector investment. When you spend more on roads and railway construction, the demand for cement and steel goes up. Government has reduced corporate tax rate for companies with turnover of Rs. 50 crores or less. They will be in a position to invest more now. So government can only give an enabling environment, conducive atmosphere and support by way of increasing public expenditure. Beyond that it is for the private sector to rise up to the occasion and invest.

http://www.livemint.com/Politics/HgQg5D74bqRBjcbjkB3MSM/We-havent-factored-note-ban-dividend-in-Union-Budget-2017.html?li_source=LI&li_medium=news_rec

5.29 Has Union Budget 2017 made India a better investment destination?

Amid global and local uncertainties, the budget resisted the tendency to be fiscally expansionist and didn't shock a system that isn't well-equipped to deal with shocks.

Arun Jaitley with his team of finance ministry officials
Photo: Ramesh Pathania / Mint

Arun Jaitley's fourth budget, his government's penultimate one, wasn't presented in the best of circumstances, global and local.

The global economy isn't in a great place. The impact of Brexit—on the UK, the European Union (EU) and the rest of the world—isn't clear and US President Donald Trump's early days in the White House have proved beyond doubt that he aims to do everything he said during the campaign—his supporters said at the time that critics were making the mistake of taking his words literally.

The International Monetary Fund (IMF) has kept its growth outlook for the global economy unchanged at 3.4%, but it is becoming clear that the estimate may not have fully factored in the impact of several things—including the extent to which the US's protectionist policies could hurt global trade in products and services.

Meanwhile, there's a sudden bullishness about oil that, if it turns out to be true, will not bode well for India, which has managed to balance its books largely on account of the bounty presented by low oil prices (New Delhi has kept end prices almost constant, taking up the tax on oil).

Locally, the latest gross domestic product (GDP) numbers indicate a slowing of growth and, more worryingly, a contraction in gross fixed capital formation; the earnings statements released by banks show that the bad loan problem plaguing the Indian banking system isn't going to go quietly; and the short-term pain associated with demonetization (the Indian government's move, on 8 November to render invalid older high-value currency notes accounting for 86% of the cash in circulation by value) had turned sentiment, both consumer and business, negative.

So, how should foreign investors rate the budget which was presented on 1 February?

One parameter for evaluation has to be the numbers in the budget itself and the philosophy behind them. Jaitley has resisted the tendency (and calls) to be fiscally expansionist and has deviated very marginally from his fiscal deficit target of 3% of GDP. He hopes to end 2017-18 with a fiscal deficit of 3.2%. This is creditable.

In terms of expenditure, though, the numbers look a little more suspect, with the government expecting a mere 6% increase in revenue expenditure. And there's no telling whether the government will be able to meet the target of Rs. 72,500 crores it has set itself to raise from divestment of its stake in state-owned companies. It will miss this financial year's target, much like it did last.

The second parameter will probably be the "Ease of Doing Business" (capitalized because of the World Bank's eponymous survey of the same name that rates countries on this), one of this government's articulated objectives.

The scrapping of the Foreign Investment Promotion Board (FIPB) will help this cause, if done the correct way. Although 90% of foreign direct investment, or FDI, currently coming into the country comes in through the so-called automatic route, this process is anything but automatic. And the government also needs to quickly clarify what will happen to the remaining 10% that needs clearances from a combination of ministries.

Tax reforms and measures play an important role in how easy or difficult it is to do business in a country; and on that front, the budget has scrapped a controversial tax on foreign portfolio investors, or FPIs, on indirect transfers. Finally, the budget makes a mention (yet again) of labour reforms and four labour codes to replace the multiplicity of labour laws (many of which are archaic). Even if nothing much happens on this front, foreign investors can take heart from the fact that the government is at least willing to talk about this politically sensitive issue.

The third parameter has to be the local economy, and what the budget does for it in terms of reviving both investment and consumption.

On the growth front, by promising almost Rs. 4 trillion of investment in creating infrastructure, the budget may have done enough to ensure public investment keeps the wheels of the economy turning till such time private investment is ready to take over. There was enough in it for housing and banks (expectedly, stocks of companies in the two businesses did very well, and drove growth in stock market indices), two sectors that have the ability to amplify, or at the least, transmit growth. And it mentioned enough initiatives and reforms in the works, including a new labour code and the scrapping of FIPB, which will make it easier to do business in India.

Relief for the farm and the rural sectors came from an increase in spending, including in farm credit and the populist rural job guarantee scheme Mahatma Gandhi National Rural Employment Guarantee Scheme, or MGNREGS, introduced by the previous government. The government spent more on the job guarantee scheme, especially in the second half of 2016-17, taking total spending in the course of the year to Rs. 47,500 crores, much higher than the budgeted Rs. 38,000 crores. The budget for 2017-18 allots Rs. 48,000 crores for the scheme. For the salaried, the relief came in the form of a tax cut of 5 percentage points for those who earn between Rs2.5 lakh and Rs5 lakh a year; a little over half of the 37 million people who file tax returns in India are in this income group, so the government's sop is well targeted. For businesses with a turnover of less than Rs. 50 crores, there is a 5 percentage point cut in the applicable tax rate to 25%. This should provide some relief to medium and small enterprises, especially those that straddle the interstitial space between the formal and informal economy and which have been hit hard by demonetization.

By far the biggest boost in sentiment, though, came from the fact that Union budget 2017-18 didn't have any unpleasant surprises in store. The sudden spike in stock markets, a classic relief rally, soon after the finance minister's speech ended, can be attributed to this, the absence of bad news. That may well be the greatest achievement of the budget: it had a little something for everybody; it didn't bloat government finances; but perhaps most importantly, it didn't shock a system that isn't particularly well-equipped to deal with shocks right now.

5.30 Budget 2017 and its Place in History

Clearly, budget 2017 is a defining moment. A lot, however, will depend on the ability of the NDA to walk the talk.

On 1 July, if all goes to plan, the country would have formally transitioned to the goods and services tax (GST) regime. By the sheer path-breaking nature of the tax reform initiative, which for the first time economically unifies the country, GST will have a special place in India's modern economic history. What about Budget 2017? For several reasons it, too, is a watershed moment.

The irony is that while the Bharatiya Janata Party (BJP)-led National Democratic Alliance (NDA) will claim credit, most of the proposals have been in the pipeline for years. It was just that no government chose to act on it previously. Alternatively, it may well be that the present ecosystem—especially the federal make-up after the implementation of the recommendations of the 14th Finance

Commission (FFC) and the imminent rollout of GST—is more conducive to such change.

Regardless, here are my five reasons.

Firstly, advancing the schedule is more than just a break with a colonial hangover. It actually gives an administration a full year to spend the money it has earmarked for various projects; of course it also means more work for our bureaucrats, who have long been used to a nine-month spending cycle.

Second, there is a fundamental reset to the nomenclature—plan and non-plan have been abandoned and instead replaced with revenue and capital expenditure. But this is much more than just a change in classification. The idea is to move to an outcome-oriented approach and the finance minister has announced that the Niti Aayog will monitor it; participating in the *Mint*-CNBC TV18 event last week, its CEO, Amitabh Kant, assured this would be done in a transparent manner.

Third, this budget is the likely template for the future. Given that GST rollout is imminent, the finance minister wisely chose not to tinker with the indirect tax rates. And most don't realize, but the movement in indirect tax rates and slabs inevitably generate the news and hype about budgets; which is probably why most people came away feeling underwhelmed.

In that sense this year's budget, sans tax rate changes, was sanitized to begin with. It focused on spending and listing out the government's priorities within the fiscal sector: social sector with a particular accent on the poorest of the poor, farmers, rural sector and roads.

Going forward, this will be the likely contour of future budgets. Not a bad thing really. After all it is time Parliament and the country focused on government spending—so far it has been in the news mostly for the wrong reasons, like misappropriation of money.

Fourth, this budget has renewed the new-found focus on agriculture; especially the emerging agriculture economy, which includes new alternatives like horticulture, dairying and so on—all of which are vulnerable to market volatility. The Indian farmer is probably the biggest risk-taker in India right now, but the least rewarded; they are a proud people who don't want largesse (as some commentators seem to think). By promising the introduction of derivatives as a hedge against price volatility and delinking perishables from the shackles of the Agricultural Produce Marketing Committee, the budget has set the ball rolling in integrating farms into the market economy (read that as the formal economy, with its attendant advantages).

Fifth, and finally, this budget marks the flowering of the federation. The FFC set the stage for the NDA to walk the talk on cooperative federalism, and the last two budgets did precisely that; GST is just another example of how the centre and states are beginning to do things in tandem. And with the shift to outcome-based budgeting (as explained earlier) the allocations of public money has moved from departments to stakeholders—like states and the third tier, panchayets and urban local bodies (though this is very inadequate the moment). Clearly then, budget 2017 is a defining moment. A lot, however, will depend on the ability of the NDA to walk the talk.

Anil Padmanabhan is executive editor of Mint *and writes every week on the intersection of politics and economics. His Twitter handle is @capitalcalculus. Respond to this column at anil.p@livemint.com*

http://www.livemint.com/Opinion/JPpnc13wedFfKTSYNh7GlM/Budget-2017-and-its-place-in-history.html?li_source=LI&li_medium=news_rec

5.31 Arun Jaitley's Budget makes a Strong Case for an RBI Rate Cut, say Economists

A conservative fiscal deficit target, as announced in Union Budget 2017, and favourable inflation numbers augur well for an RBI interest rate cut on 8 February

RBI's monetary policy committee will meet on 8 February to take a decision on an interest rate cut.   *Photo: Mint*

Mumbai: Finance minister Arun Jaitley's announcement of a conservative fiscal deficit target for 2017-18 and the low net market borrowing figure translate into a higher chance of a rate cut by the

Reserve Bank of India (RBI) when the monetary policy committee meets to review policy next week, economists said.

In his budget speech, Jaitley said India's fiscal deficit target will be limited to 3.2% for the year ending March 2018, belying popular expectation that the government would go for an expansionary budget to address concerns that demonetization will hit economic growth.

In a report on Thursday, Bank of America Merrill Lynch supported the expectation of a 25 basis points (bps) rate cut on 8 February.

"Banks have already cut MCLRs (marginal cost of funds based lending rate) after PM Modi's December 31 speech. A RBI rate cut should translate into average lending rate cuts in the April-September 'slack' industrial season," Indranil Sengupta, India economist at Bank of America Merrill Lynch, said.

It "will be an extremely close call. The 3.2% fiscal deficit figure was a positive surprise" said S.K. Ghosh, chief economist at State Bank of India.

Still, easing consumer price inflation, an increased bank deposit base and easy liquidity should also help in bringing down bond yields, which may in fact result in a lowering of interest rates without necessarily a policy rate cut, said others.

"Given that economic conditions still remain very uncertain, it is likely that the central bank will defer a decision on a rate cut till April. Although the budget was conservative, global risks are still evolving, commodity prices remain high, core inflation remains sticky, the first forecasts of monsoon will be released, among other things," said Saugata Bhattacharya, chief economist, Axis Bank Ltd.

Retail inflation decelerated to a two-year low of 3.41% in December compared to 3.63% the previous month as vegetable prices continued to contract.

RBI is targeting keeping retail inflation under 5% in the fourth quarter and 4% within a band of 2% on either side in the medium term.

While announcing the last monetary policy on 7 December, the central bank said that while a drop in vegetable prices might bring down overall retail inflation, downward inflexibility in inflation excluding food and fuel could set a resistance level for future downward movements in the headline inflation number.

The government also announced its intent to buy back about Rs. 75,000 crores worth of government bonds from the market in the New Year, pumping in some easy liquidity. "It's evident that the government wants to push the yield down, as they would like to borrow long at a good rate in the New Year. By buying back bonds, they can ensure an under supply of government securities, leading to an increase in price," a bond trader said on conditions of anonymity.

Bond yields and prices move in the opposite directions.

But others are skeptical about the government borrowing number, which is on the basis of small savings mobilization of Rs. 1 trillion.

"This is a very high figure if you look at the average levels of small savings in the last five years. If the net borrowing figure breaches the Rs. 3.48 trillion that the government has predicted, then it could result in hardening of yields later. However, we are still factoring in a 25 bps rate cut," said Ghosh of SBI.

http://www.livemint.com/Money/d2X0TgHY1KXS5rX9D0B1ZK/Arun
-Jaitleys-budget-makes-a-strong-case-for-an-RBI-rate-cu.html?li_source=LI&li_
medium=news_rec

5.32 Union Budget 2017: Demonetization's negative effects will not spill over to next year, says Arun Jaitley

By: FE Online | New Delhi | Updated: February 1, 2017 11:41 AM

Finance Minister Arun Jaitley today said that the negative effects of demonetization would not spill over to next year. The surplus cash available to banks would increase liquidity and benefit all sections of society, he said.

Jaitley praised demonetization as an epoch making decision of the government. (ANI)

Finance Minister Arun Jaitley today said that the negative effects of demonetization would not spill over to next year. The surplus cash available to banks would increase liquidity and benefit all sections of society, he said.

Jaitley praised demonetization as an epoch making decision of the government. He quoted IMF projections to press his point that the effect of demonetization would not spill over next. He said the government would continue to work for the benefit of the poor in the country.

The shock demonetization will shave off a good 0.5 percentage point from GDP growth this fiscal, pulling it down to 6.5 per cent, Economic Survey said today while predicting "return to normal" 6.75-7.5 per cent in the next financial year and calling for bold tax cuts.

Indian economy had grown at a revised rate of 7.9 per cent in 2015-16 and was projected to grow by 7.1 per cent in the current fiscal by the Central Statistical Organization, which did not account for disruption caused by demonetization.

"Over the medium run, the implementation of the GST, follow-up to demonetization, and enacting other structural reforms should take the economy towards its potential real GDP growth of 8 per cent to 10 per cent," said the Survey tabled in Parliament by Finance Minister Arun Jaitley.

http://www.financialexpress.com/budget/union-budget-2017-demonetisations-negative-effects-will-not-spill-over-to-next-year-says-arun-jaitley/532121/

5.33 Budget 2017: Jaitley reduces income tax rates for individuals, companies

Arun Jaitley in his budget speech announced a reduction in the tax rate in the income tax slab of Rs. 2.5 lakh to Rs. 5 lakh to 5% from 10%

The budget proposals announced by finance minister Arun Jaitley focused on rewarding honest taxpayers, taxing the rich and bringing to task economic offenders.

The budget for 2017-18 announced tax sops for the middle class and small companies while increasing the tax liability of the super rich. It also sought to bring to task people like UB Group chairman Vijay Mallya, who has fled the country while cases are pending against him in various courts.

Jaitley proposed to reduce the tax rate for individuals in the income tax slab of Rs. 2.5 lakh to Rs. 5 lakh from 10% to 5%, giving some relief to the middle class. He also proposed a simple tax return form for this category of taxpayers.

The finance minister also sought to reduce tax rates for small and medium-sized companies as part of an earlier promise to gradually reduce corporate tax rates and phase out exemptions given to companies.

The tax rate for companies with an annual turnover of up to Rs.50 crores has been brought down to 25% from 30%. This will benefit 96% of the 6.94 lakh companies filing tax returns, Jaitley said.

Income slabs	Number of taxpayers who filed their tax returns in 2015-16 (in million)
Less than Rs2.5 lakh	9.9
Rs2.5-5 lakh	19.5
Rs5-10 lakh	5.2
Rs10-50 lakh	2.23
Above Rs50 lakh	0.17

Source: 2017 budget speech

However, there was no respite for big corporations as the tax rates for them remained unchanged with the government seeking to correct an anomaly wherein companies making a profit of less than

Rs. 1 crores pay tax at an effective rate of 30.26% while those making a profit above Rs. 500 crores pay tax at an effective rate of 25.9%.

The finance minister announced a surcharge of 10% on individuals earning between Rs. 50 lakh and Rs. 1 crores while retaining the surcharge on those earning above Rs.1 crores at 15%. He also proposed to bring in a law to confiscate properties of economic offenders who have fled the country.

"In the recent past, there have been instances of big-time offenders, including economic offenders, fleeing the country to escape the reach of law. We have to ensure that the law is allowed to take its own course. Government is, therefore, considering introduction of legislative changes, or even a new law, to confiscate the assets of such persons located within the country, till they submit to the jurisdiction of the appropriate legal forum. Needless to say that all necessary constitutional safeguards will be followed in such cases," Jaitley said.

These measures are a reiteration of the National Democratic Alliance's intent to focus on the poor and marginalized. The provision of benefits to farmers, the poor, and salaried middle class while taxing the rich is also aimed at dispelling the tag of *"suit-boot ki sarkar"* given by the opposition.

"That (super rich) segment will not turn away from the Bharatiya Janata Party just because of this. They may not be hurt by this increased tax and this will not affect them as much. The finance minister in his speech made sure that a clear message was sent that the government is getting tough with economic offenders," said

Sandeep Shastri, a Bengaluru-based political scientist and pro-vice-chancellor of Jain University.

http://www.livemint.com/Politics/zSykIuCx17LmSXDN8HB9ZP/Budget-2017-Jaitley-reduces-income-tax-rates-for-individual.html

5.34   Budget 2017 Gives Clues about Demonetization Deposits in Banks

About Rs. 10.38 lakh crores in demonetized currency was deposited in 2.57 lakh bank accounts, showing that a large chunk of the amount came from the super-rich.

New Delhi: One of the biggest expectations with Union Budget 2017 was that the government would divulge details of how much money has come back to the banking system after demonetization. While the budget has disappointed in terms of giving overall statistics on this count, it does give an idea about the extent of money which has come in deposits of Rs. 2 lakh and above.

The figures as disclosed in Union Budget 2017 also tell us that 31% of total value of demonetized currency has come back in individual deposits of Rs.80 lakh or more. Photo: AP

This is what Arun Jaitley had to say in his budget speech: "After the demonetization, the preliminary analysis of data received in respect of deposits made by people in old currency presents a revealing picture. During the period 8th November to 30th December 2016, deposits between Rs. 2 lakh and Rs. 80 lakh were made in about 1.09 crores accounts with an average deposit size of Rs. 5.03 lakh. Deposits of more than 80 lakh were made in 1.48 lakh accounts with average deposit size of Rs. 3.31 crores."

The total amount which has been deposited under these two categories can be calculated by multiplying the number of accounts with the average deposit figures mentioned by Jaitley. This gives a figure of Rs. 5.48 lakh crores for deposits worth less than Rs. 80 lakh and Rs. 4.89 lakh crores for more than Rs. 80 lakh. The aggregate deposits under the two categories amount to Rs. 10.38 lakh crores. This works out to around two-third of the total value of demonetised currency, which was valued at around 15.44 lakh crores. These figures also tell us that around 31% of total value of demonetised currency has come back in individual deposits of Rs. 80 lakh or more. These figures show that a large chunk of the demonetized currency which has come back into banks is from the super-rich.

How much of the deposits reflect unearthed black money?

According to Jaitley, there are more than 3 lakh companies which show profits. There are 76 lakh individuals who report annual income greater than Rs. 5 lakh. Out of this 56 lakh individuals belong to the salaried class, which means that their avenues for tax evasion are extremely limited. The rest 20 lakh individuals include businessmen and professionals.

It is possible that several of the high-deposit accounts belong to those who are already in the tax net, and have legitimate reasons for holding on to cash. The finance minister has not said anything about whether these are individual or business accounts. In the latter category, a lot of cash could be classified as cash in hand for business purposes, and it would be difficult to say whether these deposits reflect unearthed black money.

However these numbers point to one unequivocal conclusion: most of the super-rich did not flush their cash stocks down the pit. Instead, they have chosen to park their money with banks, fully aware that this might invite scrutiny from taxmen. It is therefore likely that they will have good answers ready if and when the taxmen come to ask questions. There is very little reason to hope that the post-demonetization data mining exercise will help unearth a significant amount of black money. This should not come as a surprise to those who have taken even a cursory look at the findings of taxmen on black money, who have reported in the past that <u>cash is the least preferred way of holding unaccounted money</u>.

<u>http://www.livemint.com/Industry/zhdFUJDvLzNJNFe0puDjbO/Jait leys-budget-speech-gives-a-clue-about-currency-notes-de.html</u>

5.35 The Math of the Union Budget

The finance minister should allocate more resources for building the capabilities of local institutions.

The frenzied anticipation of the Union budget in the Indian media has faded. Now it is time for post-mortems, like this one. This one looks at the mathematics of the budget: its arithmetic, its geometry, and its algebra.

First, the arithmetic; Do the numbers add up? What will be the fiscal deficit? It will be 3.2%, according to the budget. The debate on whether or not the Union finance minister should have stuck to the 3% goal at a time when the economy needs a nudge will continue. With the effects of goods and services tax and demonetization on government's finances uncertain, the future will tell whether or not the revenue projections are correct.

If arithmetic is the counting of the trees, geometry is the shape of the woods. The finance minister listed 10 thrusts which shape the geometry of the budget. Together, they intend to nudge the economy into a better shape. The need to focus more directly on the creation of more jobs and livelihoods has been accepted. The thrust of the budget is to strengthen the bottom of the pyramid, focusing on the poor and underprivileged, farmers, the rural population, and youth. Small enterprises and labour-intensive sectors will be promoted.

Some companies and economists were disappointed with the budget. They wanted the finance minister to give more incentives to the top and reduce corporate tax rates to attract investment: to pursue the trickle-down model of economic growth. Some were also critical of the attention to small enterprises. They say the government should focus on creating more "good" jobs—such as those in large factories and in the large IT companies.

The trickle-down model of growth has been tarnished around the world. The wealth of those on top has been increasing much faster than benefits to people at the bottom. Inequalities within countries, especially India, are at very high levels. Populism (Donald Trump) and socialism (Bernie Sanders) are on the upsurge, even in the US. Moreover, the era of the large-factory model of formal employment is passing. New, Internet-driven business models and automation are altering shapes of enterprises and patterns of work in the manufacturing and service sectors. India should grab the future, not hold on to the past. The geometry of the budget hopes to nudge changes in the geometry of the Indian economy towards a more inclusive economy for people.

Algebra combines "x"s and "y"s—different types of factors—into one equation. Allocation of budgetary resources is one part of the solution to improve the shape and size of the Indian economy. Effective implementation is the other part that produces outcomes from allocations. Implementation is improved by strengthening institutional capabilities at many levels of the system, bottom to top.

Economists know that institutional capabilities matter, and that the quality of implementation—its speed and precision—improves the productivity of resources. Unlike financial and physical resources, institutional capabilities are not easily quantified. Therefore, they are not included in the arithmetic of budgets.

The finance minister has included "public service" as one of the 10 themes in the geometry of the budget, and also pointed towards stronger institutions in the financial sector. Thus, some "y"s has appeared along with the many "x"s. Nevertheless, a criticism of the budget is that it has done too little to strengthen institutions. For example, there is no reference to the urgency of implementing the comprehensive administrative reforms that were recommended by the Second Administrative Reforms Commission in 2009.

The devil, they say, is always in the detail. The finance minister's headline explanation of the theme of public service is, "Effective governance and efficiency of service delivery through people's participation". Most of the details are about the "efficiency of delivery of (government) services", with the use of IT, etc. There is too little about "effective governance through people's participation". There is great need and great scope for improving the efficiency of delivery of government services with IT. The vigour with which the government, led by the prime minister himself, is focused on this is most welcome.

However, the government must do much more to improve the capabilities of local governance institutions. People participate directly in the governance of their affairs through local institutions. Effective local governance ensures that results are produced on the ground to fulfill the needs of people. The 73rd and 74th amendments to the Constitution, for strengthening the roles of local governance institutions in villages and cities, were passed by Parliament 25 years ago. Since then, there has been no more than lip-service to increasing their capabilities. Central and state governments bypass them, with the excuse that there is an urgency to get results.

Until people's institutions on the ground are empowered with financial resources, and simultaneously trained to deliver, they will not develop their capabilities. The finance minister should allocate more resources for building the capabilities of local institutions. The amounts required are very small and would hardly change the arithmetic of the budget. However, they will improve the geometry and algebra of the economy, to create an economy for the people with governance by the people.

Arun Maira served in the erstwhile Planning Commission.

http://www.livemint.com/Opinion/f9qkDIPgtxNHBKuZeuFKdI/The-math-of-the-Union-budget.html

5.36 Budget 2017: Impact of demonetization transient; India will go above 7% next year, says Shaktikanta Das

Speaking at a post-Budget 2017 session organized by FICCI, Shaktikanta Das expressed optimism in the next fiscal year, the Indian economy will grow above 7%. "The GDP growth for the next year will be upwards of 7%," he said. (IE)

Budget 2017: Reiterating what Finance Minister Arun Jaitley said in his Budget speech this year, DEA Secretary Shaktikanta Das today said that demonetization will have a transient effect on the economy. "The impact of demonetization will be transient and we do not expect it to spill over to the next year," Shaktikanta Das said.

Speaking at a post-Budget 2017 session organized by FICCI, Shaktikanta Das expressed optimism in the next fiscal year, the Indian economy will grow above 7%. "The GDP growth for the next year will be upwards of 7%," he said.

According to Das, many people have now moved to digital transactions post demonetization. "We can no longer see queues outside bank branches for cash. A large part of the economy is now moving to digital transactions," he said.

Das cautioned against global headwinds in the coming quarters. "Global headwinds have become stronger," he said. Talking about the various Budget proposals, Shaktikanta Das said that the huge amount of public investment announced in the speech will propel growth. "The public investments announced by the government will have a multiplier effect," he said.

FM Jaitley on February 1 presented the Union Budget for the fiscal year 2017-2018. The Budget largely focused on increased public expenditure, especially in the rural areas and on infrastructure. Industry analysts and markets have largely given thumbs up to the Modi government for its Budget. The Union Budget was special this year, not only on account of the fact that it was proponed, but also for the government's move to combine the Railway Budget as part of the main Budget. Indian Railways has been allotted Rs. 55,000 crores from the government for the upcoming fiscal, while the total Budget for the Railways is pegged at Rs. 1.31 lakh crores.

http://www.financialexpress.com/budget/budget-2017-impact-of-demonetisation-transient-india-will-go-above-7-next-year-says-shaktikanta-das/537422/

5.37 Note Ban Impact on Gold Buying Will Wane after Budget 2017: WGC

IANS | New Delhi January 24, 2017   Last Updated at 12:54 IST

It also said demonetization will have a positive impact on the gold industry in the long run.

India's demonetization drive has impacted gold demand in the short term but buying is showing signs of revival and post the presentation of the national budget on February 1, the market will be back to normal, says the India chief of World Gold Council.

"In November and December (during the demonetization drive) certainly there was some impact. But people have started buying again. We hope soon after the budget, buying will normalize," Somasundaram P.R., Managing Director, India, World Gold Council, told IANS in an interview.

He also said demonetization will have a positive impact on the gold industry in the long run as it will curb grey market trades substantially. "Overall impact of demonetization will be positive -- industry will come under organized business. Of course the transition will take some time," he said.

"Business during the demonetization period was hurt as people were mostly busy exchanging old notes and genuine buyers stayed away, fearing they might come under the tax scanner."

The World Gold Council (WGC) on Tuesday also launched the report titled "India's Gold Market: evolution and innovation", providing an overview of the industry in the last 15 years. The report also said demonetization will have a significant impact on the economy in the short-term.

"Rumours over caps on gold holdings and buying added fuel to the fire. As tax authorities probed some jewelers who had immediately after demonetization created opportunity to convert old notes currency for fake or back-dated sales, the resultant panic ensured that genuine gold buyers were reluctant even to buy wedding jewellery," the report added.

The WGC had forecast India's full year gold demand between 650-750 tons for 2016. Till the third quarter (July-September) of 2016 the demand was at 443 tons. It is forecast that India's average gold demand will be 850-900 tons per annum by 2020.

In 2000, around 90 per cent of India's gold retailers were "unorganized". But by 2020, the organized share of the market will rise to 35-40 per cent. At present, there are around 400,000 jewelers in India, said the report.

The report said gold demand responds more to income than it does to price.

"Our econometric analysis of data from 1990 to 2015 revealed that income levels are the most significant long-term determinants of consumer gold demand -- 1 per cent rise in income boosts gold demand by 1 per cent," he added.

But if prices go up by 1 per cent then demand falls by half a per cent only. "Thus gold demand responds more strongly to income growth than price." The short-term gold demand largely depends on four factors -- tax, price, monsoon and inflation, said the report.

It said in 2015, plain gold jewellery accounted for 88 per cent of purchases in rural India. In urban India the figure was 57 per cent, with gem-set pieces accounting for 35 per cent of gold jewellery bought. Around 60-65 per cent of jewellery manufactured in India is handmade.

It said India's gold stock is around 23,000-24,000 tons, valued at over $800 billion. Southern India has the highest market share for gold demand at 40 per cent, western India at 25 per cent, while northern and eastern India have 20 per cent and 15 per cent share, respectively.

"Given that weddings are a key occasion for buying gold and the fact that 500 million of the population is under the age of 25, the number of weddings and subsequently the occasions for buying gold are likely to be higher," Somasundaram said.

"The outlook for jewellery demand is favourable."

http://www.business-standard.com/article/economy-policy/note-ban-impact-on-gold-buying-will-wane-after-budget-2017-wgc-117012400288_1.html

5.38 Budget 2017: Arun Jaitley Says Decision on FRBM Review Panel Report In Due Course

Jaitley in his Budget speech said the FRBM review panel has provided for 'escape clauses', for deviations up to 0.5% of GDP, from the stipulated fiscal deficit target

New Delhi: The report of the FRBM (Fiscal Responsibility and Budget Management) review panel, headed by former revenue secretary N.K. Singh, will be carefully examined and appropriate decisions will be taken in due course, finance minister Arun Jaitley said on Wednesday.

"The report of the committee will be carefully examined and appropriate decisions taken in due course," Jaitley said in his Budget 2017-18 speeches. The committee had recommended debt-to-GDP ratio of 60% by 2023 and fiscal deficit at 3% for next three years.

Jaitley said the committee has also provided for 'Escape Clauses', for deviations up to 0.5% of GDP, from the stipulated fiscal deficit target. "Among the triggers for taking recourse to these Escape Clauses, the committee has included 'far-reaching structural reforms in the economy with unanticipated fiscal implications' as one of the factors," he said.

Although there is a strong case now to invoke this Escape Clause, Jaitley said, "I am refraining from doing so."

"Nevertheless, I take note of the fiscal deficit roadmap of 3% recommended by the committee for the next three years," the minister added.

Jaitley said that considering all these aspects, he has pegged the fiscal deficit for 2017-18 at 3.2% of GDP (gross domestic product) and remain committed to achieve 3% in the following year. "With this gradual approach, I have ensured adherence to fiscal consolidation, without compromising the requirements of public investment," he pointed out.

http://www.livemint.com/Politics/9cApi8YtlPzXHrPTqIHnmO/Budget-2017-Arun-Jaitley-says-decision-on-FRBM-review-panel.html?li_source=LI&li_medium=news_rec

5.39 FRBM Report Is Out. This Is Why It Matters To You

We seldom worry about the macro part of the budget—about terms such as fiscal deficit and tax-to-gross domestic product (GDP) ratio.

The Fiscal Responsibility and Budget Management (FRBM) Committee submitted its report on 23 January 2016, a bit over seven months after it was set up. Read more on the origin of FRBM here: bit.ly/2klLFki. Though the report is not public, news reports say that the panel has recommended fiscal consolidation, but not at the expense of growth. Reports say that it tells the government not to worry if the fiscal deficit stays at, or just above, 3%. If your eyes are glazing over, unglazed them, because we'll find out what this means and how it affects our lives.

Priyanka Parashar / Mint

What is the fiscal deficit and why should we worry about it, especially at budget time? As households, we usually worry about individual tax rates and prices of goods as they change in response to taxes that the government levies. We seldom worry about the macro part of the budget—about terms such as fiscal deficit and tax-to-gross domestic product (GDP) ratio. It may be a good idea for us to understand what these mean and how changes in these two numbers finally do affect us, though in a roundabout way. But affect us, they do. A government runs what is called a fiscal deficit when it spends more than what it collects as revenue. Revenue is the sum total of taxes (personal income, corporate, excise, customs to name a few) the government collects. If revenue is equal to the expenditure, the government's budget is balanced, but most governments run on a 'deficit' or spend more than they collect. How does it finance this deficit? It borrows. Market loans in Budget 2016 were Rs4.25 trillion or 21% of the budget of Rs19.78 trillion. Fiscal deficit for 2015-16 was at 3.9% of GDP, with a target of 3.5% for 2016-17. FRBM targets are 3% fiscal deficit and a zero revenue deficit. Very quickly: look at a revenue deficit as your credit card debt that finances current consumption—it is a bad loan—and look at fiscal deficit as your home loan that leverages future income to build an appreciating asset. A fiscal deficit of 3%, when revenue deficit is zero has been seen as the magic formula for the government to borrow responsibly.

Why does the government need to borrow so much? Fiscal deficit was 6.6% in 2009-10 and the government's borrowing programme zoomed. One reason that the government borrows so much is the poor tax-to-GDP ratio of 16.6 in India, as compared to the emerging market economy average of 21% and OECD average of 34%. Tax on income (what you and I pay as income tax) in Budget 2016-17 was Rs. 3.53 trillion, or just 18% of the budget. The numbers of taxpayers tells a story. Just 1% of the Indian population pays income tax and the number of people who say they earn Rs1 crore or more is around 48,000. Looking around at the luxury houses and luxury sports utility vehicles (SUV) purchases around, the numbers tell their own story of tax evasion.

We know that people don't pay taxes, why should it matter to me? Large government borrowing programmes usually lead to financial repression (other than in countries like the US, where the appetite for US Treasuries is global). Financial repression is the ability of the government to attract cheap household saving to it by fixing the rules of the game. Ever wondered why you get just 4% on your saving bank deposit and why the rate of fixed deposits is usually below that of inflation? Look deeper into the return from your traditional life insurance policy and be horrified to see a return of about 3% a year over a period of 15-20 years. In order to finance the deficit, the government needs to borrow. By fixing the investment rules of banks and insurance firms, it can have a steady pipeline of funds that are forced into G-Secs.

Did you know that at least 24% of total bank deposits are invested in government bonds due to the way rules are framed? Did you know that investment rules of life insurance companies ensure that a large part of your premium is invested in government securities? According to the Insurance Regulatory and Development Authority of India (IRDAI) annual report for 2015-16, life insurance companies had an investment of Rs. 8.3 trillion as of 31 March 2016 in central government securities. This is only for traditional products, and not including unit-linked insurance plans.

This is why reforms in the capital market have been much easier than in banking or insurance. There are no fixed investment rules that suck household money through mutual funds or other market-related products. The government worries when bank deposit rates slow down. It worries when premiums of life insurance companies begin to fall. At stake is the sale of government bonds. A higher tax-to-GDP ratio will usually mean lower reliance on borrowed funds for a sensible government not in election mode. Remember that the 2008-09 United Progressive Alliance budget squandered away a rare moment of fiscal consolidation through its farm loan waiver programme. Read this column from that year: bit.ly/2iYI63c

A high fiscal deficit that goes to service current government consumption or pre-election freebies needs to worry us, as should a low tax-to-GDP ratio; because the final bill is paid by us – the tax paper, the investor and the inflation-hit consumer. What will work? A government that commits to the FRBM targets, no matter if it is a pre-election year or not, the setting up of the public debt management authority (PDMA) that takes the conflict of managing the government borrowing programme out of an inflation-targeting central bank. Better tax compliance that lifts the tax-to-GDP ratio. The presence of the

FRBM limit stops a government from spending away the advantage. Once this is in place the ground is ready to end financial repression that is today carried out through banks than insurance companies. We need to worry if the government spends too much of its tax revenue on itself. We must worry when too many people evade the tax net and buy fancy SUVs out of undeclared incomes. We must understand that macro numbers relate to our micro lives.

Monika Halan works in the area of consumer protection in finance. She is consulting editor Mint, consultant NIPFP, and on the board of FPSB India. She can be reached at monika.h@livemint.com

http://www.livemint.com/Money/0e4iui04A4u6DCeZCqb22O/FRBM-report-is-out-This-is-why-it-matters-to-you.html

5.40 Budget 2017: Good Economics, Good Politics, or Bit of Both?

For Budget 2017 to deliver the perfect score, the government will have to address the obvious challenges facing the Indian economy.

Every Union budget is shaped by the backdrop in which it is conceived; this year more so than others.

On the one hand, you have a fragile global economy with an unreliable US as its nucleus; domestically, India is still measuring the aftershocks of demonetization even as corporate India continues to struggle with its funk, precluding new investments. On the other hand, this budget, to be presented on 1 February, comes just three days ahead of the latest round of elections, which includes the biggest prize— Uttar Pradesh. Clearly, the stakes are higher than normal.

It is very likely that the Modi-Jaitley combine will accelerate the massive re-plumbing and rebalancing exercise between India and Bharat.   Photo: HT

So what will Finance Minister Arun Jaitley opt for in what will be his fourth budget? Good economics, good politics or the perfect score—a mix of both?

Whatever the answer, it will shape the remaining tenure of the government (which crossed its midpoint in December) led by Prime Minister Narendra Modi. On any way we look, this undoubtedly will be a defining budget and this is the metric with which it will eventually be measured.

The first two budgets of Jaitley were panned by critics, pining for big-ticket reform commitments (like his predecessors were often wont to do, though never delivering on it—an example being the promise of rolling out the goods and services tax). The third budget, however, seemed to have drawn grudging praise; not sure how much of it was because it was well crafted/presented and how much because his critics finally got the message.

For this year's budget to deliver the perfect score, it will have to address the obvious challenges facing the Indian economy—and this is not just about investment; it is essentially delivering jobs-friendly economic growth. It is very unlikely, as feared by those lobbying for its delay, that the budget will devote itself to addressing the coming elections through a burst of populist initiatives.

For one, it will be too little too late; Goa and Punjab vote three days after the budget is presented and the other three states will be in the throes of hyper campaigning—the noise from which will drown out benefits accruing from any complicated policy maneuvers. In any case budget euphoria is always short-lived. Second, it will fly in the face of the defining ideology—empowerment over entitlement—of the Modi-led government. Third, Modi has so far demonstrated, as with demonetization, his willingness to gamble his hard-earned social capital on unpopular decisions.

Instead, it is very likely that the Modi-Jaitley combine will accelerate the massive re-plumbing (demonetization would be an example) and rebalancing exercise between India and Bharat (which some mistakenly view as robbing Peter to pay Paul and hence a redistribution of income). In that case, one can safely expect a fresh raft of measures to spur financial inclusion, the shift towards a digital economy, strengthening of the social safety net and so on. And if they are to stay true to their commitment to empowerment then expect several measures towards rebuilding Bharat, as defined by *Mint*'s budget tag line, 'Rebuilding Bharat'. Bharat is still defined by agriculture (accounting for 48% employed) and the pathetic socio-economic statistics, something which cannot be fixed overnight—but a blueprint to fix the problem will be a welcome first step.

A boost to agriculture (which by the way is no longer just a food grain economy) will not only help alleviate the pressures of a prolonged period of rural distress but also be a short-term palliative.

But more enduring will be steps ensuring development programmes survive the last mile and reach the intended beneficiary. The buzz is that the budget is likely to see a radical recast of public spending to fix this problem by introducing a social registry. The ecosystem today—largely because the 14th Finance Commission made states equal stakeholders—is far more receptive to this recast.

For the salaried middle class, no doubt bruised by demonetization even while it was dealing with a post-boom economy, the FM would have something, just like corporate India can look forward to further ease of doing business and some tax relief. But in all likelihood the FM will finely balance these with other development measures to manage the optics to avoid being dubbed a "suit-boot sarkar" (a government for the rich); but then only to be accused by critics of being populist. You can't win them all.

Clearly, content alone won't matter; the crafting of the speech will be equally important. The suspense will be over in a little over two weeks from today.

Anil Padmanabhan is executive editor of Mint *and writes every week on the intersection of politics and economics*

http://www.livemint.com/Opinion/LC8HXUdPN0WZk7xTrCriVN/
Union-budget-Good-economics-good-politics-or-bit-of-
both.html?li_source=LI&li_medium=news_rec

5.41 Budget 2017: Move to Formalize Economy will create More Jobs, Says Team Lease Chairman

Bloomberg | *Quint* Bloomberg Quint – Thu 2 Feb, 2017 8:06 PM IST

GST and demonetization will go a long way in creating jobs, says Manish Sabharwal.

Budget 2017 may have failed to remove the regulatory hurdles that hamper creation of jobs, especially in the education sector, according to the chairman and co-founder of one of India's leading human resources services providers, Team Lease. Budget 2017 did nothing to bridge the gap between degrees and skills, nor did it remove the ban on online higher education, Manish Sabharwal told Bloomberg Quint's Menaka Doshi in an interview. But the move to formalize the economy, will eventually create more jobs, he added.

Prime Minister Modi's attempt to formalize the economy through the Goods and Services Tax and the demonetization drive, could be the only solution to India's jobs problem, said Sabharwal.

Here are the edited excerpts of the conversation:

You wrote for us, a column that identified the six interventions that you expected the finance minister to make in Budget 2017 to help the jobs economy. Not one of those has featured in the Budget. Are you a disappointed man?

The six things that I pointed out are in the nature of regulatory cholesterol for ease of doing business in any economy and in educational reform. If you step back from the jobs problem, we don't have a jobs problem, we have a wages problem. Everybody who wants a job has a job. They just don't have the salary they want or need. So at a certain level, formalization, urbanization and industrialization in human capital are what any Budget can do if they decide the problem is wages. If you think the problem is jobs, you do a Mahatma Gandhi National Rural Employment Guarantee Act (MGNREGA). We've spent Rs. 2.5 lakh crores on MGNREGA since the programme started and I know this Budget has a large allocation for MGNREGA. But MGNREGA is never going to solve the jobs problem and nor is it going to create skills. So if the one thing that I would be disappointed about was that this was just not enough regulatory cholesterol was gotten rid of in the education sector. So we didn't see new connectivity between degrees and skills, we didn't remove the ban on online higher education. But that said, a ten year plan for jobs is not 10-one-year plans. So what I am delighted with is formalization. I think the thrust of formalization is the only solution to India's problems.

The two big economic efforts of the Budget were towards housing and a tax break for Micro and Small Medium Enterprises (MSMEs). These measures have been praised, across the board, as measures that will help achieve economic growth and also help create jobs. Is that how you see it as well?

It'll achieve formal jobs. I repeat myself, our problem is not jobs, it is good jobs. We have 6.3 crores enterprises in India. 1.2 crores of them don't have an office and work from home. Only 85 lakh enterprises have any sort of tax registration, only 10 lakh are companies but most tragically, only 18,000 companies in India with a paid capitalization of more than Rs. 18,000 crores. So 6.3 crores enterprises in India means nothing if it only translates into 18,000 companies with a paid up capital of more than Rs. 10 crores. So it's not just the tax reduction for MSMEs, it's also the cap on paying more than Rs. 3 lakh in cash and following up on Goods and Services Tax (GST) implementation and demonetization, if the government stays the course on formalization, this what the government can do for jobs. The world is a hostile place right now with Trump and Brexit. When China started thinking about jobs in 1978, they saw a super cycle of global growth, global openness for trade and global manufacturing. We don't have that. Domestic consumption is our ticket and formalization of enterprises is the only way we are going to accomplish it. They did ten things on formalization and I think they all take us towards the direction of better jobs.

In which case even though the six interventions you had asked for were not met with, the big effort or push towards formalizing several elements or aspects of the economy should make you a happy man at the end of this budget exercise except for the fact that I think skills building may not have found as much mention in this Budget, so I think there are many out there who believe that this in not necessarily something a government can do in any direct fashion. Would you agree with that?

The role of the government is not to set things on fire. It is to create the condition for continuous combustion. I think they are obsessed about regulatory cholesterol in ease of doing business, formalization. I think that there obsession has to translate to getting rid of the regulatory *'ayatollahs'* (high ranking religious leader) like University Grants Commission (UGC), All India Council for Technical Education (AICTE) who are today preventing connection of skills to college, fixing school education, they did talk of learning outcome. So my sense is if the Budget is evolving to towards becoming an accounting statement, then we got the wrong expectations, maybe that's what it is supposed to be. But I think following GST, demonetization and their formalization with massive changes to the regulatory cholesterol in human capital would be nice over the next few months.

Beside GST and limit on cash transactions would you like to list some of the noteworthy ones?

Differential tax rate for the companies, I think that's really the kick for formalization and I think the lower regulation, the revamp of the human capital in the tax department. I know a lot of people missed that. People have been worried about tax terrorism but the move to data driven algorithm is a move towards rule of law...We need to move from deals to rules for everything in India to formalize. One of India's tragedies is somebody follows a rule they feel like they have missed a deal so I think there was a lot in the budget sort of moving away from deals to rules so whether you think about what they are doing for the tax department, whether it's about the threshold that they did for reopening the cases, I think there is a lot of plumbing...your campaign is poetry, but how you govern is prose. I think this Budget was an overdue dose of prose in ease of doing business.

https://in.finance.yahoo.com/news/budget-2017-move-formalise-economy-143650214.html

5.42 How the Modi Govt. is struggling to Defend Note Ban in Parliament

Nearly three months after demonetization was rolled out, people are still waiting for the Narendra Modi regime to coherently explain what the exercise was for. In keeping with the public mood, MPs have been asking a lot of questions about it over the first two days of the ongoing Budget session. The responses to the questions show the government is struggling to defend the move.

Over a dozen questions have been asked in the Lok Sabha about note ban and related issues. These range from details of the government's assessment of the move to details on cash withdrawals and from irregularities by bank officials to deposits in Jan Dhan accounts.

On 3 February, a group of MPs asked whether the government had assessed the success / failure of the "scheme". To what extent had it achieved the stated objectives of "flushing out black money and counterfeit currency, curbing terror and insurgency financing"? Also, the MP asked, have the dreams of "conversion of cash-based economy into a digital economy and higher tax revenue" been realized.

Interestingly, a significant number of the MPs who have asked questions about demonetization are either from the BJP or parties that are supporting it. They include BJP's Sanjay Shamrao Dhotre, Satya Pal Singh and Dushyant Singh, Shiv Sena's Rahul Ramesh Shewale, YSR Congress Party's Avinash Reddy, TRS' Kotha Prabhakar Reddy.

The MPS have also sought to know the details of the programmes being run by the government to "restore normalcy and provide relief to the cash-based industries, unorganized sector, farmers, labourers and other affected/aggrieved persons".

And what was the response?

On the assessment of demonetization and what objectives were achieved, the government said "demonetization seeks to create a new 'normal' wherein the GDP would be bigger, cleaner and real" and that the exercise "is part of the government's resolve to eliminate corruption, black money, counterfeit currency and terror funding".

The list of achievements provided by the government is this:

- "More than 1,100 searches and surveys were conducted and more than 5,100 notices were issued by the Income Tax Department".
- "Seizure of valuables of more than Rs. 610 crores", including cash worth Rs. 513 crores.
- Seizure of cash in new currency notes worth about Rs. 110 crores.
- Detection of undisclosed income worth about Rs. 5400 crores till 10 January.

The government conveniently sidestepped the question on the realization of the objectives regarding black money, counterfeit currency, terrorist funding, digital economy and higher tax revenue. All it has given are the statistics quoted above and some steps that were taken much before demonetization was announced. These include:

- Constitution of the Special Investigation Team on Black Money.
- Enactment of the Black Money (Undisclosed Foreign Income and Assets) and Imposition of Tax Act, 2015.
- Amendment to the Benami Transactions (Prohibition) Act, 1988.

Different question, same answer

A nearly identical response was given to another question by a different set of MPs, who sought to know:

- The value of black money in form of old / new currency notes and gold seized during demonetization move.
- The total value of notes demonetized, the demonetized currency returned back as on date.
- Whether the government has seized new notes as part of its operations against black money hoarders during the course of demonetization.
- The amount of black money and undisclosed assets unearthed during these raids.

The government's response is a repetition of the statistics quoted in the previous answer, plus some more numbers:

- As on 8 November 2016, there were 17165 million pieces of Rs. 500 in circulation.
- There were 6858 million pieces of Rs. 1,000 in circulation.
- The value of Rs. 500 and Rs. 1,000 returned to the RBI and Currency Chests amounted to Rs. 12.44 lakh crores as of 10 December 2016.

Once again, no details about black money, terror funding, fake currency.

More evasion

Another question asked on the same date by another group of MPs asks:

- Whether any study / survey was conducted or experts / stakeholders consulted by the government to assess the possible consequences of demonetization prior to its implementation.
- Whether the government had made any assessment of the estimated quantum of black money in the economy before the implementation of demonetization.

The government's reply is baffling. It doesn't answer whether any study was conducted or any experts consulted. On assessment of the amount of black money unearthed, the reply quotes "the white paper on Black Money, dated May 2012", which, in turn, refers to data from 1976 and 1984. It also refers to a World Bank report that put the shadow economy estimate at 20.7% of the GDP in 1999 and 23.2% in 2007.

These answers make it clear that as the curiosity over demonetization is peaking, the government is struggling to give an adequate response and defend the move. Is the day coming when somebody in the Modi regime or the ruling party will admit that note ban too, like Achche Din, was a jumla?

https://in.finance.yahoo.com/news/modi-govt-struggling-defend-note-134512550.html

------------------------- END -------------------------

ABOUT THE AUTHOR

Award winning Key Note Speaker at International Level, Professor Ajit Kumar Roy is an acclaimed researcher and consultant. Prof. Roy obtained his M.Sc. degree in Statistics and joined Agricultural Research Service (ARS) of Indian Council of Agricultural Research (ICAR) as a Scientist (Statistics) in 1976. In recent past was engaged as National Consultant (Impact Assessment), for East &North Eastern States of India at National Agricultural Innovation Project (World Bank funded) of ICAR. Prior to that he had served as a Consultant (Statistics) at Central Agricultural University, Agartala. Earlier had served at CIFA, ICAR, as Principal Scientist and was involved in applied research in the areas of ICT, Statistics, Bioinformatics Analytics, and Economics. At International level he served as a Computer Specialist at SAARC Agricultural Information Centre (SAIC), Dhaka, Bangladesh for over 3 years.

The author with over 45 years of research and teaching experience in Statistical Analysis, Analytics, and information & Knowledge management edited eighteen books and several conference proceedings. Besides, published over 100 articles in refereed journals. His recent best-sellers are Facts and Figures of Demonetization in India-Reactions, Views and comments; Big Data and Data Science Initiative in India- Upcoming Job Opportunities: Big data Job Opportunities in India (Big Data-Series-4 Book 1);'Applied Big Data Analytics'; 'Impact of Big Data Analytics on Business, Economy, Health Care and Society'; 'Data Science - A Career Option for 21st Century';' Self Learning of Bioinformatics Online'; 'Applied Bioinformatics, Statistics and Economics in Fisheries Research' and 'Applied Computational Biology and Statistics in Biotechnology and Bioinformatics'; Emerging Technologies of the 21st Century.

He is a Member, Organizing Committee Board for the 6th International Conference on 'Biometrics and Biostatistics' to be held during, November 13-14, 2017 Atlanta, Georgia, USA. Editorial Board Member, Jacobs Journal of Biostatistics, Jacobs Publishers, 900 Great Hills, Trail # 150 w, Austin, Texas. He now works as Visiting Professor, question setter and examiner of four Indian Universities.

www.ingramcontent.com/pod-product-compliance
Lightning Source LLC
Chambersburg PA
CBHW051625170526
45167CB00001B/63